The Lion and the Tigress

Helen Rayson-Hill

Glass House Books
an imprint of IP (Interactive Publications Pty Ltd)
Treetop Studio • 9 Kuhler Court
Carindale, Queensland, Australia 4152
ipoz.biz/glass-house-books/
ipoz.biz/ipstore

First published by IP in 2022

© 2022 Helen Rayson-Hill, and IP

All rights reserved. Without limiting the rights under copyright reserved above, no part of this publication may be reproduced, stored in or introduced into a retrieval system, or transmitted, in any form or by any means (electronic, mechanical, photocopying, recording or otherwise), without the prior written permission of the copyright owner and the publisher of this book.

Printed in 12 pt Book Antiqua on 14 pt Avenir Book

ISBN 9781922830029 (PB); ISBN 9781922830036 (eBook)

A catalogue record for this book is available from the National Library of Australia

For my family,
Glyn Rayson-Hill
Freya, Tristan, Ingra, Jojo and Pippa
Jonathan, Simone, Charlie and Madeleine

Acknowledgements

Cover image: *God Speed!* by Edmund Blair Leighton
Book design: David P. Reiter

What started as a spark has taken hold. To those who introduced me to Eleanor of Aquitaine and to those who applied the bellows to the fire I am more than grateful. They have my heartfelt thanks. But above all, my gratitude goes to that amazing little girl who was born in 1122, 900 years ago and grew to fight for her right to be heard, to have her education and intelligence recognised against the powerful male elite of her times. Even as a Queen of both France and England she had to prove herself.

My introduction to Eleanor of Aquitaine began through a production of the play *The Lion in Winter* by James Goldman. I wanted to get into Eleanor's head, so I started reading historical biographies about her life starting with *Eleanor and the Four Kings* by Amy Kelly, *Eleanor by the Wrath of God, Queen of England* by Alison Wier, then biographies by Ralph V Turner and Marion Meade whose books about Eleanor kept my interest firing. To these authors and the membership of The Historical Novelists' Society of Australasia, and The History Quill, I am thankful.

For years, Eleanor ran round my head till I was given a mighty prod by author Toni Jordan who said that if I did not get my ideas on paper I never would. I am also indebted to the Lyceum Club of Melbourne's Writers' Circle who have listened patiently to my readings of early drafts, who have encouraged me, continue to give me the confidence to keep writing and who convinced me that my first volume in the series *Eleanor, the Firebrand Queen* could be published. Irina Dunn again ran her conscientious editor's eye over *The Lion and The Tigress* and is an inspiration.

Dr David Reiter of Interactive Publications, I thank for his faith in my work and for his ongoing commitment in publishing the Series and to bring alive Eleanor of Aquitaine's tumultuos marriage to Henry II, King of England and to send it on its way.

To all my friends and family who have put up with my lectures on Medieval History and Eleanor in particular. Also, to my friend Pearl Longden, who ran her eagle proofreading eye over the final drafts of the first two novels, not missing an ill-placed comma or apostrophe, my appreciation.

Lastly, my love and thanks to my husband Glyn Rayson-Hill, my computer guru, who calms my fits of despair, through corrupted USB sticks, my general lack of computer knowledge and horrors when the screen goes black or when some other minor glitch occurs without losing patience or his sense of humour.

Glass House Books
The Lion and the Tigress

Helen Rayson-Hill trained as an infant teacher, and taught in country Victoria, Melbourne and the UK. Later, she became a drama teacher following a long interest in the theatre.

After a family transfer to Brisbane, she was appointed Queensland Manager of the Australian Elizabethan Theatre Trust. For two years she co-ordinated National Arts Week in Brisbane working closely with the Queensland Government's Ministry of the Arts and Brisbane City Council.

On returning to Melbourne, Helen held a position at the Victorian Arts Centre in the Membership and Fundraising and Development Department. For two years she was an adjudicator for the Victorian Drama League.

Helen has also performed both on the stage in Melbourne and Brisbane and on television in *Neighbours* on Channel 10 and *Something's in the Air* on the Australian ABC network.

Writing has always been an interest of Helen's and she is a member of the Writers' Circle at Melbourne's Lyceum Club. She has written plays for her drama students as well as sketches for amateur theatre. Also an artist specialising in oils, Helen has held several successful exhibitions at several Victorian galleries.

Helen's short stories and memoir pieces have been published in anthologies, and she has written a children's book, *Kid Detectives*. The story was inspired by her grandson who wanted to know how children entertained themselves before electronic devices filled their lives.

Helen has long been interested in Medieval history, especially in the life of Eleanor of Aquitaine. After many years of research, inspired originally by the play *The Lion in Winter* by James Goldman, Helen was motivated to write about Eleanor's amazing life. Consequently, *Eleanor, the Firebrand Queen* became the first in a planned series of historical novels about this Medieval feminist.

Glass House Books
Brisbane

Contents

Chapter 1. London	1
Chapter 2. Regency	33
Chapter 3. Aquitaine Christmas	58
Chapter 4. Owen Pendragon	71
Chapter 5. Chancellor Becket	86
Chapter 6. An Awkward Talisman	107
Chapter 7. The Disgruntled Lion	121
Chapter 8. Rebellion Looms	151
Chapter 9. Duchess Or Queen?	167
Chapter 10. Archbishop Becket	212
Chapter 11. Estranged	235
Chapter 12. Heir Apparent	254

Genealogy

Eleanor: Queen of England, Duchess of Aquitaine, Countess of Poitou, and Gascony 1122/23 – 1204 (birthdate sometimes disputed).

Mother: Aenor de Rochefoucault (deceased). Died when Eleanor and Petronilla were about two and three, respectively.

Uncle: (Mother's brother) Lord Ralph de Faye.

Mother's family - Grandmother: Dangerosa de Rochefoucault (deceased).

Mother's family - Grandfather: Aimery de Rochefoucault Viscount of Châtellerault (deceased).

Father: William X Duke of Aquitaine (deceased).

Father's Youngest Brother: Raymond Prince of Antioch (deceased) was only six years older than Eleanor.

Father's family – Grandfather: William IX Duke of Aquitaine (deceased).

(Dangerosa and William IX were lovers living openly together in the Maubergeonne Tower, part of the Palace of Poitiers.)

Father's Mother: Phillipa of Toulouse (Rightfully, Eleanor was also Countess of Toulouse).

Sister: Petronilla (also known as Nilla) Countess of Vermandois – husband Raoul.

Brother: William Aigret (died as a baby).

***

Henry II (Plantagenet) King of England, Duke of Normandy, Count of Anjou (1133–1189).

Genealogy

Mother: Empress Matilda, Dowager Duchess of Normandy (Cousin Stephen of Blois deceased – son Eustace deceased).

Father: Geoffrey Plantagenet, Duke of Normandy (deceased).

Brothers: Geoffrey and William, half-brother (illegitimate) Hamelin. Mother said to be Adelaide of Anjou.

Eleanor's 1st husband: Louis VII of France. (their daughters were Marie and Alix).

***

Children to Eleanor and Henry:

William, 1153-1156

Henry (Hal) – the Young King, 1155-1183

Matilda, 1156–1189 (Queen of Saxony)

Richard I (The Lion Heart) 1157-1199

Geoffrey (Duke of Brittany) 1158-1186

Phillip died at birth (date not recorded; I have invented one).

Eleanor (Lenore) (Queen of Castile) 1161-1214

Joanna, 1165-1199 (Queen of Sicily and Countess of Toulouse – second marriage).

John, 1166-1216 (became King of England after Richard's death.)

Geoffrey Fitz Henry 1152-1212 (the bastard) Henry II's illegitimate son (historians believe mother's name was Ykenai).

Chapter 1. London

We celebrated the birth of Christ in Westminster Abbey. It felt odd after all the pomp of our Coronation to be back in the that mighty house of God, but also a relief the concerns and nerves leading up to that momentous day were over. However, the ritual, the spirituality and solemnity of the occasion would remain forever in my heart.

What a fateful year it had been for Henry and me. Stephen of Blois and his evil son Eustace were no longer. Henry's mother, Empress Matilda was at last avenged, and England her rightful inheritance, returned to its dynastic roots.

The year of 1154 was carved like an inscription on a monument in my mind. Judith's prophesy all those years ago in Antioch had provoked within me every emotion from doubt to anger. Now that it was coming true, I wrestled still with its predictions: *You will marry the love of your life, you will bear him many sons, but your life will be tumultuous. You are destined to become a great queen.*

***

This morning while we knelt in Westminster Abbey, I glanced at Henry with his head bowed and I pondered what his thoughts might be. The responsibilities of his kingdom lay heavily on his young shoulders even though his mother had groomed him for this role. I prayed not only for God's guidance of our onerous future, but to endow Henry and me with the wisdom to unite this war-torn nation. Henry was a natural leader of men, a soldier, a valiant knight, but not a patient diplomat. I prayed I could provide that influence.

After we returned to the old Saxon Palace of Bermondsey, our temporary home, our families enjoyed themselves and were able to relax. Our Christmas court was informal, allowing us to partake in simple fun. We exchanged little gifts, drank mulled wine, and ate goose and other fowl such as grouse and pheasant. With sticky fingers we relished sweetmeats made from dried fruits and nuts flavoured with spices and laced with honey.

This would be the first Christmas little William would remember; such a joy. My Aquitainian court was as excited as puppies with the appearance of snow. Laughter and sport took place in the fairyland-like gardens as we made snowballs and hurled them in all directions. It became quite a joust with the Plantagenet men trying to outdo each other. Henry's brothers, Geoffrey, and William were as competitive as he was. Nilla's children ran about squealing with joy, for the first time since their father Raoul's death. Wrapped up in furs, my sister and I looked like cuddly bears. We joined in the fun. But the cold eventually won as flurries of snowflakes sent us indoors to the warmth of the braziers, but not before I hit Henry on his ear with a snowball, dislodging his cap. He whirled around.

'What the… Eleanor!'

I saw him wrestling with his thoughts – should he retaliate with someone in my condition or not. But, with a peel of laughter and speed that surprised him, I had shot indoors before he could hurl his handful of snow.

Henry caught me puffing up the stairs. He backed me into a corner. My expanding belly was no barrier as he forced the snow down my neck. My shrieks brought everyone to see what the commotion was. With a fiendish chuckle, Henry picked me up despite my protests and carried me to the great hall.

'No! Henry, stop. Put me down!'

To get my own back, I shoved my freezing hands under his tunic.

'Ahhh! God's teeth Eleanor. Your hands are freezing!'

Sir Robert de Lucy Henry's squire who was standing with a goblet of mulled wine in his hand and a mischievous look in his eye, quipped, 'Oh, dear oh dear! Such questionable behaviour from the King and Queen of England!'

'Ah ha, de Lucy! Enough cheek from you.'

Henry and I pounced on him and thawed our freezing hands on his face and neck. Our attendants thought we had lost our senses.

Mulled wine soon warmed us as we collapsed into chairs or onto stools, still laughing and panting. Nilla and I were reminded of our childhood Christmases at Poitiers or L'Ombrière, though snow was almost unknown in the Aquitaine. Nonetheless, Christmastide was always a time for family festivities as much as a day to celebrate Christ's birth.

Our first Christmas day in England was a joyous event, a reprieve from the obligations to come. Later in bed, Henry and I reflected on his plans and dreams for our kingdom and our lands across the channel.

We talked of London. The contrast with Paris, full of students and learning combined with the piety of the French court of my first marriage, was profound. London was so different, full of burghers and commerce. The wide river Thames carried ships from as far away as Venice and Syria. The city was bustling, recovering from years of economic uncertainty, but many buildings were in poor repair after Stephen's reign, and many people were destitute from years of deprivation. It was the same in the provinces where castles, manor houses and whole villages had been destroyed. Barons' lands were covered in brambles where crops should be thriving. Abbeys and monasteries were hard pressed. There was still dissent among certain members of the nobility that spread to their serfs. We spoke long into the night. Henry said as soon as possible we must undertake a royal progress across the land, to restore law and order. The rebellions that took place between my Aquitaine vassals from time to time were mild compared to what had happened in England.

Stephen's invasion had thrown it into civil war. The barons had taken sides. There were those who supported Empress Matilda, others Stephen, and the unscrupulous played one hand off against the other. From prosperity, England had fallen into anarchy and ruin. Henry must repair the damage and unite the country. As he snuggled up to me, I said,

'Henry I will do everything in my power as your wife and queen to assist you. You have my promise. I will do my duty.'

Henry stroked my bulging stomach.

'I think you are already doing your duty.'

'Yes, but… I want to do more than just have babies. There is much I can offer.'

'Hmm! Indeed… you already do.

Henry chuckled lasciviously. There are times no matter how much I loved him; I wanted to swat him.

***

The New Year – 1155 I recorded – was full of anticipation. Henry and I made several trips across the Thames to survey the state of the Palace of Westminster. The outer structure was blackened and scarred, but, like the palace at Winchester, the damage was worse in certain sections of the building. The living quarters were the least affected, but the great hall and audience chambers needed rebuilding. Broken windowpanes had to be replaced with new glass to keep out the weather as well as the pigeons which were roosting everywhere. It will be an excellent opportunity to introduce the new Gothic architecture and to fit fireplaces, a novelty in Britain. This will be expensive. I will need to convince Henry, and Uncle Ralph for that matter, to loosen the Aquitaine purse strings. If Gothic influences are introduced, I will have to source architects and engineers from France and, as much as it sticks in my craw, from St Denis, Abbé Suger's old stronghold. His cruelty within the French court when I was Louis's young queen still haunts me. I hope he rots in hell!

I was relating my plans to Henry when he interrupted, 'Eleanor, I think you should attend to your condition rather than taking charge of the refurbishment of our London residence as originally planned.'

'Henry, being with child is not an illness. I can still give instructions. Dear God, I am not carrying bricks. Anyway, I asked Sir Robert to do a few errands for me. I have a list of stonemasons, glaziers, carpenters and other artisans I need to interview whom he can summon on my behalf, so stop fussing.'

'Darling, I need Robert to travel with me to Canterbury. I will appoint Thomas Becket to your services instead.'

'Becket, that sanctimonious fellow I met at Winchester? He is rather too intellectual for such pursuits is he not? What rapport would he have with carpenters or others of the craftsmen's guilds?'

'Get off your high horse, Eleanor. Becket is a Londoner, born and bred. He has an eye for fine workmanship and more importantly, knows how to bargain.'

I was still not so sure. I found Becket – odd.

Henry was impatient to leave for Canterbury. The weather, however, came to my aid, keeping him close at hand with Archbishop Theodore and others who were bound for Kent.

***

By early February, work was underway at Westminster. The pigeons were driven out once the new glass was in place. The kitchens though not damaged, needed renewal. New spits, pullies and grates were installed. I was impressed with the diligence of the men employed to rebuild and renovate. Now that peace was spreading throughout the land, they could follow their crafts without fear their work would be destroyed by another wave of rebellion.

During one of my visits to the palace, I met Becket. I had ascended, albeit slowly from the lower levels after inspecting the kitchens, to meet with stonemasons and brick layers who were working on the fireplaces. They had some interesting tiles they wanted to show me, sourced from an ancient excavation near the Thames, possibly Roman. I was admiring what the men were showing me when Becket interrupted my discourse. The two craftsmen froze as I turned towards him. Becket did not immediately recognise me. I begged his pardon to ask why he was interrupting my dialogue.

He looked down his nose at me and smirked, 'I believe I have priority here. I am King Henry's supervisor of the restoration of the Palace of Westminster, and I need to speak to these craftsmen.'

'Indeed! Well, *Master* Becket, as King Henry's wife and your queen, I am perfectly capable of making decisions regarding my future home. Your services today are no longer needed.'

I resumed my conversation with the artisans. Becket remained where he was, huffing and flapping his robes, so again I turned. 'Master Becket, you are dismissed.'

To my amazement, Becket stood rooted to the spot. The cheek of the man! 'You may leave.'

I understood that Thomas Becket had a quick and clever mind, as well as a deep understanding of English law, but I did not think he had much to do with women, especially one as erudite as I was. I think he found me intimidating, not knowing how to relate to a mere woman who could possess an intelligence better than his. My dear maid, Amaris reported hearing him sneer to a petty clerk that *I had been the errant, adulterous Queen of France and, if it were not for my dowry, the king would never have married me.* Unfortunately, there were clerics and others with connections to Île de France ready to gossip and spread misinformation. Becket would need to guard his tongue if he wanted to continue in our court.

Chapter 1: London

***

I had pride escorting Henry around Westminster when he arrived back from Canterbury. He was impressed with the progress made: in another four weeks or so, I thought we could move from Bermondsey. Our quarters were almost finished, the connecting galleries now had their parquetry floors repaired, and the fireplaces were completed where they were most needed. Although the weather outside was inclement, our carpenters and stonemasons could work safely within. Some of the public areas, like the great hall and grand staircase, would take longer. When Henry asked the whereabouts of Becket, I told him what had transpired, adding that, until the chancellor knew his place, he was not welcome in my company. Henry rolled his eyes but said he would speak to him.

***

Late February arrived with a snow and sleet. Thank God, Henry was in London preparing for Oxford and not on the road. Unable to sit still for a minute, it was frustrating for him, but I was enjoying having him to myself for a few days. It was most pleasant sitting together while he studied some maps and I embroidered for our new child. I had just put aside my stitching when I felt the familiar but unpleasant sensation in my back and lower abdomen. It had been niggling on and off all day. The baby's arrival was nigh, and despite my previous successful births, I still feared what could happen. Irrational I know, but too many women died in childbirth and the thought of William being without his Maman tore at my heartstrings.

With an intake of breath, I heaved myself out of my chair. Henry looked up as I made for the door.

'Are you off somewhere?'

Before I could answer, I was clutching a table as the first belt of severe pain shot through my body. The waters had not broken but I knew they were the next likelihood. I

The Lion and the Tigress

did not want to embarrass myself in front of my husband, but I could not move. Henry suspected something was amiss and was by my side in a flash.

'Do not touch me!' I hissed. White knuckled, I gripped the table.

'I will fetch Renée. Do not move.'

Henry tore through the door pursued by my groaning and curses.

By the time they got back to my side, I was in a puddle on my knees, moaning. Renée called for a litter. I yelled at her in dialect, *'I can walk!'*

Henry had gone white. I struggled up and lurched dripping towards my chamber, the whole palace privy to the beginning of my labour.

In the early morn of the 28th day of February in the Year of Our Lord 1155, I gave birth to our second son. We named him Henry, baby Hal. His father was beside himself with joy. Although ecstatic, I was exhausted. Baby Hal suckled at my breast, which gave me great comfort. Even euphoria, however, could not keep me awake. Henry smothered me in kisses and tenderness. I hoped he had forgiven my colourful language as I called every man in Christendom names indescribable during the baby's delivery. Sir Robert was heard to utter in amazement that one of my breeding should know such language. I admired Sir Robert's jocularity. His beloved wife Isabella died with their baby daughter when the child was born.

I awoke to Henry beside me smoothing my hair. 'My darling, how are you? I feared for you. I love you so much. Are you well?'

'Yes, Henry, I am well. Is he not a bonny boy?'

'Yes, he is beautiful like his mother.'

'Henry my love, what have you done to your fists?'

'I had a fight with a door.'

'Oh, Henry.'

'You were in such travail, and I could do naught but listen to your – your struggle. You know, I believe you can out swear my knights!'

What could I say? I felt embarrassed but consoled by his feelings and hoped his bruised and bloodied knuckles were not too painful.

It was heralded that Louis's new wife Constance had produced a daughter and I prayed the French court would allow her to keep her child. Henry and I having another son must be galling beyond belief for the French clergy, let alone Louis. It was a shame Abbé Suger, Louis' pious mentor was no longer of this world. He once accused me of being incapable of having sons because I was educated and thus unwomanly. How I would have loved to gloat.

Our new boy seems to resemble my side of the family. I saw much of Papa in him. I hoped this was so. William was suspicious, not sure whether he loved or hated his little brother. I reassured him I had enough love in my heart to share with many children.

***

The weather had improved, and a watery sunshine broke through the clouds. This was a relief because Henry's patience was wearing thin. He was eager to travel to meet with barons at Warwick, Oxford, and Coventry. Now he and his men could gallop out of London. In his usual manner, he would arrive rattling their portcullises before they knew what had struck them. I would very much like to accompany him, but even a mad woman would not take a newborn out in this fickle weather. Spring was approaching so I must be patient.

Nilla wished to return to the Aquitaine with her children. The cold of England, she complained, was chiselling her bones into buttresses. She had responsibilities regarding Raoul's estates which she must attend to as well. I would miss my little sister. She had become a supportive influence during all the stress and excitement of Henry's and my coronation though she mourned her husband. But I had to make another heartbreaking farewell. Renée was not coping with the cold and damp, either. Her age was catching up with her, and as much as it broke my heart, I understood I must send her home. I knew she would not want to leave me. She had been a mother to Nilla and me since our *Maman* died when we were tots, as well as having to juggle her daughter Clotilde, who in later years she had to leave in L'Ombrière to perform her duties on my behalf. To sail for home with Nilla would help her. She would be able to attend to my sister and her children and not worry about me. Millicent, William's nurse, was invaluable. She knew she could never supplant my little *Maman* and did not expect to because she honoured and respected Renée's standing within our family.

Henry was also sad Renée was leaving us, Nilla, and her children too. Although ready to ride west he waited to farewell them for my sake. We said goodbye on the Thames docks. They left on the tide, their ships billowing down the river. I struggled with my emotions till I returned to Bermondsey where I could no longer contain the sadness I felt. When would I see Renée again, feel her arms wrapped around me in comfort, encouraging me to prosper, reining in my impetuosity, caressing the hurts, chiding me? I knew I would see Nilla, but Renée was aging.

Henry calmed me in his strong embrace. He empathised because he had hated leaving Maud, who was his nurse and who had nurtured him. William was also sad. It was hard to explain why Renée had to go home as well as *Tante Nilla* and his cousins who had become his playmates.

***

After Henry set off to Oxford, I travelled across the Thames to check on the progress at Westminster. I was delighted that the palace was finally habitable. The repairs and renovations were not complete, but we could move away from the drafts and chills of Bermondsey which were getting everyone down.

Chapter 1: London

It was exciting to watch the carts, drays, wagons, and carriages transporting our belongings across the bridge. Larger items were ferried by barge. Treasured items from Poitiers and L'Ombrière could now come out of storage.

The kitchens were fired up. Henry and my quarters were aglow with magnificent Byzantium carpets. The luxurious tapestries from my Aquitaine homes were hung, their silken threads gleaming. Papa's old chests sat proudly in our chambers, being practical as well as beautiful. William and little Hal had a comfortable nursery with separate bed chambers for Millicent and our new wet nurse, Agnes, who looked after Hal at night.

One absolute indulgence was the installation of a bathing room adjacent to my bed chamber. It took quite a lot of explaining to the carpenters and the masons who installed the fireplaces. Amaris, who was well acquainted with these delectable bathhouses from her childhood in Constantinople, was indispensable. The result was not exactly a hamam more of a garderobe, but we had established a room in which to bathe all the same. Hot water for the tub would be heated from the fireplace within. Churls would not have to carry scalding water from the kitchens, a blessing for them as well as for me and my maids.

Becket, thank God, had been assigned duties with Archbishop Theodore, who was counselling him for the church hierarchy. Before they left for Canterbury, he attended me in my audience chamber. Henry must have insisted he apologise, not that he was looking contrite when the page let him into my chamber. I kept him waiting till I finished my writing and applied the pounce to my journal.

'Ah, Master Becket, and to what do I owe this unexpected pleasure?'

'I believe I was remiss during the repairs to Westminster. I was unaware who I was addressing on the day in question and may have spoken out of turn Your Ladyship, for which I must apologise.'

He stood as stiff as a pike staff. I believed the words practically stuck in his throat.

'Indeed. Well, as you now do know me, I am certain you will afford me greater respect in the future. Furthermore, Master Becket, I would be most careful about what else might spill from your lips regarding the Queen of England if you wish to remain in our court.'

I could see his brain ticking over, reddening as the realisation his malicious gossip had been overheard and reported. 'If there is nothing else... You are dismissed Master Becket.'

He gave a tight nod of his head and backed towards the door. I feared Becket may yet be trouble. He had delusions above his station.

***

I was increasingly intrigued by London. It thronged with people and bustled with activity, with languages spoken from places far and wide. It was much less austere than Paris, in fact some of the activities would make, I think, even naughty Grandfather William blush. London might not be the intellectual centre Paris was, but it had several famous schools as well as scores of churches. When I moved amongst the people, I found them generous with their love and respect.

One Sunday, on leaving the Abbey, Henry and I decided to walk, much to our guard's concerns. But I felt no threat from the people. A woman thrust a child at me. She told me he was named William, after our son.

I beamed at her showing my pleasure and pressed a coin into her hand. The people accepted my odd English even when I got my tongue tangled. It was a joy too that the Londoners did not judge me by innuendo, or misinformation regarding my so-called 'black' past. They were pleased that Henry and I were prepared to walk

Chapter 1: London

amongst them. I wished, though, that the narrow-minded members of the nobility and the church would look past gossip and rumours and judge me instead by my abilities and deeds. The Aquitaine, after all contributed generously towards the repair of the damage caused by England's civil war. Also, I wanted to be recognised by more than a breeder of heirs. I would like those men to accept that I was intelligent, but of course, that would mean admitting I was more so than most of them.

In France, Louis put me on a pedestal and then ignored me. Abbés Suger and Bernard de Clairveaux, thenceforth, knocked me down because I did not comply with their ideal of womanhood. To them I was the incarnation of Eve, or the wicked, salacious witch from the lascivious House of Aquitaine, the queen who committed incest with her uncle. Louis owes me the honour of speaking out against what he knew was a malicious lie, but it still suited his purpose and jealousy to say nought. Thank God, Henry believed my so-called adultery with my Uncle Raymond was manufactured to discredit me so the French could get their hands on the Aquitaine.

***

When Henry returned from his progress to the west, our court, William, baby Hal and I were housed in the comfort of Westminster. The great hall was close to completion with the warm odour of newly carved wood redolent in the air. It gave me great pride to take Henry on a grand tour from sculleries, kitchens, and servants' quarters to our own chambers. I kept the great hall for the final surprise. Sawdust had been swept away from its beautifully crafted parquet floors and the sun shone through the gleaming, diamond shaped glass of its new Gothic windows. It looked vast. When furnished it would be able to accommodate a great number. Two large fireplaces were installed, one on either side of the room. Minstrel galleries would soon be alive with music and song. Henry was amazed. As we descended the grand, staircase he asked,

'Can we afford such splendour?'

'Henry, I do not think you need to worry about the costs. After all, the Aquitaine has given mightily. I am ignoring Uncle Ralph's grumbling. My treasury is not his personal fiefdom. Anyway, we need to have one opulent abode for grand occasions and that should be here in London, our seat of power.'

'Hmm! There is a lot of imported stuff. The Thames was clogged with your ships from as far abroad as Venice and Byzantium.'

By now Henry was sounding like Uncle Ralph – annoyingly so!

'Look, Henry, if you want something to last it has to be of quality and excellence. That is why the glass comes from Venice. It was on the inventory.' Sometimes I wondered if he ever reads anything he signs. I continued, 'As Papa used to say, a thing of beauty comes at a price, so stop nagging.'

I needed to take a deep breath. We diverted to the nursery. Baby Hal was fast asleep in his crib. Agnes and I warned Henry not to wake him; there would be plenty of time for cuddling later.

We then went to watch William ride his pony. He looked so adorable with his chubby little legs sticking out on either side of the pony's rotund girth as one of the grooms led the little animal in circles near the stables. William nearly fell off with excitement when he saw Henry, so he trotted around one more time to show Papa how he could ride. Henry lifted him out of the saddle, throwing him into the air, with William squealing with pleasure, delighted to see his father after his weeks away from London.

We dined together simply without ado. With the children in bed, Henry moved to my chair where he stood behind me. His hands slid down the front of my bodice. I

Chapter 1: London

leant back as his mouth found mine.

My maids were dismissed. Undressed, we fell onto the bed, abandoned to our passion.

***

It was necessary for me to accompany Henry north. His barons and the people needed to get to know me. Also, as far as I was concerned, there were a few smouldering fires of intrigue about my past that needed to be extinguished. We travelled to Woodstock which was to become a significant household for us. Fortunately, it missed most of the attacks laid by or against Stephen. Woodstock was also convenient to Oxford.

I was a novelty. Everyone wanted to see Henry's wife. My reputation, glamour and wealth had travelled before me. God knows what Henry made of it. For someone who once complained about the number of gowns I possessed, he had become most particular in what I wore, never wanting me to appear in the same robe twice. He drove my maids and me mad hovering in the background before banquets to see what I had chosen. As *he* often looked as if his beautiful tunics had been thrown on him from beyond Normandy, this was more than annoying.

'Henry, as I go to a lot of trouble to look like the queen you expect me to be, at least you could try to look like the King of England.'

'What is wrong with what I look like? I do not have time to primp and preen like a woman.'

I shook my head and took Sir Robert aside suggesting he made sure Henry left his chamber looking neat and tidy rather than a beggar. Robert rolled his eyes and said he would do his best.

To make matters worse, Henry sometimes repaired his own clothes. Frugality was one thing, but his workmanship was a lot to be desired as he frowned with his tongue out the side of his mouth poking away with thread a league long and a needle more suited to stitching a hessian sack. My maids would do a far better job.

From Woodstock, we were to travel the many leagues north to York. Of course, Henry was impatient to arrive before he left.

'Henry, you have to make allowances for William and baby Hal. It takes time to attend to their needs.'

'Well, leave them at Woodstock with their nurses. You are slowing me down Eleanor.'

'I am still suckling Hal, for God's sake, Henry!'

'Can you not wean him?'

'No!'

'You are the most pigheaded, obdurate woman in Christendom.'

'And, of course, you are a saint! Well, you have a choice, Henry. I can continue to give your baby son my breast, or you can sleep in your own bed!'

I stormed out and slammed the door. I did not want to become pregnant again just yet but explaining that to Henry would lead to another argument because he wants more children – and fast. So, William and baby Hal travelled with us.

***

Sometimes it was easier getting blood out of a stone, than obtaining information from Henry. I was most interested in his plans to right the injustices caused by England's civil war. Eventually, after much nagging, he informed me he wanted to reinstate the kingdom's system of taxes made inequitable during Stephen's reign. Stephen used tax as a form of bribery. Non-compliant barons were extorted. They would lose land or goods, even castles, if they did not obey his irrational expectations to feed his greed. There were nobles too who supported Stephen's practices for their own benefits. Henry was determined to punish the lawbreakers.

As it happened, Henry had already accomplished

much with surprise visits to some of the barons favoured by Stephen, who had dispossessed nobles loyal to Empress Matilda. Stephen then granted Royal charters to his privileged followers. Thus, many unscrupulous barons had accumulated great wealth.

Henry was loved by those whose lands he had returned, or who were being over-taxed, but was as popular as the pox with those who had been caught out. The nobility who had followed Stephen and changed their allegiance from Empress Matilda to her unscrupulous cousin, were in for a nasty surprise. Henry was looking quite gleeful. But many took to hiding their wealth. Such behaviour Henry saw as a challenge to his authority.

Laws of the land were another of Henry's priorities. Under his great-grandfather and grandfather, English law was strict but fair. From the lowliest serf to the ruling hierarchy, people knew what was expected and respected the justice system. Stephen had manipulated the laws to suit himself, so the country fell further into anarchy.

The night before we left Woodstock, we were seated near the fire in Henry's chamber. Henry and Sir Robert were playing chess while I watched. Henry seemed to be leagues away in thought and not concentrating. He still avoided playing me, having not forgiven the thrashing I gave him when we first met at L'Ombrière. I whispered a move in Robert's ear, but Henry noticed. He yelled at me not to interfere. I ignored his rudeness and asked what was on his mind; after all, he was not paying attention to the game.

'The Earl of Rothley if you must know.'

'Are you going to elaborate, or do you expect me to read your mind?'

Henry sighed. 'The earl is one of the nobles to whom I want to pay a swift surprise visit.'

'Tell me more.'

'Rothley is despicable. He played both sides against the other during the civil war. It is purported he is sitting on a fortune of misappropriated goods. Also, he and his wife were involved in every iniquity conceived by Eustace up until his death. Now you are going to damn well slow me down.'

I chose not to fire back. I had an idea. 'What is Lady Rothley like?'

'Vain and ambitious, I hear.'

'Is she educated?'

Robert hooted as Henry continued, 'I have heard both husband and wife are incapable of stringing two words together in Latin.'

I fetched the flask and poured us more wine then sat back by the fire. I wondered what Lady Rothley had heard about me. Nothing good, I imagined, *The French Whore*, no doubt. Would she have heard about my learning? Probably. My wealth, yes. My features would have been bandied about. For once, my face could be useful. She could be afraid her husband might pay me too much attention. Would she find Henry's queen intimidating, or would she want to prove she was better? I wanted to do something to justify myself and my children's presence on this journey, which Henry seemed to be regretting, as well as to prove I could assess a situation for our benefit. I heard Henry and Robert push back their chairs. Robert excused himself, taking leave for his bed. Henry joined me by the fire, hitching up his tunic to warm his derriere.

'Henry, I have thought of a way to locate Rothley's stolen treasure without having to search for it or strike a blow.'

'Oh, yes?'

'Instead of looking sceptical you could listen.'

'All right, I am all ears.'

'Rather than arriving unannounced, I suggest you send a courier alerting Rothley that you will be attending his pleasure, accompanied by the queen and the princes, on whatever day we will be in his domains.'

'And give Rothley time to conceal everything,

including his horses?'

'I disagree. I guarantee Lady Rothley will deck her table with gold plate, her hall with expensive furnishings, dress her servants in ornate livery, and lay on the finest of furniture, furs, and drapery in our quarters. She herself will be dripping in jewellery and wearing her finest gown.'

'Hmm! I will think about it.' He dropped his tunic and moved to my chair pulling me out of it.

'Come on, I can think of better things to do with our time.' He kissed me and pressed me to him. Would he ever take me seriously?

***

After riding beside me to Leicester when I was kept none of the wiser, Henry did employ my method. Just as I had predicted, Lady Rothley had flown into a tizz, and had prepared a sumptuous banquet, the table more ornate than the Pope's. She appeared festooned in jewellery and draped in a gaudy robe. I wore a simple black velvet gown with a gold beribboned girdle. My white veil was held in place by a plain gold diadem. Lady Rothley was short in stature, a beady-eyed woman with a pinched face, while her husband was of a stocky build with a paunch that had seen much good living. Both fawned over us in an obsequious manner.

During the banquet while the pair grovelled, Henry's men followed a devised plan to take control of the poorly manned castle. Henry appeared calm during the evening and was his delightful Plantagenet self. I too am adept at seeming charming regardless of what might be going on in my head. I noticed Lady Rothley glance at me from time to time not sure as to how to behave towards me, as well as keeping an eye on her husband's reactions.

I had much to lose if my tactics failed during this operation. Henry would never trust my judgement again, so I was nervous, though well practiced at concealing my emotions when necessary. There were no sounds

The Lion and the Tigress

of anything untoward from beyond the great hall. Sir Robert did excuse himself briefly and returned smiling to the table uttering what a beautiful night it was. A signal perhaps? Henry squeezed my hand.

The Rothley's had consumed a considerable amount of the Bordeaux wine Henry had gifted to them – his clever idea not mine – and so went merrily to their beds unaware of what was occurring around their bailey and castle walls.

By morning, the castle was ours and I breathed a sigh of relief. The expressions on the Earl and his Lady's faces next morn were something to behold when they realised their past misdeeds were discovered and their castle overwhelmed while they snored under the influence of one of Bordeaux's best vintages.

Stolen goods were recovered, returned to our coffers and an appropriate tax was applied to the Rothley estate. The Earl was accused of adverse possession, *Novel Disseisin*. A baron, Lord Reyland Drury, had petitioned our courts to recover his land and to be granted damages to compensate for the wrongful seizure. He had been divested of his properties during Stephen's rule by Eustace, who then bestowed them on Earl Rothley. Documents discovered in Rothley's quarters were found to be titles to the estates owned by Lord Reyland. Rothley and his wife were arrested. Rothley's grovelling protestations and his wife's hysteria fell on deaf ears as they were led away in chains.

I felt satisfaction Henry used my methods. After all, I was brought up in the Aquitaine where meticulous planning and clever tactics are preferable to bloody battles. That was why I was an excellent chess player. As far as Lady Rothley and her husband were concerned, they deserved the judgement they received. I felt a certain thrill my scheme was successful. Henry rewarded me with a beautiful ruby and emerald ring.

Word was soon heralded amongst other rebels to be

Chapter 1: London

on their guard. By the time Henry's unexpected arrivals had searched their manor houses, they knew not what to expect and gave up what was illegally gained from those loyal to Matilda, right down to their wives' earrings.

But this was only one narrow strip of the country. There was much more to be attended throughout the kingdom.

***

We made our way north. York was inspiring with its magnificent cathedral and early Roman influences. Archbishop Roger was an astute man of high intelligence. Henry, he found to be of a similar intellect, but was surprised to find me equally well-educated. Even so, I was relegated to the background except when 'decoration' was needed, much to my disgust. So, I concentrated my time on William and Hal.

After Henry had completed his many meetings in York with local barons and clergy, it was time to return to London. A week before we left, I suspected I was carrying another child. I woke one morning, ate a couple of mouthfuls of my breakfast and had to dash to the privy. My poor maids panicked. I knew it was going to be a long miserable ride back to London without Renée's potion to ease my mornings and Amaris unable to procure the ingredients. By Woodstock, I said enough was enough, but Henry insisted I do my best to continue. It sounded like he was unsympathetic, but he cradled me when I was feeling wretched each morning. The Palace of Westminster was a relief as we approached the Thames.

***

Henry had taken wing towards the west where there was trouble on the Welsh border, so I had time on my hands. I gazed at my journal, procrastinating. I was out of sorts. My stiletto lay on my desk. I was absentmindedly stroking the bejewelled hilt when the Italian Cardinal who gave it to me flashed into my mind. He was an unusual man for a Prince of the Church, far more enlightened I seem to remember. He did not look down on me. Louis had received the Oreflamme of France at the Cathedral of St Denis to carry to Jerusalem, and Cardinal Benedetti was one of many high-ranking prelates in attendance sent by the Pope.

We were discussing the up-and-coming Crusade when he said, 'I see Milady you are a true Crusader by the jewelled cross pinned to your gown but what other protection do you have other than God when you venture into Outremer?'

I think I replied, 'I will be well protected by my men.'

That night at the banquet celebrating the Crusader knights who had pledged to carry the Cross of Christ, the Cardinal surprised me by giving me this long slender blade.

'And why, Your Eminence would you be giving me a *misericordia*?'

'Ah, my dear Lady Eleanor, more for your defence than to dispatch the mortally wounded. But in Italy we call it a stiletto.'

'Indeed, is that so? Quite a musical sounding name for a beautiful blade. I will, therefore, also call it thus – a stiletto.'

I smiled at the memory and thought, as I returned it to the scabbard on my belt, 'I have not slain anyone with it, but it has certainly broken the seal of many letters.'

***

I was resenting this pregnancy. Somehow my plans for another child did not work. I conceived whilst still suckling Hal. I was not stupid, I knew breast feeding was hit and miss, but I supposed I did not believe it would happen to me. As much as I loved Henry, and as much as I found making these babies an exquisite pleasure, I wanted more time to look normal without another bulge.

Chapter 1: London

I missed Renée, I was tired of this cold gloomy climate and disappointed that Henry rarely consulted me regardless of my success over the Rothley estate. Too often I was finding myself like the 'ornament' I was on Île de France. At banquets and royal occasions, there I was with some dribbling, panting, overzealous baron or exulted bishop, trying to be charming and witty. Too often I found them fools.

I was also finding some of Henry's actions condescending. For instance, he gave me several manors, but the profit from the estates went directly into the revenue of the English treasury.

So, I challenged him. 'Henry, I applaud your generosity in granting me these estates, but I see it does not include the income they produce. May I ask why?'

'Treasury matters are the responsibilities of men.'

'Oh, really! As I can successfully rule my Duchy and lands from Poitou to Gascony, I am more than capable of running a couple of farms. And I should be allowed to decide how *my* income is best distributed.'

'Eleanor, you already countersign all transactions from the Aquitaine treasury, so stop complaining. Anyway, you are hardly short of a sou.'

'What is that supposed to mean?'

'That I have better things to do with my time than arguing over petty nonsense!' Then he stomped off muttering. 'Women!'

My tisane mug bounced off the closing door.

***

Boredom drove me to wander around like a lost soul. I ended up in Henry's quarters. I had ordered the churls to light fires in his grates to control the damp. When checking they had not stacked the wood too high, because we did not want to burn the palace down, I found myself by a long trestle table Henry used as a desk. Stacked on shelves behind in higgledy-piggledy rows were scrolls of velum. I knew I was snooping but I could not contain my curiosity. One by one I rolled them out to read. They were not in Henry's hand; these documents were far older than our reign. I discovered they were the original scrolls of the Common Laws of England. Henry was working diligently to reinstate these laws, but on discovering how inaccurately these scrolls were scribed, I was worried. The Latin in some cases was crude and misspelt. This meant some laws could be misinterpreted or twisted to suit a clever advocate. Papa was pedantic when Nilla and I were taught our Latin. We had to be perfect not only in speaking the language but writing as well. When Papa employed tutors, they continued to hammer it into our heads.

At last, I had a project of interest. Eagerly, I collected velum, ink, and quills. I did not make mistakes. Not only would I rewrite the scrolls in correct Latin, but I would also be able to increase my knowledge of English Common Law.

As I progressed, though, I had a horrible thought that, by correcting the Latin, I might be altering how the law was interpreted. Cicero sprang to mind, but how would an ancient Roman advocate apply to Britain? The Romans left six hundred years ago. I found I was arguing with myself. Was there a copy of Cicero in Westminster? I doubted it. Why did I not bring mine from Poitier? I consulted our chaplain. He thought Bishop Belmeis of London might have one. I requested he find out if he could borrow it for me? He looked at me strangely, maybe thinking my condition was sending me out of my wits.

Bishop Belmeis had just what I wanted and said I could keep it. Not that Cicero solved my dilemma. I recalled Papa discussing with me and a bored yawning Nilla how Cicero *articulated an early abstract idea of rights based on law and custom.*

I continued my work on English Common Law, deciding in the end that corrected Latin would not change

Chapter 1: London

the law; instead, it would clarify the intent, making it simpler to make a judgement.

After rewriting all twelve scrolls, I was mightily pleased with myself. They were well penned with nary a blot or mistake. My enterprise taught me much about English Common Law. I piled the corrected scrolls, neatly rolled and beribboned, next to the originals which I stacked in an orderly manner. I disliked mess. All I had to do now was face Henry who, I was told, had reached Winchester.

My task kept my mind occupied so I did not worry about this child who would arrive sometime after Christmas, but I was neglecting Hal and William who were demanding my attention. It was time to be Maman again.

***

Henry returned in his usual pandemonium of exhausted horses and men. I was so pleased to see him.

'Mmm!' he said. 'God, you have expanded. A man cannot get his arms around you, and I was hoping for more than a cuddle. Can you order something I need to bathe?'

'I suggest cold water.'

'Very funny.'

I sent for a repast to be served in Henry's quarters. He reappeared smelling of soap. I poured wine for us both. Henry propped his feet on the fireplace and grinned,

'You look like a galley in full sail.'

'When are you planning to ride to Windsor?'

'Anon.'

'Tell me about the Welsh border? I overheard Sir Robert say some of the fighting was brutal.'

'Pendragon is a cunning, conniving, swine. He employs no rules of chivalry in warfare, and his men attack willy-nilly. We lost a few knights, and the bastard knocked my standard to the ground.'

'What!'

'Calm down. The standard was trampled and some of my men were a bit confused because I was in the middle of the melee. A few thought I had gone down with the pennant.'

'Oh no! No – you could have been killed.' My horrified expression startled Henry.

'Oh, my darling. Look, I am here I am not hurt! Jesus Mary and Joseph!'

I had dropped my goblet as I clutched my chair, a feeling of dread coursing through my body as wine splashed everywhere. Henry ignored the puddle as he knelt before me, consoling me.

'It would take more than a Welsh rat to knock me off my horse.'

Maybe it was my condition, but the panic I experienced after the horror of the crusade can, without warning, assert itself if sparked by familiar memories. I found myself shaking, clutching his head to my bulging stomach, my fingers locked in his still damp curls. I could no longer speak.

Henry's muffled voice beseeched me, 'Darling, let me stand. You are suffocating me.'

'I could not live without you.'

'My darling, I do not have so much as a scratch. Owain lost men too. Next time we clash, I will not be surprised by his guerrilla tactics.'

'Henry, surely diplomacy would be a better option than trying to kill each other. Talk is less lethal, after all.'

'Eleanor,' he laughed. 'As far as I know, we have no common language. I think he only speaks Welsh.'

'Then why in God's name do not you ride with an interpreter before I kill you for not using your wits?'

My fear for Henry's life turned to frustration. While I sulked, the children were brought to their father by their nurses. Henry played with the boys, though he could be a little impatient with them. We dined together as a family, then when the boys went to their cots, we planned our journey to Windsor. I managed to convince him to rest for a week before leaving, to give him time to read missives that had arrived from all over the countryside, as well as from Normandy. I was surprised he had not noticed the extra pile of scrolls next to the old ones now tidily stacked behind his trestle. In case he flew into a temper at my interference, I decided I would confess after Christmas.

***

The Christmas court was a combination of festivities and services. The service was conducted by Archbishop Theodore, who seemed not as sprightly as when I first met him. He joined us for our Christmas feast. William enjoyed the celebrations. Henry gave him a saddle for his pony. Much to our amusement he calls his pony 'Horsey' after his beloved felt toy, never far from his possession. Hal, at eleven months old, slept though the service – a relief. Babies, I had found, could not stay still if awake and found prayer boring.

Through the Bishop of Westminster, I located a magnificent volume of Tacitus's *Historiae* for Henry so he could indulge in his enduring curiosity about Roman history. He was delighted, then with a quirky look on his face, he said he thought his present might have been a volume of Cicero. Oh dear! Although I had said naught about the scrolls, I had a feeling he had discovered my enterprise after all. I had left the copy of Cicero next to them. I blushed to the edge of my veil.

His gift to me was a bejewelled Celtic Cross hanging from a simple black ribbon. I donned it immediately. Everyone admired it. My maids were given fine linen fabric and Henry and I gave dear Robert a new saddle also. His old one had seen better days. He was constantly repairing it, but the last straw was when he lost a stirrup on the return from Wales.

***

By the end of the day, everyone was sated, some dozing, including the archbishop. Henry was reading his new tome. I was thinking of taking myself to my bed, but the thought of leaving the warm chamber to venture down cold galleries to my quarters was unappealing. Windsor was mightily draughty. Today, it had not snowed, but a cold sleety wind was blowing through every crack and crevasse in the castle and dripping water had turned into stalactites. Sir Robert rose to put more wood on the fire stirring Archbishop Theodore who begged Henry to take his leave, thanking us for our kind hospitality. After he left, Henry told my maids they were dismissed. Amaris said she would repair to my bed chamber to make sure it was warm and would wait to undress me.

By now, Robert, Henry and I were the only members of the Christmas party left to toast ourselves. I shooed Robert off to his bed. I had to admit to Henry about the scrolls, so it might as well be while he was in a benign mood. I blurted out my confession. Carefully he closed his *Tacitus,* leaving a ribbon in the page where he was reading. Without speaking, he looked at me, his face expressionless. If not so cumbersome, I would have been hopping from one foot to the other. Henry took a heavy breath and exhaled with deliberation.

'So, it was not some ghost of scribes past.'

He was about to reopen his book as I huffed at his gibe. 'Well?'

'You write very prettily in excellent Latin.'

He turned a page. If he had not been cradling such an exquisite tome, I would have thrown a log at him. He looked up and saw my expression.

'By Our Lady, I suppose, Eleanor, you are now an expert advocate in British Law!'

His eyes twinkled. He was teasing me, and I was not in the mood. I pouted,

'I learnt much. Yes!'

'I can see next time I am away, I had better make certain

you are gainfully employed.'

'Next time you alter, improve or introduce a new law, you can consult me... for a small fee.'

Henry shut his book and stood grinning, ignoring my humour. He asked when I thought this baby was due, totally changing the subject.

'Soon.'

I flounced towards the door, and he caught up with me, turning me around and passionately kissing me. His child came to my rescue with a hefty kick.

'God's teeth, it's wearing boots.'

***

Just a week into the New Year, on the 6th of January in the Year of Our Lord, 1166, I gave birth. When I pushed the babe from my body, and they said it was a girl, I was worried about Henry's reaction. There was no need – he was thrilled. He cuddled her, smothered her in kisses, and told her he hoped she would grow up to be as beautiful and clever as her mother. She looked at him wisely as babies appear to do. Henry was besotted. We called her Matilda after his mother.

William was happy with her. Hal was too young to care, but he grinned his two-toothed smile and grabbed at her with his pudgy hands. While I wrote, she slept in her crib beside me. But I had a lump in my throat as I remembered Marie and Alix, my lost daughters from my first marriage, whom I had never so much as held. What did they know about their mother? Nothing good I suspected. The French court and Louis, I feared, would not be truthful, or pleasant if asked. Now they were older I had thought of writing to them, to tell them of the love I carried in my heart, to tell them about William, Hal, and Matilda. I put this thought to Henry who, although sympathetic, believed such an action would only stir up trouble, so instead I dreamt of a miraculous day when we might meet.

At the end of the week, we were to travel to Wallingford Castle. The Constable reported problems within the shire. He suspected the local sheriff could be misusing revenues from crown lands for his benefit. I was now over Matilda's birth, and so well enough to ride.

***

It had been weeks since I held a quill. Why? Oh why, oh why? To write his name was more than hell. God took my William, my baby boy. Why? Was this punishment for loving Geoffrey, or Abraham? But why Henry, Hal and Matilda? Within my womb there was another. Would I live through this birth? Terror wracked me. I was being rebuked by God.

I knew not for how long; I could not eat. I heard voices outside my head, like eerie echoes.

'You must let him go, Milady. We must bury him, Eleanor. Milady, he is in God's arms. He is chosen.'

In my mind's eye, I saw Henry, weeping. In my head, I heard screaming.

'Where is Horsey?'

'He cannot go without Horsey. William cannot not sleep without Horsey. He will be cold without his Maman. Do not take him from me. He is frightened of the dark.'

But they took him. I could not remember who. They placed him at the foot of a man he does not know in Reading Abbey. Even Henry did not know his grandfather, Henry Beauclerc. Will he look after William? Why does God hate me so much? Am I so evil I must be punished like this? My maids, I think, told me I fainted and had to be helped to the carriage.

Robert came. Amaris was talking to me. I feared to touch Hal or Matilda in case God took them too. Someone, Matthias our physician maybe, told me Henry grieved also. Was he in pain like me? Was his heart cleaved into pieces? My head ached. I banged it against a stone wall. Blood poured down my face and soaked my hair, hair I tried to tear from my head. The wailing in my head echoed across the universe.

Robert told me I had to go to Henry. He mourned and needed me. Amaris tried to raise me from my corner, but I was trapped in anguish, rocking, rocking. But Robert said it was imperative I go to him. His grief was as great as mine.

Amaris and Marion half carried me to my bed. Some days later, I knew not when really, I begged Henry to forgive me for not helping or holding him when he needed me, so bound was I inside my own hell.

Henry was with his justiciars. Ruling had to go on, writs signed, charters issued, laws renewed, and passed. I allowed Marion, Celeste, Millicent, and the others to dress me. They told me Amaris was exhausted. Except for this new swelling, my laces had to be tightened. The gown was plain white. I wore Henry's beautiful cross. The bracelet of the lion that celebrated William's birth, I could not touch any more. Lucille walked with me down the gallery to Henry's audience chamber. She sent a page to announce I wanted to speak to my husband.

The door opened. All the men around Henry almost knocked over their chairs to rise as I entered alone. I excused myself, requesting their indulgence to interrupt their conference to speak to the king. He dismissed them, telling them he would send for them anon.

Henry looked gaunt. God knows what I looked like. He put his arms around me. Neither of us spoke. There were no more tears. We had run dry.

I whispered, 'Forgive me for neglecting you.'

He held me tightly. 'There is nothing to forgive. That you have regained your wits is all that matters. I feared for you. I feared I had lost you as well.'

'When they told me Papa had died, I thought that was the worst moment of my life. Then when Louis took Marie and Alix away, particularly Alix, I was mad with grief.

I grieved for your father. But nothing, nothing prepared me for the death of our little boy.'

'Me neither, Eleanor, me neither.'

'Henry, I hate God. Now I will truly rot in hell, but it can never be as bad as the hell in which I now live. I have tried to pray. But I cannot. I cannot accept this awful decree. I should confess my hatred, but I do not want to be told this is God's will. I will never, ever accept God's cruelty.'

Henry was silent, speechless at my heretical protests. When he found his voice, he said

'All I pray, is that one day we will heal.'

I was hoping that, by finding the courage to write it all down, I would scourge my soul of this aching pain. My confessor, Brother Peter, I could not face.

Chapter 2. Regency

Henry must return to Normandy. His mother had couriered missives detailing governance problems only Henry's presence could solve. I knew he did not want to leave me, but it was paramount that he calmed a potential rebellion amongst his vassals on the Vexin border, as well as threats from damn Louis, who still could not forgive us for marrying.

I was surprised but honoured he was making me his regent during his absence. He said he would be back well before our next child's predicted arrival in early Autumn. He believed I was well enough to take on the responsibility. Was he more perceptive than I thought, wanting to keep me busy, so my mind would not dwell on William? It helped. Not that my grief was obliterated, far from it, but I now had a purpose, a resolve to follow my destiny as my Papa had trained me. All my copying of the laws of the land would now hold me in good stead.

So, I picked myself up – scraped myself off the dungeon floor would be a better description – to fulfil my role as Queen of England. The onus entrusted on me gave me a feeling of renewal. At the bottom of my being, I still questioned God's will, but I was ready to move my sorrow into that special recess in my heart reserved for Papa and Henry's father.

Like Henry, I mounted my horse to travel where I was needed. I wore gowns to disguise my condition. I wanted to be taken seriously and not be condescended to because I was carrying another child. It was necessary, though, to leave Hal and baby Matilda with their nurses. I would miss them. It was hard being queen and Maman at times. Trying to put on a smile, I reassured them that I would be back soon. They cried as I rode away.

***

To begin with I was a novelty. The general population who, from time to time caught a glimpse of their king as he rode through their towns and villages, were not used to seeing Henry's queen. I roused people's curiosity, so, instead of riding through at speed, on the spur of the moment one day I dismounted. It threw my guards into a panic, but I never felt threatened or had concern for my safety. My muttering guards were forced to follow behind, hands on their sword hilts, eyes on the backs of their heads.

I found a word here and there enabled me to discover the mood of our people; how they were faring, how they were treated by their overlords and sheriffs, if crops were thriving and many other small details. Word spread I showed an interest in the occupations and wellbeing of ordinary townsfolk, as well as serfs. To listen to tales of their lives and concerns I found rewarding. It shook me out of my self-pity.

One day, in Lincoln, when I was on my way to my accommodation for the night, I was stopped by a woman who looked wretched, not unlike the poor creature near Winchester when I first set foot in England. She grabbed my sleeve. In her arms she held a tiny mewling babe. I thought of giving her alms and moving on, but something, I could not say what, stopped me.

'Milady, thou hast lost thy son. Let me give thee mine. I owe my freedom to thee and Lord King Henry, allow me to give thee this gift.'

I froze. My heart felt it was being gripped in a vice. The sacrifice this poor soul was ready to make for me, privileged beyond any of these people's wildest imaginings was incomprehensible. Regardless of my accented English, I had to answer.

'Why? Do not thee love thy child?'

'Aye, that ist why I desire to give him to thee.'

This offer plunged my mind back to memories of

Chapter 2: Regency

William that I was trying to suppress. It was hard to control my emotions.

'Thy name, what dost they call thee?'

'I be Winifred, Milady.'

'Mistress Winifred, there be no pain so bad if a child be taken. Our conscience canst not take from thy loving arms this babe. Some other way we will find. Where dost thou reside?'

Winifred hung her head, too embarrassed, I think, to tell me. Most likely the streets. I arranged for her to be taken into the refuge of the church. It was obvious she was trying to give me her baby because she could not afford to look after the child. A gold coin, I realised was not enough, only temporary. Winifred and those like her needed more.

Outside Lincoln there was a Dominican Abbey run by nuns. I needed to speak to the abbess. Many orders took in abandoned or orphaned children, but were any of them providing training for mothers to work as bondmaids such as seamstresses, laundresses, or cook's assistants where they could be employed in a household? This would enable them to support their children, who could also be trained for useful lives in service or the church.

***

By the time I reached York, I had made it my business to visit as many abbeys and convents as I could along my route. I spoke with the abbesses. They all thought my idea possible if they had the funds to achieve my objectives. I explained I would provide them with alms to put my plans into practice. When some appeared dubious, I said with heartfelt experience, no mother should be separated from her child, citing my own anguish when Marie and Alix were taken from my care and of course, William's death.

Many of the abbesses were of noble birth, sadly some the result of brutal marriages, some widowed. Several had little ones whom they had lost to the cruel system of our society in which their status placed them. As a result, their children, especially their daughters, were brought up in households where they were betrothed to a young heir or used to barter peace between warring nobles or, more often for their dowries.

Reverend Mother Joan was one such woman. We sat in her small cosy office, and she told me a little of her life.

'I was married without my consent with no say in who my husband was to be. He was a cruel tyrant. I was very young, only fourteen years old. He beat me and I was far from home. After two years I could take my life no longer, so I ran away. Near our estate there was this convent run by the Dominicans. Praise God, the community took me in.'

I nodded as she went on with her tale.

'I came with some education and set my mind to increase my knowledge. The simple life of devotion suited me. I continued to learn and eventually I was chosen Mother Superior. But my decision came at a price, because I was forced to abandon my baby daughter to others.'

She dabbed the tears from her eyes and took a hasty swallow of her tisane.

'Mother Joan, I understand. I was married at thirteen to Louis Capet. It mattered not that I was Queen of France. My French daughters were taken from me at birth. I never held them.'

Mother Joan took my hand and gave it a sympathetic squeeze.

'In many ways our lives have similarities. You found compassion within the walls of this convent. I ran into the arms of others.'

She did not condemn me, for which I was grateful.

'I believe I am being punished for my adultery, in the cruellest possible way, by having my little boy taken from me by God. Would I do the same thing again if I were as miserable as I was married to King Louis? Who can say?'

Chapter 2: Regency

We sat quietly engulfed in the events of our past.

'Lady Eleanor, I like your idea to help women like Winifred, I fully support your plan. I will put your wishes to my sisters. I promise assistance should they agree, and I see no reason why they would not. But will Lord King Henry approve? Because no matter how generous we feel, a sizable distribution of alms will be necessary to put this scheme into action.'

'That will not be a problem. I have access to the treasury of the Aquitaine with or without the king's approval.'

Mother Joan looked surprised. I was not about to enlighten her that I had my grandmother's fortune, unbeknownst to Henry. Should he object, I could still go ahead. But I did not think he would disapprove.

***

My next destination was York, where I was welcomed again by the archbishop. It was good to relax and leave my horse in the stables, to catch up with my journal and read my awaiting missives.

Henry was making progress in Normandy. He hoped to return to England in the next few months. He asked about my health. He sent his love. I sat in my quarters within Archbishop Roger's palace in a warm glow.

The next epistles had seals I did not recognise. Their contents were from two different sources relating to the same disturbing subject. The King of Scotland, Malcolm, had been deposed and imprisoned by his nephew, David, who was aged fourteen or fifteen years. Henry had mentioned David was one of the nastiest, most evil young men in Christendom. King Malcolm was respected by his people, though at times a thorn in Henry's side. His nephew, however, was a cruel barbarian.

The author of one of the letters, Douglas of Stirling, feared Malcolm could be assassinated by his nephew, and this would throw Scotland into civil war. The other letter was from the Bishop of Melrose Cathedral, in which he said the same thing, adding the king was being held in the dungeons of Melrose Castle. I had to think and plan carefully. I was not travelling with a large army except for my loyal Praetorian guard and a contingent of Henry's men, all excellent knights, but that was all. I spoke to my most senior knight, Antoine.

I informed him it was imperative to have Malcolm restored to his throne and David brought to justice. Did he think it was possible to surprise the young usurper? He thought the chance was slim. Together we assembled my men. Without mincing words, I told them what had transpired and the urgent need to free King Malcolm. I said I had an idea at the back of my mind and would appreciate their opinions when I had my thoughts in order. I requested they be patient, even though we needed to move to cover the distance from York to Melrose on the Scottish border as swiftly as possible.

We left at dawn the following morn. Except for Lucille who rode as well as I did, I insisted the rest of my maids remained in York. Amaris was most unhappy, but she and the others were not horsewomen. I decided to ride a different mount leaving highly visible Rebel in York in favour of a bay destrier. Like Henry, we moved at speed, and, like the men, Lucille and I rode astride our horses. We covered many leagues in good time.

We spent the second night with the Archbishop of Durham, then onto a monastery short of the Scottish border. The monks there were most informative regarding Melrose Castle. The crusade all those years ago might have been a disaster, but I learnt much from our wily foes. I agreed with Antoine we could not make a surprise attack on the fortified castle where David was lauding it over Malcolm's subjects. My men and I gathered around a long table in the refectory. A map of Melrose Castle from the good monks' archives was rolled out in front of us, and I explained my plan.

I told my men I would make our arrival formal, a

Chapter 2: Regency

royal visit. With much pomp, we would follow a courier heralding England's queen. While I was using my well-practiced charm on David, a selected group of men would take up strategic positions throughout the castle. I was hoping my over-lauded 'beauty' would distract the young upstart's followers enough to allow this operation to be easy. Antoine, however, said he would not let me out of his sight, and Roger concurred, so I agreed they and Lucille would always be in my company. I couriered missives to the Bishop of Melrose and to Stirling, giving them enough information about our strategy, without exposing our overall scheme should the epistles fall into the wrong hands. Side saddles were now found for Lucille and me to arrive "regally".

***

It was not exactly a fanfare I received. The Scots have a peculiar squawking instrument they prefer to use for ceremonial occasions, sounding a little like a shawm. By this means I was greeted. I hoped the egotistical young David would think my formal arrival would legitimise his position. I was welcomed into the great hall of the castle where there was quite a to-do as the young upstart's followers and minions fell over each other to welcome or get a glimpse of the infamous Eleanor. It was one of the few times I felt smug about my reputation.

David, I noted, did not seem to know whether he was supposed to pay homage or act as an overlord. We progressed down the great hall to the end of a long trestle table where two throne-like chairs were placed. The pipsqueak sat in the most ornate. If the situation were not so dire, it would have been laughable; I am tall, David short. I towered over him by almost a hand span. He was not unpleasant to look at. His hair was straight, dark in colour, falling to his shoulders, but his eyes were a hard, cold, greyish blue. His mouth had a sneering twist; trustworthy, I perceived him not. He wore the far too large, usurped crown. I had difficulty keeping amusement from my face, because, if not for his ears, it would have sat round his neck like a dog's collar.

The hall was crowded. It was difficult hearing his conversation, so I smiled in my most beguiling, eyelash fluttering manner. Speaking with him was difficult. I have no Gaelic and his English was uttered in such a strange accent it made mine sound perfect. His Latin was most ill. But in some ways, this worked well in my favour. He was so busy trying to impress me, with the people around fawning and gawping, my men outside were able to move easily throughout the castle.

We had timed our arrival for late after the noon day bells, so my men could strike in failing light. Out in the bailey, they milled around as if preparing their horses to be stabled. At the first opportunity, they moved to take over the battlements from the soldiers left as sentinels, and so on throughout the castle, working their way on silent feet to the dungeons. Malcolm's guards were slurping their gruel. I was told by Simeon that they knew not what had befallen them. Malcolm was released and removed to the stables where horses were readied should he need to flee.

We had agreed on a pre-arranged signal whereby Simeon would enter the great hall with a missive, supposedly from Henry, when their work was done. I was getting anxious. I felt I had been making small talk to this idiot boy for hours. Torches were lit and food was presented, but apart from the fresh salmon, was heavy. A fiery drink was served which I did not like. One sip almost took my breath away. Lucille caught my eye and gave a reassuring nod.

Then to my relief, the far doors opened. Simeon begged the indulgence of the guard and made his way towards me, managing to look like a weary courier. Roger, Antoine, and I glanced from one another. With a quick nod, Simeon addressed me in Langue d'Oc as he held out a scroll. I broke the seal, scanned the page, and feigned concern.

'I do apologise, Lord David, but I need to prepare to leave first thing on the morrow as urgent tidings from my Lord King Henry need my attention.'

'Lady Queen Eleanor, I insist on escorting you. We Scots are not the barbarians some below our borders think we are.'

As I rose to leave, I gave David the most cloying, simpering smile I could muster. I had little choice but to tower along beside him. Less than a yard from my hem walked Roger and Antoine, with Lucille a step behind. All of them had their hands readied on sword or dagger. Mine was neatly disguised in the folds of my gown, my right hand grasping its hilt.

The doors were opened. As soon as Lucille had stepped through, they were slammed shut and bolted, letting no-one follow. I was surrounded by my men. David realised he had been trapped. He made a grab for me but faced my blade.

'Little boy, unless you want to be skewered like a pig on a spit, I suggest you step out of my way.'

Roger grabbed him. In the ensuing struggle, his usurped crown fell from his head to be collected by its rightful owner, who had appeared from the stables. He was accompanied by Douglas of Stirling, the Bishop of Melrose Cathedral, and others loyal to the King of Scotland, who had answered my letters. A frightful racket was going on within the great hall, as David swore while trying to break free from Roger's powerful grip. His struggle was fruitless as he was manacled.

'Now you show your true colours, you black witch. Satan's whore is too good a title for you.' David bellowed.

'Lord David, it is hard for me to comprehend the notion that sent you on this foolish quest to commit treason against your anointed king. I pray God will forgive you.'

His baying followers were also arrested. Next day, David and his supporters were tried for treason and executed, a sorry end to a foolish young man.

I was housed most comfortably in the bishop's palace where Lord Malcolm and I met formally. I found him likable. He had more wisdom than Henry gave him credit for. I did not think he would give England too many problems in the future. He was full of praise for the clever plan that restored his crown with little loss of blood. He swore to be *'My Liege Lord of Life and Limb'*. I wondered what Henry would think of that. I could not wait to tell him about our incursion to restore King Malcolm to his throne. It would also give me joy to discuss my plans for religious orders to take in needy mothers and children. We would have much to share.

***

In York, we were welcomed back, our victory celebrated by Archbishop Roger. He said he had worried about me galloping into a situation which was, he thought dangerous. My safe return with my brave men was an answer to his prayers.

After I luxuriated in a tub of soothing warm water, Amaris wrapped me in towels while she attended to my wet hair.

I had not stopped burbling on about our swift, incredible success at Melrose, so I felt a little shudder at the seriousness of her tone when she asked, 'Milady, can I be frank with you? There are things I have mulled over while you were in Scotland.'

'Go on, Amaris.'

'You have been more than good to me since you rescued me from the slave traders so long ago in Antioch. My gratitude is heartfelt.'

By now I was waiting for the BUT! I feared she was about to say enough is enough. I know I can be difficult, impatient, overly meticulous about myself and my belongings. Then there was my temper, and my moodiness. Amaris has had to bear the brunt of my flaws often, maybe she yearned for peace. I held my breath, nodding for her to go on. She paused, then in a rush she said, 'Milady, I am concerned at times about your swings from joy, vigour, and happiness one minute to the depths of despair the next.'

I inhaled as William's little face flashed before me. Amaris guessed my thoughts.

'I do not mean your grief when Prince William died. That was natural. What worried me was the intensity, like your desolation after Princess Alix was born. Also, I was afraid you might lose control when Lord King Henry's father died, that perhaps you would betray your deep feelings for him.'

By now, I knew not what to say.

'Are you criticising me, or do you think I am mad?'

'No definitely not. But I wonder if, when you were knocked out on our ship returning from the Holy Land, you were more wounded than we thought. For weeks, you knew not who you were. I feared you were going to die.'

I was puzzled because that episode was so many years past. Amaris took a deep breath and continued.

'Then hard on that incident your life became more anxious with your pregnancy with Princess Alix. When you needed calm and rest, the French Court took her way straight after her birth. No sooner had you recovered from that grief, you feared your unhappy marriage to King Louis would not be annulled.'

I wanted her to stop but I could see she had more to say.

'Go on, Amaris.'

'I know the late Duke of Normandy and you were… close, but you fell out. One calamity followed another. Even your relief from being freed from your marriage to King Louis almost ended in disaster with your near abduction on the way to L'Ombrière. Then there are those terrible nightmares you still have from the horrors witnessed during the crusade.'

'How long have you thought – noticed – this?'

'I watched your marriage of *"necessity"* to Lord King Henry turn to love. Never have I seen you so happy and I thought all was now well. But when Prince William was taken, you plunged back into despair. Everyone including King Henry thought you had lost your wits.'

'By the sound of your words you did think my grief for William is – was – excessive.'

Amaris stopped speaking and stared at the floor. Then she whispered, 'No. I know how you felt. It was what I experienced when I lost my family, the unbelievable terror and grief was worse than hell. Then there were the slave traders, the death of my baby. But you rescued me. I will never forget that day.'

'Neither will I.'

'Milady, you helped me to heal physically and mentally. You gave me a new life for which I am eternally grateful and which I love. But you have responsibilities over and above what I have, and you think more deeply than anyone I know. Forgive me for saying so, but I think you have difficulty accepting life outside of your control.'

What could I say? I ordered I be dressed, I was getting cold, then I dismissed Amaris and tried to make sense of *'me'*. Judith's words about my life being tumultuous rattled around in my head. Could some of the turmoil be caused by my being knocked out cold on that storm-wracked barque? My fingers went to my head where I could feel the healed scar from the injury, I inflicted on myself by banging my head on the granite wall of Wallingford Castle. No wonder they thought my wits had deserted me.

The fires in the braziers were burning low, which after the success in Scotland was how I was feeling. Damn Amaris! She took my triumph and flattened it. A churl, as if reading my mind from a distance, appeared with wood, followed by Lucille who was still grinning with delight. I had arranged rewards for my men, but I had not given a thank you gift to her.

Chapter 2: Regency

As she entered, not knowing of my exchange with Amaris, I hoped her gaiety would enthuse me again. I walked to a nearby chest, returning with a ring of gold, rubies, and sapphires I knew Lucille admired. I gave it to her and thanked her for the support and faithful duty she had bestowed on me to and from Scotland. She boosted my low morale with her thanks and laughed she had never had so much excitement in her life. After that I could not remain gloomy. But recording Amaris' conversation made me look at myself, to wonder…

***

The long ride home found me quieter than expected. Everyone, I think, put it down to my burgeoning shape, presuming I was tired. There was no way I could disguise my condition anymore. I was no longer angry with Amaris, but I believed her timing was ill. She could have picked a better moment to air her concerns.

I was now back in the comfort of the Palace of Westminster. My reunion with Hal and Matilda was joyous, which cheered my disposition. How they had grown! Matilda wondered who I was, which pulled at my heart strings. She screamed when I picked her up, wriggling to be returned to Agnes. Hal did know me, which was a relief. Her brother's delight calmed little Matilda. Soon we were all playing together on the floor of the nursery. My little girl could crawl like a demon, which sent us into fits of laughter. As the centre of attention, she put on an extra spurt with squeals of delight. She adored Hal and he her, which was wonderful to see. Hal no longer asked, 'Where is William?'

***

My conversation with Amaris gave me concerns. Twice I knew I had lost control when faced by severe, tragic moments. I was not always so afflicted. Papa's death was heart-rending, but maybe it was Renée who had the right maternal touch during that time which helped the pain, and I had Nilla who I had to be strong for, and Jerome and Clotilde. For the terror that consumed me when it involved my children, they were not there. Perhaps I could not face the truth of what happened. Maybe I needed to discuss my problems with our physician. Matthias joined Henry's and my entourage shortly after we came to England. Henry's mother never liked him. I had employed him to tend Geoffrey, Henry's father who was dying after I dismissed the ancient family apothecary. Henry, as a result asked Matthias to come to us. But he could not save William and had to suffer my uncontrolled hysteria and abuse. I hoped he had forgiven me.

At the end of the week, we were to leave for Winchester. I took Amaris to one side. I had been rather frosty towards her, which was becoming obvious to all my maids.

'Thank you for being frank with me, I know you have my best interests at heart. I am going to speak to Matthias. Will you come with me to hold my hand?'

'Of course, Milady.'

'You have witnessed all my highs and lows, and you will be able to jog my memory about incidents I cannot recall.'

We spent an hour talking to Matthias.

'Milady, the severe bang to your head during that frightening storm during your return from Jerusalem could have weakened your ability to cope with events you cannot control.'

'Please elaborate, Matthias.'

'Lady Eleanor, you are blessed with exceptional intelligence and because of your status, you are used to being obeyed.'

'Matthias, when William died, I felt impotent that I could not save him. To hold him and watch him convulse and die in my arms... Never have I felt such fear... and – and panic.'

'As hard as it is, you must accept that death is part of life.'

The conversation paused. By now I was feeling worse, not better. I felt I was falling into an abyss. Matthias must have detected something in my demeanour. He took my hands in his, and his eyes were intense.

'My dear Lady Eleanor. I tried everything to save Prince William. I have castigated myself I did not do enough. I have asked myself repeatedly what more could I have done? Then I had to turn my attention to you. William had gone but you were in dire need. King Henry was more frightened than I have ever seen a man. He was on his knees begging me to save you. In the end, you prevailed because of your own inner strength.'

Amaris gave me a goblet of brandy wine; I took a gulp and my breath slowed along with my nerves.

Matthias went on, 'Although you are Queen of England, you are still human. If you cut your finger, you will bleed like any peasant or churl. Also like them, you must accept God's will.'

I wished he had not said that! I was still struggling with God's 'will'. Brother Peter, my confessor, had worn out his knees praying for my wretched soul and apologising to God on my behalf.

I felt powerless when Louis had Marie taken away, more particularly when Alix was removed, because that act of cruelty magnified the original anguish over Marie, tipping me over the edge.

I have tried to make sense of my behaviour. I know I must use all my determination to overcome this weakness, perhaps caused by the accident on the barque. I searched my soul, too, regarding my past adultery. Would I do the same again? Under the circumstances – most likely. From no love to love was too strong an aphrodisiac. I must therefore try to accept no-one could have saved William, and I know Louis was too weak to fight his miserable mentors to allow me to be a mother to our daughters. Maybe among the Greek philosophers there is an answer. Who knows?

***

I was as excited as a child at Christmastide when the palace at Winchester came into sight. As fast as my bulk would allow, I dismounted. I had not been here since the final restoration work was completed. Previous visits were like living in a carpenter's or stone-mason's workshop with dust and wood shavings in every crevasse, including a film over one's wine. I asked our stewards to take me on a guided tour.

I could not have been more pleased with the workmanship. Each chamber, gallery and stairway were a work of art. No more cracked glass. There were fireplaces to warm our quarters, and the carved lintels, newel posts and windowsills had transformed this beautiful old palace into its former glory. I was agog. But for me the pièce-de-resistance was the library. It was in a parlous state when we first arrived in England. Many books had suffered Stephen's and Eustace's wrath. Many were rescued by the Archbishop of Winchester, who returned them as soon as he saw the restored library. I sat and breathed in the familiar odour of leather and parchment. It is a sunny chamber with tall windows – so welcoming. I found a magnificent old desk in one of the lower rooms, and had it cleaned, polished, and installed where I could look out the window. My belly was a little in the way, but that was a minor annoyance as my small incumbent beat its own rhythm on its rim.

I was most impatient for Henry to arrive. His galley had been sighted off Plymouth, so he would dock within hours and be here first thing on the morrow. In our quarters, I had hung tapestries brought from Poitiers, purloined from the Maubergeonne Tower. I was sure Grandmother Dangerosa would not mind. They looked so well with the light from the new Gothic windows dancing on the silken thread. I thought Henry would be impressed.

***

Chapter 2: Regency

Henry arrived with foam-flecked horses, his men almost falling to the ground in relief. It was so good to see him. He roared to a stop in front of me, realising there was no way he could lift me off the ground to whirl me in circles. Instead, he fell to his knees and buried his head in my bulky middle. Laughter, joy, and tears engulfed us both.

Henry gave me some wonderful news. 'My darling I am the advance party, but guess who is plodding sedately in a carriage behind me?'

'I have no idea, Henry. Stop teasing.'

'Renée.'

I let out a shriek of joy.

'She will arrive at Winchester after the noonday bells. When she heard about William and this latest baby, she insisted she return with me. I have another surprise, too, but you will have to wait for that one.'

'Henry please!'

'No.'

He grinned like a gargoyle and my pouting was fruitless. I knew to pursue questioning would be a waste of my breath, so I diverted his attention to the children. Matilda was all eyes agog wondering who this hirsute fellow was. She could walk now but clung to my leg. Hal was shy, hiding around my gown, clinging to my other leg. Henry had to coax them out with some funny faces till they worked out it really was Papa who, I had been telling them, would be home soon.

I had ordered a light repast for myself and a more substantial one for my ever-hungry lord. We talked about his campaigns in Normandy. The French had been barking at the Norman borders. God be praised, foolish Louis had withdrawn for now. Henry hoped the treaty signed at Gisors would be more lasting. He said his mother though aging was still feisty. His brother Geoffrey was aggravating, but younger brother William had been accommodating and would visit us anon. He hinted there was a way for achieving peace between him and Louis that would also be mightily beneficial for the future of the two kingdoms, but he had much to formulate before he could discuss it with me. I realised I would have to be patient.

I was about to give him my report on the Scottish rebellion, but he pre-empted my news. God's teeth, he already knew, by the expression on his face. He was like his father; he had spies everywhere. To be honest I was peeved.

'If you know so much, you tell me.' I sounded like a petulant child.

'I heard you placed Malcolm back on his rightful throne, but I have little detail as to how you achieved it.'

After I elaborated on our success, he chastised me as if I were a child. He huffed and puffed.

'Eleanor, you could have been killed or taken hostage. You had no idea how evil that little piece of dog's turd David was.'

'For your information, I knew exactly who I was dealing with, having been well informed, which was why I appealed to David's vanity, outsmarting him with nary a drop of blood spilled amongst our men. It was an easy checkmate, *'enri Plantagenet-a!*'.

Henry glared at me. He hated it when I alluded to chess tactics.

I told him about my plans to endow convents to take in needy women and their children. Henry approved as I thought he would, agreeing it was an excellent idea. I will now courier the news to the abbesses I had spoken to. Alms will be distributed in the New Year.

I heard carriages arriving in the courtyard below. As fast as the incumbent would allow me, I dashed down the stairs into Renée's embrace. At first, words were impossible for both of us. When I found my voice, I welcomed her, telling her I had accommodated her in the sunniest chamber nearest to mine with a large fireplace, so she would be warm. It was then I heard a discreet cough behind me, and turning I was amazed to see Jerome looking so elegant in his dark Benedictine robes. My old playmate was a handsome figure of a man. I threw my arms around him in an extended hug. He stepped back, examining me from head to toe and commented how well I was blooming. Here was my family, except for Nilla. They both fussed over Hal and Matilda and produced little keepsakes for their amusement.

***

The evening was a noisy reunion. We caught up with the news of the Aquitaine, Poitou, Angevin and Normandy. Some births, some lives ended, except no-one mentioned William, his death a leaden spectre hanging over the joyful party. Jerome broke the tension by calling for his recorder, Sir Robert rushed to find his rebec. Henry and I had our lutes, though mine I found difficult to balance on my belly. In the end I opted to sing, handing the lute to Marion who played well. Amaris kept a good rhythm on the timbrel. Much to my embarrassment, the men all knew Grandfather William's risqué compositions and poems, and even, to my horror, Jerome. When I chided him, he said my father taught him the words when he was quite young. Really? But he said his comprehension of their innuendo was, at that age, innocent.

After a few goblets of wine, a few crazy jigs were attempted as well as the Moresque from Amaris's birthplace. Celeste's mad attempt to try the steps had her falling over her hem and onto her derriere, much to everyone's amusement. When the candles started spluttering it was time for all to take to our beds.

Henry still wanted to sleep in my bed regardless of the bulge. It could be frustrating under the circumstances.

'Henry! Your feet and hands are freezing.'

'And you are so nice and warm.'

We would be off to Oxford in a week to stay at Beaumont instead of Woodstock which was just as comfortable. It looked like this baby would make its arrival there.

***

Our journey started with Henry and me arguing.

'You are not riding that horse.'

'Who says?'

'I do. In your condition it is dangerous. Get into the carriage with Renée. She can keep an eye on you.'

'I hate carriages. I find them uncomfortable. Some people experience *mal de mare*, I suffer from *mal de chariot*.'

'Eleanor, I am sure you exaggerate, stop being so bloody stubborn.'

'All that swaying, and lurching makes me sick.'

'God's teeth, you are so pigheaded! At times you are impossible!'

After we screamed at each other for half an hour, Henry galloped off in a huff. Well, damn his eyes, I rode.

***

Robert and Henry arrived ahead of everyone. I took the journey easily. Galloping apace was not a choice in my condition. But Henry was not there to welcome me, so I presumed he was still fuming. I settled Hal and Matilda with their maids and toys and took to my quill and ink. If Henry wanted me, he could find me.

Renée wanted to know when my confinement would take place. She was trying to organise my life as well as Henry. I thought soon, in a week or so. I looked like a whale and was mightily uncomfortable. This baby was bigger than the others, which was not pleasing me or helping my disposition.

A knock on the door brought in Henry, grinning, which was a relief, though I was still grumpy. Next, he was nagging me to eat with him. After our repast, somewhat silent on my part, he insisted I rest. What had got into him? If it was not Renée, it was Amaris; both, I think, have passed their agitation to Henry. I wanted to hide.

For a short time, I managed to escape to the orangery.

Chapter 2: Regency

The surrounding gardens here were beautiful, with many beds of bluebells, lupins, and hollyhocks. I thought the flowers of England strange to begin with, but now I was enjoying a new diversity. Violets I adore, not only for their sweet perfume but for their colour. They matched some gowns I wore. I wondered if our *parfumier* could extract an essence to produce a fragrance.

***

I was in the library when letters arrived from Petronilla. Her youngest child was sick with an ague causing a high fever and might not survive. She would be about seven years old now. I was distraught for Nilla, praying her little girl would live. The news brought the memory of William flooding back. Renée and Jerome tried to pacify me. To make matters worse, my baby was overdue. I had twinges, but nothing had transpired. I was being dragged down. My ankles were swollen, my temper was most ill. Everyone was avoiding me except Amaris, who came to me this morning wanting a word. What she had to say was interesting. She told me that in the harems of the east, women in my state sometimes recruited their husbands to lay with them which encouraged the overdue baby to be born.

    I was willing to try anything, but would Henry comply? We were barely speaking to each other of late because of my foul moods. The last thing on his mind would be intimacy. He yelled at me before today's hunt, that I was pricklier than a hedgehog. But I was desperate. This baby was getting bigger by the minute, exacerbating my terror of giving birth. This child felt like an elephant.

    Henry arrived back in a jovial mood, which was a relief. He seemed surprised to find me in his chamber. I told him I wanted to speak to him alone. He dismissed Robert, Martin and Roger and a few others. They were going to enjoy a few ales; he said he would be with them anon. Unusual for me, I found this conversation with Henry embarrassing. I explained how I needed to try to encourage our child to arrive and how we could perhaps hurry it along. Henry was aghast. He insisted nature should take its course, but when he saw how distressed I was, he agreed.

Now came the interesting bit. Being naked, as far as I was concerned at this stage of my pregnancy, was not attractive. My distended belly was grotesque. Henry said he had never known me to be prudish. I stood there in my shift like a sail billowing on a galley. Henry was wearing a silly expression. I could tell he was in two minds whether to strip me and throw me onto the bed, not a good idea under the circumstances, or to entice me in some other way. By now both of us were in fits of laughter. I told him to shut his eyes as I scuttled to the bed, threw off my shift and hid under the bed linens which, with an evil look on his face, he threw off. My belly button stuck out. Henry thought it was hilarious and tried to poke it back. He said he could hang a Plantagenet pennant from it. None of this was helping what we were there to do. Finding a position was a novelty. Both of us were in stitches. Eventually we managed. Henry was gentle, tender, afraid he might hurt me. He forewent the ale as we lay side by side on his bed holding hands. There was a little blood afterwards but nothing else. I was beginning to think Amaris was wrong, but I had not asked how long after making love the child would move, so I had no idea what to expect. Henry fell asleep. I swung my feet to the floor.

***

Well, it worked. I had barely taken two steps from Henry's bed when the waters broke, and my labour began. I managed to leave my sleeping lord without moaning like a sick cow to stagger to my bed chamber. I threw my maids into a panic. I clung to the bed post unable to move

Chapter 2: Regency

as the contractions became more frequent. I swore at them all as they insisted, I get into my bed. Without a winch, HOWWWW!?

Eight hours later, the fastest of all my babies, on the 8th day of September, in the Year of Our Lord 1157, I had another boy. He was huge. We called him Richard. He looked like he was already four weeks old. We stared at each other, his eyes not moving from mine. His skin was a little tan. Renée said it was because he was late. He had a mop of red hair like a young lion. He took one look at Henry when he held him and screamed. What lungs! Henry told him he helped him to arrive, so he should be grateful, but no, Henry had to give him back. Richard snuggled into my breast, suckling, closing his eyes in comfort. Henry gave me a look. I think he was jealous. Matilda thought she had another doll, while Hal said I could send him back to God. Oh dear!

***

We returned to London. Richard was now eight weeks old. He was growing mightily fast. It took me a little time to heal from his birth because of his size, but I felt well. Henry, who had gone onto Westminster ahead of me, was thrilled to see us, especially as I could be his lover again. I was still feeding Richard, so I hoped it would slow down the likelihood of another baby for a while. *Doigts croises*, fingers crossed.

Henry decided I should return to the Aquitaine for a short visit and to spend Christmas in Poitiers. It was almost five years since I arrived in England. I was overjoyed. Poor Nilla lost her little girl, the youngest of her three children, so we would be able to commiserate with each other. I was worried about Renée also who, although determined in her outlook, was aging. Clotilde was going to spend Christmas with us, so that would be a delight for both. I felt guilty. Renée had spent more time mothering me than her own daughter.

***

In my library at Westminster, I was brooding. It was more than a year since William died. Dear God, how my heart still hurt and ached. My mind was leagues away when a light knock on the door pulled me from my melancholic trance. It was Jerome. He knew by my expression I was not happy. I questioned if I would ever come to terms with William's death.

'Jerome, I struggle. I blame myself as William's mother for not being able to save his life. I feel I am being punished. I have difficulty accepting God's decree in taking my baby boy.'

'Elly, you are not being punished. William died of an incurable illness, typhus, which produced a high fever and convulsions, Lord Henry told me. You cannot go through life blaming yourself or God. Why would God want to punish you?'

'My lurid past is probably a good reason. Worse, I know I would do the same again under the circumstances because, although Louis said he loved me, it was not how I believed a man should love a woman.'

How could I explain to a celibate Benedictine monk that my first husband found my body abhorrent?

'Louis' love was for an object, a possession, my Duchy. Now I am being punished for finding happiness with – others.'

'Do you still love these men?'

'They will always be remembered fondly and deeply. I have put them aside in a special part of my heart. Henry is the love of my life, not them.'

'Then there is no need for God to punish you, Elly. Why should you not mourn for your boy any more than you should not mourn for your Papa, or I for my family? Even so we both have much to be thankful for, to God. Think on that Elly.'

'Did you ever want to marry, Jerome? Have you ever been in love?'

'Once… I suppose. But she was not for me, never could be. My feelings for her will never alter though.'

'Who?'

'She is a secret between me and God.'

Jerome stood and gave me an odd look, as he left the library.

I picked up my quill, puzzled, then a dawning penetrated my mind. Surely Jerome did not mean me. We were always close as children. Papa's death cleaved us apart, I to marry Louis, and he to the church. But my love for him was for that of a brother. Maybe his, too, was nothing more than for a sister.

Also, this was the first time I accepted the word *typhus* or could write it down. Bless Jerome, the only person who could utter it in my presence because he empathised. The same disease that took William, took his family.

Chapter 3. Aquitaine Christmas

What a flotilla! I think it took as many ships to take us back to Barfleur as it took for my arrival in England. Diablo, my prancing hispano stallion, was there to meet me. He remembered me, whinnying, and nudging me with his head. He had been brought from Rouen at my insistence and looked magnificent caparisoned in my livery of purple and gold. He had been with me since he was a foal, before I met Henry, but I had left him in Normandy, mostly because Henry had a fit about me riding a stallion. Men!

Our entourage stretched for leagues on our long journey south to Poitiers. Throughout the towns and cities *en route* we were cheered and welcomed. To hear my native tongue again brought tears to my eyes. And the warmth! I had forgotten how the sun felt on my back. My arrival in Poitiers was hallooed from street to street. My people! How proud I felt, how honoured, how loved. Not that I was treated ill by the common people in England; I was well respected, but home is home. I suppose I was being parochial.

After greetings from my dear sister, who had travelled to Poitiers, Guillaume, Guile, Saldebreuil and Uncle Ralph, plus the whole palace family from pages to churls, I entered the familiar old palace, with its stone walls, its tall, beautiful windows, and infamous Maubergeonne Tower. The first thing I wanted to do was to come here to Papa's library where I stood surrounded by memories. The windows overlooking the west courtyard below reflected diamond patterns on the floor in the afternoons – so familiar.

I dawdled along the shelves of books, running my fingers along their spines, breathing in their special odour. These shelves contained my education, Greek philosophers, dramatists, poets and story tellers, Romans in lyrical Latin, my beloved Aeneid, Cicero, Suetonius and so many others, Ovid, too. Stacked in one corner were scrolls from my Troubadour Grandfather: beautiful poems, and music, along with the funny, and the wickedly naughty. This was where I was brought up, where my love of learning began, where I was encouraged to think, to argue, to find laughter. Dear Papa, I thanked from the bottom of my heart for this gift. Here I felt so close to him, as if his safe, loving spirit were smiling down on me still.

My desk, where I had penned my deepest thoughts, recorded my highs and lows, and where I had learned and practised Latin and Greek, was like an old friend. This was where I could simply be Eleanor without being the freak, a learned woman in a world of men, and ignorance.

The gardens of the Palace of Poitiers had always been a favourite place to play. As children, Nilla and I would spend hours climbing trees, much to Renée's annoyance because we were always tearing our smocks. We played games of hide and seek and pestered our patient gardeners to help plant seeds. My love of gardens started there, as well as at L'Ombrière. I could not wait to take Hal and Matilda out to play amongst the flowers and shrubs with Nilla's children, Ralph, and Eloise, while Richard slept in his baby carriage. We clucked and laughed as our children tumbled together, both of us trying to push the sadness of the missing little ones from our minds. Today I was letting nostalgia and remembrances take importance before I had to attend to the seriousness of duties. Queen of England and Duchess of Aquitaine were today mother and sister.

We sat reminiscing about our childhood.

'Remember Simian, Nilla?'

'I suppose, Elea, I should be sorry I let him loose into the audience chamber on the day you met King Louis, but I am not.'

'It was hilarious. The terror on his face when he thought your monkey was Satan was something to behold.'

'The looks on the guards' faces were a study as they tried not to split their sides after I fetched Simian. You were trying to keep some decorum I recall.'

'What a fool of a man. Thank God that era of my life is over.'

We laughed in fits as we recalled the debacle caused by her pet. She wiped her eyes. 'I am delighted you and Lord Henry are so much in love regardless that he is younger.'

'I am not so chuffed about being reminded of my age thank you very much.'

Nilla ignored my comment.

While we were soaking up the wintry sunshine, I took the opportunity to examine my younger sister's face. Yes, there were laugh lines around her eyes, a few on her forehead and a hint of one when she frowned, but her skin was soft, and she was still pretty. Her body was plumper, but that made her look voluptuous, womanly. But the difference in Henry's and my years niggled. I was terrified of aging; afraid he would tire of me.

'Do you think I look old? Tell me, be honest,' I blurted out.

Nilla turned and stared at my face. Neither of us were veiled so our hair could be examined, too. She did have a few grey ones, but her hair was darker than mine, so they were more obvious. I felt as if her eyes were raking me from head to toe, then she pouted,

'You know, Elea, it is not fair. Your features have changed little, and you should not compare yourself to Henry. He is no longer looking boyish. If people did not know, they could easily think you were the same age.'

She grabbed my head to examine it as if looking for nits. 'Damn you! You do not have any grey either. It is darker, though, more brownish than honey coloured. And you are too skinny.'

'I am not skinny Nilla!'

'Yes, you are.'

'I am not. I am just tall. But my body is not as firm as it used to be. After I wean Richard, I fear my breasts will be saggy. And the skin around my stomach is a map of fine lines. I am terrified Henry will notice.'

Nilla hooted. 'Your belly will be the last thing on Henry's mind if your reputed love making is anything to go by.'

Nilla could not stop sniggering. It was time to round up the children so I could escape.

***

Before our Christmas observances, I spoke to my almoner about monies to be distributed to Reverend Mother Joan and other convents and abbeys who were to take in poverty-stricken women and their children. Without fuss, this was achieved, and Uncle Ralph was happy to loosen the Aquitaine purse strings for such a worthy endeavour. It was a wonderful Christmas present, not only for the needy and their administrators but for me as well.

I had been able to visit Fontevrault Abbey on our journey south to Poitiers and had a wonderful reunion with Henry's Aunt Isabella. She fussed over the children and spoiled them with small gifts the good sisters had made, early Christmas presents. A dolly for Matilda, a stuffed dog of felt for Richard and some beautifully carved and painted toy soldiers for Hal. I renewed the amount of alms we gave to the Abbey – increased their stipends, too. Henry and I had discussed that they should start an order in England. I put this suggestion to Mother Isabella, who agreed.

***

I left Nilla in charge of the Christmas celebrations to concentrate on meetings with my justiciars. They were running my duchy with such proficiency, I told Uncle Ralph it seemed I was not needed. He kindly said it was my diligence prior to my leaving for England that allowed them to follow my orders with ease. He reported a few of the known troublemakers had territorial disputes from time to time, but when it was put to them that they were letting me down in my absence, they muttered and grumbled but put away their siege engines. Guile said they were so terrified of Henry descending on them in dire wrath, it made them think twice about their petty rebellions. I told them I preferred diplomacy rather than Henry's *casus belli* (all-out war), perhaps with a little cunning, unless there was no other way to quell an insurgency.

I was concerned, however, about threats to the north of Poitiers between the County of Poitou and the Angevins above the Loire. These disputes were trying. Louis had no hope of placating them. Henry, being Angevin through his father and educated in Angers, had more success. As Christmas and winter approached, at least the protagonists were recognising a truce. I intended to write to bishops and the local justiciars on both sides of the border to jog their consciences to see if we could keep them apart – permanently. On my side, I hoped the Poitivins would continue to obey their Countess. That I was now Duchess of Normandy, however, would do me no favours in the eyes of some. Normandy was aligned with their supposed enemy, the Angevins.

Uncle Ralph also brought up the County of Toulouse, which hung like a storm cloud. It was my inheritance through my father's mother Phillipa of Toulouse. The county was usurped from her by Alphonso Jordan's family but reinstating it to the Aquitaine without an all-out war was impossible. That I had done without it for so long was not a priority for now. I intended to relax and enjoy Christmas.

***

Though I was missing Henry and the children too, Christmas was delightful. Oh, the wine, bliss. I would like to take some vine cuttings back to England. Surely there were parts of the countryside where they would grow, perhaps Kent or Surrey. If we can grow citrus fruit in orangeries, there must be a way to produce grapes. Some vines had been planted but did not produce the quality of Bordeaux – a challenge for one of our monasteries or estate gardeners, I was sure.

With sated stomachs, Nilla and I sat warming our toes by the fireplace in the great hall. Clotilde joined us. She had come from L'Ombrière with her family to spend Christmas with Renée. All the children were playing some noisy game in the background overseen by Renée, who was referee for squabbles. Amaris, Marion, Celeste, and Lucille, I suspected, were in their cups having imbibed a little too freely of the Bordeaux wine. In another corner, Uncle Ralph was softly strumming a lute. He was another of the family's fine musicians.

Clotilde was like another sister. I asked her how life fared at L'Ombrière. Beautiful, was her straight reply. Nilla and I sighed, then as one we said we must take the children there before I returned to England. L'Ombrière was a second home after Poitiers. As children, we had travelled throughout the Aquitaine with Papa, visiting all our estates – Châtellerault, Sanzay, Thouars and de Faye, and relatives and friends – on official progresses as well as for pleasure. L'Ombrière, had always been a favourite, second home despite the bittersweet memories of being told there about Papa's death followed by my disastrous marriage to Louis. But it was also where I met Henry. I smiled at the memory, both of us were reluctant wooers. He fell in love before I did, but in time I was captivated. Plantagenet charm overcame the necessary political alliance to protect me from dubious adventurers.

Clotilde suggested we return with her. She then broached another subject, Renée.

'Lady Eleanor.'

Oh, dear, this was serious. Clotilde had no need to use my title, and I never expected it. I waited, knowing what she was going to say. Renée was her mother.

'My mother is getting on. All the travel expected of you as part of her duties is exhausting for *your petite Maman*; therefore, she should not be expected to continue – she should retire. What is more, she needs to get to know her blood grandchildren. She, Milady, has been your nurse long enough.'

Clotilde had always been blunt. I heard Nilla take a deep breath, waiting for *her imperiousness* to explode, no doubt.

'I know... Clotilde I will talk to her.'

Renée took her duties seriously. It would not be easy for either of us. But I had to face facts and insist that she stepped down to be with her child and grandchildren. Nilla and I would go to L'Ombrière, then say goodbye.

***

L'Ombrière was beautiful. The sun shone while we were there, flooding the palace with warmth. In the gardens, there were still flowers blooming. The parfumier concocted the spicy fragrance which Nilla loved. I preferred the floral perfume he infused for me from jasmine and damask roses. I wore it for the first time the night Henry and I broke the Commandments in Dangerosa's folly. It drove Henry wild. It could almost be called an aphrodisiac. I kept it for special moments, wearing simple rose ester, or lavender at other times. My heart longed for him. Nilla could see I had gone all misty eyed, so we wandered off to the temple ruins of Aphrodite, which did not help one bit. I was missing Henry and decided to return to England sooner than I had planned.

To take my mind off Henry and my parting with Renée and Nilla for that matter, I took the time to visit the harbour master. The new sea wall and clever groyne were successfully controlling the build-up of sand during tidal

Chapter 3: Aquataine Christmas

changes. The entrance and exit for the fishing smacks was now safe and predictable. Since their completions, no boats had capsized, and better still, no fishermen had drowned. I was mightily pleased.

I must also *nail my courage to the sticking post* to visit Cousin Nanette. That was, of course, if she would want to see me. We parted with such bad blood she may not. It must be five or nearly six years since I refused her alms for her convent's damn relics. The argument she sparked almost undid me marrying Henry. I wondered if she still considered me a whore. Possibly. If I took Nilla with me for protection, she may control her tongue, not wanting to offend my sister. I sent a courier announcing my intentions. I signed the letter as Queen of England, so she could hardly refuse.

Nilla baulked, 'Nooo! There is no way I am going near Nanette. She used to bully me when we were children.'

'I cannot remember, but it would not surprise me. Nanette has always been domineering, but I cannot recall her doing the same to me.'

'She would not have dared, because your tongue was worse than Nanette's.'

Sometimes, my sister made me squirm with her frankness.

Nanette did not refuse my request but was frosty all the same. Her nuns were pleasant, however, spoiling me with sweetmeats and a honey-laced, spicy tisane. They gave me some of their exquisite lace, a little too reminiscent of my trousseau when I married Louis.

My visit was brief. I left alms for new buildings, which softened Nanette a little. She congratulated me grudgingly on my marriage, ascension, and lovely children, ending my visit by saying she would pray for William's immortal soul and my depraved one. She could not resist one gibe, Queen of England, or no. I reminded her she might be Mother Superior, but I held the purse strings, to which she had to demur, no doubt fuming.

On my return, I seethed and ranted about what had taken place.

Nilla nodded. 'I told you Nanette is a bully, and yet you still gave her alms for her convent. Well, I suppose you got the better of her in the end.'

'Maybe. She is probably sticking pins into my effigy as we speak.'

At least we could laugh.

Nilla was sad but understood my decision to return to England. The two older children needed their Papa, and Richard too. He was such a bonny boy with a serious disposition, but when he smiled the world lit up around him. He was Maman's boy though, at times a little clingy when he went to Agatha, which was why I was still suckling him. Agatha reminded me I was going to have to wean him sooner than later. I would as soon as we were back in England. I dreaded the thought of engorged breasts. I must take one of Renée's physics with me to help dry my milk or I would have to resort to Agatha's shivery, cold, cabbage leaves.

I must also visit Rouen and Empress Matilda before my return. Today I sent a courier, warning her I had put forward my planned arrival. She had yet to meet her namesake and other grandchildren. I hoped she found them likeable. She was not the least maternal, hardly ever holding William. But she was good to Henry's illegitimate boy Geoffrey, whom I must bring back to England at his father's request. God knows what Matilda had told the child about me. He was quite small, little less than two years when I saw him last when he regarded me with suspicion. I had however promised Henry that I would always treat him as my own, so I hoped we would get along.

***

It was hard saying goodbye. Nilla and I had a good cry, but with Renée it was heart wrenching. Words could not

Chapter 3: Aquataine Christmas

express what I owed her. I had written repeatedly what she meant to me and to my family. Clotilde was more than aware of the sacrifices Renée made when her mother became nursemaid and Maman to the two privileged daughters of the Duke of Aquitaine. Once she called me a spoilt brat. She was probably right. I put to her that if she ever desired to be my apothecary, I would be delighted to have her join my household. Clotilde thanked me but repeated her duty was to her mother in her twilight years. That was it. Whatever control I had on my emotions dissolved with the realisation I might never see my petite Maman, my beloved nurse, again. Clotilde did her best to comfort her almost twin sister. Clotilde is only nine months older than I. She told me in her gruff way to pull myself together, as Elea, Duchess of Aquitaine. I had expecting her to say – grow up! She promised she would look after Renée with all her being. I then went to Renée and hugged her till she protested she could not breath. I wept all the way back to Poitiers, Nilla too.

***

It was a long trail of baggage and retinue that entered the castle at Rouen. Matilda had come up from her palace to greet us. She surprised me by kissing me on both cheeks. Maybe because she could see England progressing, and knew I could govern in Henry's absence, albeit as much as Henry would allow, that she no longer thought of me as some sort of over-educated, outspoken treasury. Though, without my dowry, her son would be hard pressed to achieve what he had done. Heirs to continue her heritage helped, too.

When we gathered in the old assembly hall, I introduced Empress Matilda to her grandchildren. Hal cheerfully greeted his Grandmaman. Sweet-natured little Matilda was happy to meet her too. True to form, Richard bawled, clinging to me with chubby fists. I managed to coax him to turn his head to look at his grand dame. He gazed at her with huge soulful eyes, snotty nose, and tears as large as waterfalls running down his face. Richard let go with one fist, so he could shove his thumb in his mouth, head on my shoulder.

'Well, Eleanor, I can see who he looks like.'

'Yes, Milady, Henry's hair and determined chin. I think his eyes will remain blue.'

'Hmm! Henry sucked his thumb, too, I remember. Drove his father mad.'

I took note of that for when Henry nags about it. Although there was a little Aquitaine about Richard in build, I saw more and more Plantagenet in his features.

Matilda then called for young Geoffrey to be brought into our presence. He had of course grown since I last saw him at Henry's father's funeral. He was quite a striking looking boy. Matilda was fond of him and he her. I felt sad that Henry wished to bring him to England because Matilda would miss him. Geoffrey was quiet. I knew not whether his reticence in reacquainting himself with me was shyness or suspicion.

'Hello, Geoffrey,' I said. 'How tall you have grown. Let me introduce you to your half-brother, Prince Hal, your half-sister Princess Matilda and baby Prince Richard.'

Geoffrey smiled, but, before he could utter a word, Hal pulled at my gown and said, 'Maman, is he William?'

'No, darling, he is Geoffrey. He has a different Maman.'

'Where is his Maman?'

'In heaven, like William.'

Hal smiled brightly and said, 'Then God can give William back, and she can have Geoffrey.'

Well, that utterance set me back. 'Oh, my darling boy, that can never happen. Those who go to heaven, stay there forever.'

I was feeling bereft. What Empress Matilda made of the exchange I knew not. She did speak a little English. I just prayed she did not catch on to Hal's babbling. The situation was becoming awkward. Hal looked like he was

Chapter 3: Aquataine Christmas

going to cry, little Matilda's bottom lip was trembling, but Richard came to the rescue with a sudden gurgle of joy and grabbed handfuls of Geoffrey's hair. We had to disentangle the poor boy, but they bonded just like that. Richard found a friend in his big half-brother.

***

I spent a week in Rouen. Matilda told me over dinner on our first evening that the rebellions Henry had quelled, and the treaties that were signed when he was last in Normandy, were holding. Henry's youngest brother, William, was coming to England with us and would meet us at Barfleur. When I asked about Henry's middle brother Geoffrey, she said she thought he was in Paris. I said naught but I knew if so, it would be nothing but trouble. Empress Matilda asked me to say nothing to Henry until she was certain of his whereabouts.

A few days later while I was scribbling in my journal, I was interrupted by a page who informed me there was a courier in the bailey with letters addressed to me. Poor man had been following me round the countryside, having first ridden to Poitiers. I rewarded him mightily for his trouble and diligence.

Back at my desk, I saw one was from Henry who said he must ride again to the Welsh border. There had been incursions by the Welsh King near Shrewsbury with disputes over certain lands as well as tax disagreements. I tried not to worry, after all Henry's last encounter with Lord King Owain had him close to being defeated. He said he would be staying with a loyal baron and his wife close to Shrewsbury; Huw, and Margaret Grenvale. I knew them not, but Henry was pleased they could accommodate him and his men. He sent love to me, his mother, and the children. My letter about my early return appeared not to have reached him yet.

The next seal seemed familiar. I slid my stiletto under the wax to find the epistle was from King Malcolm of

Scotland. The contents had me mightily concerned. He warned me that Henry could be walking into a trap in Shrewsbury. How Malcolm knew this he did not say, except he cautioned that the Grenvales could not be trusted, informing me that they often plotted with Stephen and Eustace as well as with King Owain. They had no scruples and played one side off against the other, especially Lady Margaret who was a manipulator. He says she was a distant relative of Owain Pendragon's late wife. I decided to leave immediately to warn Henry.

The next day we bid a hasty goodbye to Empress Matilda. Without going into details, because I did not want to worry her, I said I or Henry would send her further information anon. Matilda gave me missives to take back to Henry.

Chapter 4. Owen Pendragon

I was impatient to arrive in England. The weather, thank God, was in our favour with steady winds and good seas. By the morrow we would be in Portsmouth. I was more than worried trying to work out when Henry would have left London for Shrewsbury. I had letters ready to courier the moment I set foot on dry land. I wrote them in *Langue d'Oc*, so, should they fall into the wrong hands, they would have had to find a translator who understood my dialect – unlikely on the Welsh border. Henry will get the gist. I intended to leave immediately for Shrewsbury, a part of England I had not visited and taking the children. This was risky, but I wanted people to think I was joining Henry. We would pick up the dogs and more guards at Winchester. I had already informed Antoine and my Praetorians about the situation. Henry's brother William and young Geoffrey would travel onto London.

***

After many weeks, we were back in Westminster. What occurred in Shrewsbury almost ended my marriage. As soon as we disembarked at Portsmouth, we hastened to Winchester. Amaris and my other maids rushed around and readied us for travel. Some of the old Roman roads that once had tentacles all over Britain had been repaired by Henry and restored to use. For the greater part of the journey, we could use these old routes and move with speed. Except for the urgency of the situation, we could have been on progress. I collected the overjoyed family mastiffs. They were excited, galloping in circles and full of doggie exuberance, but if a stranger approached my children, they would go for the throat.

It took several days of intense riding and many changes of mounts to reach the Grenvale's Castle stronghold on the banks of the River Severn. Surrounded by my guards, I entered the fortified bailey. Where were their guards? It was suspiciously quiet. Antoine told me not to dismount in case we had to retreat in haste. My maids and the children were approaching at a safe distance and would only be summoned if there was no danger. It was most odd; the castle seemed deserted. I was about to send Antoine to find an attendant when an elderly, rather stately gentleman appeared looking hot and bothered. He introduced himself as John the castle steward, but he was not sure who he was welcoming. He said he was not expecting visitors other than the king, who was with the hunting party. That was a relief. He apologised he was not there to greet us, but everyone was out on the hunt, and he was in the cellars organising wine to go with whatever game was brought home – venison he was hoping. Antoine introduced me from my lofty perch on Rebel and helped me dismount. The steward was amazed as if I had sprung out of thin air.

    I told John I was puzzled he knew not of our coming because I had sent letters in advance informing my Lord King Henry and Lord and Lady Grenvale of my imminent arrival with our children. The poor steward seemed confused, and I was beginning to wonder what had happened to my courier who I feared might have been accosted. A flustered John said he would take me to King Henry's quarters. A couple of curious pages appeared who were ordered to prepare for the Princes and Princess and the rest of my entourage.

    Time went by. My children and maids were settled, and the dogs sprawled. Richard was not happy – his teeth I suspected – so only I could comfort him, with my breast. He did not want Agatha. So much for weaning him. Afternoon was approaching. I found a game of chess to play by myself and a book Henry was reading, but I could not stop worrying about what had happened to the courier and my letters. Tiredness from our frantic travel eventually overtook me. I nodded off in the chair, still wearing my crown, until awoken by the sounds of horses and activity below in the bailey. Ah! Henry at last. With excitement, I heard his laughter approaching. I arose from the chair. It was such a relief he was well. The door opened. I was about to run into his arms when in he came with his hand on the small of the back of a weasel-faced woman.

He froze as she said, 'Who is that?'

'That is my queen.'

I stood there. Shock followed by fury and raging jealousy roared through my veins. My basilisk eyes could have struck Henry dead even though he was smiling.

'May I introduce you to my wife, Lady Queen Eleanor. Eleanor, this is Lady Margaret Grenvale.'

'Indeed.'

She gave a little bob.

My blood was surging, pounding in my head and ears. Henry reached out his hand to me. I slapped it away.

Hauteur of rank froze my face. My height had its advantages, and I towered over her.

'You, Madam, are dismissed from our presence. You may leave.'

The weasel glanced at Henry, no doubt hoping to have my order over-ruled, then scuttled out when none was forthcoming.

I turned on Henry as soon as the door closed behind her. My anger, my hurt, consumed me. 'How dare you betray me, especially when I have come to warn you of the Grenvale's treachery.'

'Eleanor – what the... I am sorry, but, Eleanor, I do not know what you are screaming about.'

'Adultery! I come here to warn you of the Grenvale's collusion with the Welsh and I find you being familiar with that woman who is plotting your demise. I sent you letters. Where are they?'

'Eleanor, what letters? The last correspondence I received from you was penned in L'Ombrière saying you were returning to England ahead of time. That was weeks ago. I have received naught from you since.'

'I sent missives from Normandy, and latterly from Winchester, by the swiftest horse and rider.'

'I have received nothing.'

'Then it is a good thing I arrived when I did, or I would not have discovered your treachery, your betrayal of your wife.'

Henry stepped towards me.

'Upon my word, I have done nothing.'

'Then why was your arm about her? Why was she entering your bed chamber?'

'Come on, Eleanor, you are being ridiculous.'

He reached out and I slapped him away, hissing,

'Like father, like son.'

'Well, you would know!'

That sliced a wound open like lancing a boil. By now, whatever remanent of control I had deserted me. With all my strength, I pushed Henry out of my way as I ran from the chamber. I hitched my gown, took the stone steps two at a time, and did not stop till I reached the stables. Grooms were brushing down horses returned from the hunt. Rebel was munching hay. I demanded the mare to be bridled and saddled, ordering the man to make haste. He took too long. Much to the poor fellow's amazement, I managed to scramble onto Rebel's bare back. I gripped the animal between my thighs, grasped the reins of her bridle and whipped the poor mare across her withers with the leather.

We crossed the draw bridge at full gallop. Rebel thundered along an unknown path by I presumed the River Severn. Five, ten minutes into my dash, Rebel swerved, shying as a rabbit shot across our path. I ended halfway up her neck; managing to stay on by sheer luck. I slowed to a walk. The poor animal was blowing and

Chapter 4: Owen Pendragon

twitchy. I took in my surroundings. The path branched into two; one was overgrown and headed away from the river. I had no idea where I was. A low branch slapped me in the face. My heart was thumping. I came out into a clearing where a small stream, or spring, splashed into a pool with a stony bottom as clear as crystal. I slid off Rebel's back and tied the reins to a low tree branch with enough length for her to nibble the grass.

My mind was roiling with confusion, wracked with dread. I swore in dialect. In fury I tore the gold bejewelled crown of Normandy holding my veil in place and flung it as far from me as possible. A loud splash brought me to my senses. With horror I watched it sink to the bottom of the pool in an array of stars and bubbles. The silk veil slipped around my neck as I stamped my foot and cursed again, only to make Rebel toss her head and dance around her tether. I looked around for a stick in which to fish it out, but nothing was long enough. I had to cut a small branch from a nearby oak. Balanced on the edge of the sloping bank, I poked about trying to reach the crown. Frustration, combined with my infamous lack of patience, undid me. I slipped and landed on my derriere up to my knees in water on the brink of the deep pool. I managed to stagger backwards with my wet gown plastered to my legs and flung down my *fishing rod* swearing in Langue d'Oc.

Waves of self-pity overcame my fury. I wept. I was getting cold. My breasts were engorged. What had happened to my epistles? I had left my baby and little children in a hostile castle, and my husband had hinted he knew about my affair with his father, to which I would never admit, even on the rack. I suspected him of being unfaithful with a hideously ugly woman. I was lost in mind as well as in my surroundings.

I nearly leapt out of my skin as a voice spoke behind me. I backed towards Rebel. A tall, silver-haired, bearded figure stepped from the fringe of the surrounding forest dressed in a white robe. In lilting English, he chuckled,

'A golden trinket, is it you are desiring? A crown for the Queen of the Wood Sprites, I am thinking.'

Another throaty laugh followed. Who was this? He had a regal bearing.

Without another word, he stripped off his gown, boots braies, and hose and dived into the pond, emerging with his shift clinging to his well-built torso, and clutching my crown. My face was aflame. I hauled my veil from my shoulders and threw it at him.

'Whosoever thou art, cover thyself!'

My English soon gave me away as not of a native speaker. I snatched the dripping crown from his outstretched hand grasping my knife in the other. He stripped with easy carelessness, drying himself much to my indignation with my veil, then flung the gown over his head, wriggling his arms into the sleeves. Now covered, his eyes pierced mine, giving me a suggestive look. I was attracted. I was tempted. It was imperative I leave before, in my present state of mind, I did something I would regret for eternity, but there was no way I could mount Rebel easily without saddle and stirrups. It would be a graceless scramble, impeded as I was by my wet, muddy gown. Also, I would have to sheathe my slender weapon.

As if he could read my mind, he said, 'Is it a boost onto your mighty steed you are needing, my beautiful sprite. But the blade, I hope, you will be putting away.'

I had no choice but to slide it into its ornate cover. The crown dangled from my wrist. My muddy foot I placed into his cupped hand, and I was propelled onto Rebel's back. He handed me the reins. I then had to crown myself with as much dignity as possible. With flaming cheeks, I admitted I was lost, and asked could he tell me the location of the River Severn so I could return to my dwelling. He asked me to follow. I heard voices ahead, urgent, and worried. Frantic Langue d'Oeil was calling

Chapter 4: Owen Pendragon

my name. Before I surged towards the familiar, I turned to thank my saviour, but he had vanished.

Henry's voice was fretful in the distance. I kicked Rebel into a canter, emerging onto the river path. I must have looked a sight with bunched, muddy gown around my thighs, my face streaked with kohl. My veil, I realised, was with the stranger. Henry's face registered relief, his voice full of emotion, thanking God. He then berated me for riding off the way I did. I was relieved to see him, but in my fragile, suspicious state of mind, I wanted answers as to what he was intending with that woman.

Robert asked if I was all right. All I could do was shake my head. Henry and I rode side by side in silence and thus we reached his quarters. I could hear Richard howling through the walls. Henry followed as I went to him. Agatha was jiggling him to no avail. His little arms reached out to me. His face was red, streaked with tears, his nose running. Terror he had a fever wracked me, but apart from his red cheeks his forehead, praise God, was cool. He stopped screaming, burying his head in my chest then shrieked again when I could not unlace my bodice fast enough. He wanted my breast and nothing else was going to placate him. Henry looked on in disgust.

'God's teeth, Eleanor. Are you giving that boy your breast?'

'He needs me, unlike you.'

Henry's snarl scattered my maids who found chores away from our presence.

I cradled Richard who eased my pain as well as his hunger, his fingers entwined in my unravelling, plait. Henry paced, fighting emotion. Richard fell asleep exhausted from all his yelling. I eased my nipple from his lips, holding him over my shoulder. A hearty burp that could have come from a tavern issued from the sleeping baby. His thumb replaced my breast. Henry grunted with derision.

'Your mother said you used to suck yours, so do not cast stones,' I said.

I rocked our son while Henry continued to pace. He was irritating me beyond endurance.

I was about to snap, when hoarse with emotion, he said, 'It has been too long, Eleanor. I want you.'

'Jesus, Mary and Joseph! One minute you have your hand on the back of another woman, entering your bed chamber, then you presume I would want to lay with you!'

I took the sleeping child through to his cradle and Agatha, then returned to Henry. He grabbed me. I pushed him away.

'You are in danger here. Are you not interested in what was in my letters?'

I strode to my writing chest where I had carried Malcolm's missive to show Henry. 'Tame your ardour and read.'

He scanned the parchment then narrowed his eyes. 'Would you like to inform me why Malcolm, King of the Scots, prefers to pass this knowledge to you rather than me, King of England.'

I shrugged. 'Security maybe? Perhaps he could not send couriers safely into the vicinity of the Welsh border.'

I thought I was probably more approachable, but, also, he owed me his life. He could be returning his dues. Henry was stomping around.

'Henry, I fear for the life of my courier.'

'I am going to get to the bottom of this,' he thundered.

Bed was put on hold as he marched to the door. I followed regardless of my muddy clothes.

'I will come with you.'

'Then wipe your face.'

Henry fished out a crumpled handkerchief from his robe handing it to me. I wiped, not making much impression. I needed water. Henry grabbed the kerchief back, spat on it and wiped my face to remove the smudged

Chapter 4: Owen Pendragon

kohl like Renée would have cleaned me when I was four.

'Better.'

I felt chastened but followed. We descended to the bailey, where we found John in his little nook with the castle constable. They nearly fell over each other when confronted by the king and dishevelled queen. Henry demanded to know if a courier had arrived while he was away from the castle because he was expecting urgent epistles from Winchester. Both men seemed surprised and glanced at one another. John was uneasy and asked had not the Lord King received letters prior to departing for the hunt?

'No!'

John admitted a courier had arrived, that he had accepted the letters to deliver them, but as Lady Grenvale was at hand, she offered to convey them to his Lordship.

Henry glared. 'Find them! Unless you want to be strung up by your balls.'

Henry's growl had the constable and steward scurrying for the stairs. Antoine was hovering.

We waited back in our quarters. Henry wanted me to change my gown because I was shivering, but there was no way I was doing anything till the letters were in his hands. I stood by the brazier while he paced back and forth. A knock on the door brought a page with two bedraggled pieces of parchment which he thrust into Henry's hand before turning tail faster than a greyhound. Henry looked at me. The seals had been tampered with by someone who had tried to conceal the damage by remelting the wax. Henry read the contents. His face darkened with rage. He sent for Robert. The guard around our quarters was doubled. He checked the children, the dogs snarled.

Another page was sent to our supposed hosts: we would not be attending tonight's banquet. Henry wanted to know what I had brought in the way of provisions. I said there was enough. We had our own little meal, not very fancy but adequate. Henry had brandy wine, which warmed me through. Marion had managed to secure a tub, so I was eventually able to remove the muddy, damp gown and to bathe.

As I sipped the brandy wine, Henry said, 'My darling, I have no desire for that woman. I was just being chivalrous escorting her across the threshold. She was going to show me the preparations being made for you and the children. Your arrival was sooner than expected. I had told the Grenvales you were returning earlier from Normandy and would be joining me.'

As his arms engulfed me, my longing for him overcame my jealousy. My shift fell to the ground with his tunic and braies. My unplaited hair fell down my back. He carried me to his bed.

'Why would I want another woman when I have the most beautiful wife in Christendom, the most sensual of lovers?'

Nilla was right, Henry did not notice if my belly was not as taut as it used to be. His caressing hands and mouth on my breasts were exquisite. My legs circled his waist, my hands gripping his thrusting buttocks. It was a night of nights despite the atmosphere around us.

***

We met with Huw Grenvale the following day. He was grovelling, dismayed we were unable to attend the banquet. Henry told him our plans had changed, that early on the morrow we would be returning to London. Henry reminded him that he had promised to arrange a meeting with him and Pendragon. Grenvale paled when told all lands wrongfully acquired along the border must be returned. Fair taxes would be applied. Those avoiding them would be punished under English law, and a peace treaty would be agreed with the Welsh. The earl was agitated, I suspect trying to bide his time. But no matter how he hummed and hawed, Henry ordered

Chapter 4: Owen Pendragon

the earl to either harness his horse to accompany him and his queen, or have one of his men guide us to the Welsh King's camp. I had told Henry I was coming regardless of how much he protested. After much flustering and flurry, we set off. I ordered my men of the Aquitaine to guard our children and entourage. Antoine without question obeyed. Henry's elite Norman knights rode with us. Lord and Lady Grenvale would have had to be total fools not to notice that the warm humour of their royal visitor had iced over.

We followed the Severn as I had the previous day. On the way, I told Henry of my unusual encounter, describing the Druid. After my account, Henry hauled his horse to a halt. He resorted to his mangled Langue d'Oc,

'Where did you turn off the trail?'

Looking around I said, 'Further along, I think.'

Henry's guards milled about, horses jiggling their reins.

We moved along slowly till I recognised the path to the pool. 'Here, Henry. I rode down that track away from the river.'

'Right. Let us go exploring. Robert, we will continue alone along this track.'

Robert frowned. 'A bit foolhardy, Milord, especially as her Ladyship's mystery Druid, as you hinted, might not be one.'

I was puzzled.

Robert tilted his head towards Grenvale and softly said, 'What will I tell the Earl?

'Tell him that I am going to roll in the grass with my wife if you must – but keep him away.'

Though still perplexed, I did not question his orders. Henry wore an air of determination; an argument would have been fruitless.

As we turned off, Robert, the guards and Grenvale continued. This time Henry followed me. The pool with its gurgling spring was only a short distance further. I was nervous. We dismounted. We could only hear the sound of the water, the rustling of leaves and birds overhead. I stood near Rebel, ready to remount and flee if necessary.

'Who do you suppose this person is, if not a Druid?'

'Owain Pendragon, I suspect. You were damned lucky you were not abducted.'

'I did not introduce myself. He would not have known who I was.'

Henry gave me a dubious look. I did not enlighten him about what had taken place. After my fit of jealousy, he would have had his own, knowing that a naked man had handed me back the crown of Normandy after I had, in fury, if by accident, flung it into the pool.

'It is so quiet; I might have time to ravish you after all.

'Not if we are being watched by a cohort of Welsh rebels.'

Something, I know not what, made me glance over Henry's shoulder. 'Look behind you.'

My hand reached into the folds of my gown, grasping my finely-honed knife.

Without panic Henry turned as if he was going to admire the view. The tall 'Druid' was standing quietly observing us. Henry, relaxed and jovial, ambled towards the figure in white.

'Ah! King Owain, my good foe, I am delighted to see you looking so well.'

Owain Pendragon strolled towards us. He seemed to be alone and unarmed. I knew Henry was, and I was not about to sheathe the blade hidden in the folds of my gown.

Owain gave me a far too familiar look as he acclaimed, 'We meet again, Queen of the Wood Sprites.'

Henry shot me a look. I think my flaming face could have set fire to a thatch.

'Ah, um, goodness me... thank you Lord King Owain for kindly leading me to safety yesterday, when my horse and I had wandered off the path and become lost, and had I known who you were, I would not have drawn my knife.'

With chivalry of which my troubadour grandfather would have been proud, he smiled, too familiarly I thought, and said, 'It was an honour, doubly so knowing now who the lady was.'

The two kings then began their conversation on a convenient log with water trickling in the background, their only witnesses being me and the birds. I arranged myself among a field of bluebells as I listened intently to their dialogue, which was, to my surprise, in Latin. Time passed. They discussed the border: who had sovereignty over various estates, especially the Grenvales, and who owed allegiance to whom, including again, the Grenvales. Taxes were mentioned. No peace treaty, though.

The thorny question of taxes became a sticking point. I interrupted, suggesting the moneys collected from estates on the border be shared equally between England and Wales. Sheriffs in the border towns already had the responsibility for tax collection. An accounting system could be arranged whereby the sheriffs could distribute taxes to the treasuries of both kingdoms in an equitable manner.

This was greeted with silence as both men stared at me agape. Henry knew my grasp of English law had become profound. What Owain understood of me or my education, I knew not. I believed he only saw a Wood Sprite.

Henry remarked he did not know one sheriff in England who was that honest or had the capacity to be a mathematician, but of course he could not speak for the Welsh. Owain just shrugged.

This drew their conversation to a close. I felt frustrated because nothing had been finalised. Documents would have to be drawn up following their discussion. This I knew would take time and we were to leave on the morrow. All I could think was that Henry must have had a course of action in mind. They rose and took leave of each other. Henry helped me stand. My thin patience was surfacing.

In Langue d'Oc, I hissed, 'What happens next?'

'We have much to think about.'

'But surely there must be a written agreement about what has transpired or people like the Grenvales will continue to dupe you both, and they will continue to play the Welsh against the English and vice versa.'

'Nobody dupes me!'

Owain cleared his throat. Although I was doing my best to keep my voice even, he may have detected I was not satisfied.

'Well, as far as I am concerned, you have done a lot of talking, gaining nothing.'

'Eleanor, keep your voice down. We have achieved much. A rapport has been developed. You becoming lost yesterday has made many things possible, and more will be accomplished as a result. Anyway, you are always nagging that I should talk more.'

Touché! But I was aghast at the casualness of this meeting. Surely Henry did not trust the Welsh King who he had said in the past was as cunning as Nilla's old pet monkey, Simian. What of the Grenvales? According to Malcolm, they were plotting to kill my husband. Were they doing Owain's bidding? Apart from myself, there were no witnesses to the meeting. What was more, in the surrounding woods there could have been Welsh rebels ready to pounce. Under my regal exterior I was agitated, but Henry was as calm as a summer's day.

Henry and Owain shook hands,

'We will meet again Lord Owain. I thank you for your useful thoughts, I will take them to heart.

'And I yours King Henry.'

Owain bowed his head to me, taking my hand to his lips. He said with a wicked twinkle, 'If ever thou should lose thyself again, it will be a pleasure to rescue thee once more.'

Chapter 4: Owen Pendragon

I hoped Henry did not see the glint in his eyes. With that, he disappeared into the surrounding woods.

We remounted, riding back to the main path. To my surprise, Robert and several men of Henry's guard emerged from the shadows of the oaks. So, we were protected after all. Henry gave me a knowing grin.

'Why did you take the risk of talking to Owain alone?'

Henry replied, 'I was hoping the Welsh King was as enchanted by the English queen as was the Scottish Malcolm. You getting lost yesterday has opened doors. He would have known who he was assisting even though that you did not introduce yourself. Owain has spies everywhere.'

'Especially in Grenvale castle,' I muttered.

As far as I was concerned, Henry's and Owen's conversation was frustrating. I wanted a treaty on velum and signed.

***

That evening, surrounded by his guards, Henry informed Lord and Lady Grenvale they were fortunate not to be leaving their estate in chains to be tried for treason in England or in Wales. From now on they would be watched from both sides of the border. He taxed them heavily.

To my surprise, before we left the next day, he sent an armed escort to the clearing where we held our discourse with Owain Pendragon. Owain appeared as Henry expected, and his share of the geld from the Grenvale purloined coffers was given to him. My fears were allayed. At least for now, England and Wales were at peace.

That morning both husband and wife were chastened as we mounted to leave before the noonday bells. Henry took Grenvale's young son Aeled as a hostage for insurance, telling Lady Grenvale nothing would befall her son providing she and Lord Grenvale kept their agreements with England and Wales. I felt no sympathy for her at all as her wailing echoed round their battlements.

Chapter 5. Chancellor Becket

Our journey towards London was taken at a gentle pace. Henry was at times impatient to move at his usual break-neck speed, but having put aside my jealous rage, and Henry his own distemper, we enjoyed each other's company. We made quite a sight through towns and villages with our entourage trailing for leagues. In Worcester, we spent a few restful days being entertained by the bishop at his comfortable palace.

From there we wended our way towards Woodstock. But I awoke one morning to the familiar stomach-churning knot of pregnancy. One would think after so many children my body would have adapted. I kept asking myself why I had vomited my breakfast and felt so wretched.

At long last I had managed to wean Richard. He was the clingiest of our four children. He and his father did not like each other. Henry could not stand his yelling, which was lusty. To make matters worse, Richard screamed and arched his back if Henry picked him up. After we left Shrewsbury, I handed him over to Agatha. Of course, he was hungry because he would not suckle from her if he thought he could have Maman. This meant he howled and screamed. This, along with the teeth he was getting, meant he was insufferable. If I tried to comfort him, he wanted my breast. It was a nightmare. Henry's method of fatherhood was to insist I ride with him, leaving Richard in the carriages with the long-suffering maids and me feeling on edge and guilty. At least Richard slept at night, probably from exhaustion.

So far, Henry had not noticed my condition as he rose early to talk to the men, our hosts, and to ready us for the next stage of our journey. I asked Amaris for the physic I took to try to control the queasiness, but she had difficulty

Chapter 5: Chancellor Becket

locating where it was packed. After tearing chests apart, she admitted she thought it would not be needed before London.

Woodstock was a welcome relief. I was still suffering, even though Amaris was dutifully preparing the stomach settling tisane. I think the ingredients she found were a little stale. Henry drank it by mistake on two occasions which did not help. When I wailed, he wanted to know what it was, so I had to confess. He grinned like a gargoyle with happiness and praised my fecundity. I often wished he would praise my other attributes as well. Then he made all sorts of silly cooing noises till I threw a pillow at his head, which only made him jump back into bed for a wrestle. That was either going to end with me vomiting all over him or what made this child in the first place.

***

It was decided I should stay at Woodstock with the children so Henry and his men could travel at a mad gallop. There were duties of state to attend to in London. Young Geoffrey would be excited to see his father, also Henry's brother. It was pleasant being carefree for a while, not having to mount a horse for a long tiring day in the saddle. Hal and Matilda enjoyed the gardens there. The weather was pleasantly warm, with springtime flowers popping their heads up. There were crocuses everywhere, as well as daffodils forming a golden carpet. The bees in the orangery were busy.

If only I could defeat the morning sickness. I spoke to an apothecary to see if we could find something to settle my stomach once and for all. Nurses Millicent, Agnes, and Agatha put their heads together. There seemed to be as many remedies as there were mothers. Only God knew why nothing worked in my favour. Amaris reported Renée said it was because I was a picky eater. I could think of a very rude answer to that. Unfortunately, some of their physics were so foul tasting they made my problem worse. Their latest was boiled water, lemon or lime juice, ginger, honey with mint leaves steeped in the mixture. For once it tasted quite pleasant. I prayed it would work. Millicent's pure vinegar made my eyes water. Moreover, I was mightily tired of dry crusts.

***

After I arrived back in London, I was annoyed again by Thomas Becket. Wherever I stepped he seemed to be there. I was alarmed by the deepening friendship between him and Henry. Becket had been on the periphery of the court since we arrived in England. As chancellor, he was competent. Even so, I neither trusted him, nor knew what to make of him. The feeling was mutual. During my absence in Woodstock, he had wormed his way even closer to Henry's bosom, almost supplanting Robert as his confidante. This was most unsettling.

Becket made much of his features. He dressed most flamboyantly with great opulence. One would think Thomas was the king, decked as he was in all his brocaded robes embroidered in gold and fringed with fur. Whereas Henry preferred austere, plain garments. Even his capes were short for ease of mounting his horse as well as keeping them out of the dirt. *Curtmantle*, they called him in jest.

What irritated me most was Becket's flattery of Henry. Becket was from lowly beginnings, but he was out to promote himself to become a permanent member of Henry's inner circle. He was well schooled in the law, a qualified advocate. For all his education, though, his Latin pronunciation was most ill. He had spent time in Paris as a student. I discovered he was there when I was Queen of France. Archbishop Theodore was grooming him for high office in the church. I asked why, for God's sake?

Becket was alienating kind, generous Robert and keeping Henry from the task of governing, which added to my suspicions. They spent evenings carousing in inns

Chapter 5: Chancellor Becket

and taverns. Some of these places, Robert told me, were not desirable. Robert had to bring Henry home well and truly in his cups at times. Robert rarely had a bad word for anyone. He was a true chivalrous knight and gentleman, but he too was concerned about Henry's behaviour. Henry enjoyed life and liked the company of men as well as some fun to ease the seriousness of his ordained life. But he was not behaving responsibly. He was ignoring his role, his duty.

When I saw wagons and carriages entering the palace, I was shocked to find Thomas Becket moving under our roof. I went to Henry in his audience chamber where he was with his justiciars. Henry excused himself, then followed me to the quiet of the library.

'Have you lost your senses?' I demanded. 'What in God's Name is Becket doing moving into our palace? Furthermore, why was I not consulted?'

'Calm down, Eleanor.'

'Henry, I do not want that snake in Westminster. You will rue the day.'

'Thomas is my guest, not yours. He is here to help draft new laws and update some that need to be improved to suit England's new rule. The taxation system also needs an overhaul.'

'Cannot you see you are being manipulated by that fancy upstart!'

'Oh, for God's sake! Sometimes, Eleanor, you are impossible!'

Henry then stomped off as if I was some serf to be ignored. The ink pot ricocheted off the closing door.

***

I thought of taking myself and the children back to Woodstock, or to Windsor, but then who would keep an eye on what was happening? Robert and I started to put our heads together. So far there was little to report. I made a point of joining Henry in the evenings, bringing the older children, including my stepson, Geoffrey. This slowed down the quaffing of ale a little. If I really wanted to annoy Henry, I would bring Richard who would tire and start grizzling. Young Geoffrey would try to distract his little brother, but that only lasted for a while. Henry would start grinding his teeth and demand Agatha take him to his cot. As one by one they dropped with fatigue, I would be left along with Henry's die-hard men.

Often, they would play chess. A blind man could see Thomas was letting Henry win. It was all I could do to contain myself. Henry was a good player if he put his mind to it, but he bored easily if the game was drawn out, which was another reason why I won. One night, I sauntered to the table and watched Thomas' feigned shock when Henry checkmated him which was nauseating.

'Another game, My Lord?' he simpered.

I rolled my eyes, stirring Henry's wicked sense of humour. Grinning, he said, 'Thomas, you are too easy an adversary. Why not play Lady Eleanor?'

Robert and I glanced at each other. With amusement dancing round his lips, Robert raised an eyebrow adding, 'What a good idea.'

I knew not if Becket was aware of how well I played, but I did not think he would want to be beaten by a woman. He agreed with a gleam in his eye, so I was sure he thought he could humiliate me. The first moves were conventional ones I had been taught by Papa when I was four or five. Thomas should have been warned. No-one was wagering, but all were crowding round the table. He was being careful, not like when he played Henry. So far, he had done nothing risky proving he was a better player than he pretended. I waited like a spider in its web for a fly to land. My next tactic was to hesitate over his last move as if not sure what to do. He sat back in his chair looking smug, while Robert and Henry glanced sideways at each other. When at last I moved a knight, he must have thought I had no idea what I was doing, so without

Chapter 5: Chancellor Becket

thinking too much, his next move was ill conceived. I had lured him into a trap. After just five moves, it was my turn to show self-satisfaction.

'Checkmate, Master Becket, is it not?'

He was dumb struck, staring at the board.

'Let me show you where you made your mistake, Master Becket.'

I heard Henry's intake of breath. With great deliberation, I returned the pieces to the board exactly where they had been five moves back.

'Had you not fallen for the bishop, we could have had a longer game, though I doubt the outcome would have been any different.'

I rose giving Henry a look that suggested if he came to bed now, he would get more than a goodnight kiss. Giving Becket a friendly punch on the arm, he said he would see him on the morrow.

We left, peeling with laughter.

***

Henry's association with Becket continued to create arguments between us. Some nights I could not stay awake. My condition was still disguised, but I was tiring. I needed my bed. On more than one occasion, Henry arrived late in the night smelling of ale. He fumbled at me wanting sex. I do not often refuse Henry. I love him and desire our intimacy, but I told him on this occasion I would not make love to a drunkard and to get out of my bed. His unsteadiness made him easy to push out. He landed with a hefty thump on the floor. He was furious with me.

I also grew concerned about some of the entertainment being brought into the palace. Thomas had many friends who were travelling entertainers, musicians, jesters, mummers, and such. I was used to the Aquitaine troubadour tradition which could be rather suggestive at times, like some of my Grandfather William's songs and poetry, but they were clever and witty. Our mummers were professional and sophisticated in their performance. In contrast these players were from local taverns, and some were most strange in their behaviour. One night a group of mummers performed a play that could only be described as crude. Even Henry who rarely blushed, found it vulgar. My maids were shocked, so I sent them to their quarters. I remained because I did not want Henry carousing into the night. When Thomas invited the mummers, little more than riff-raff, to partake in brandy wine in his quarters. I was furious.

After Henry and I repaired to my bed chamber I was ranting about Thomas Becket's cheek. 'Henry, this cannot go on. Who gave Becket permission to bring those people here? Where did they come from?'

'I gave him permission, Eleanor, but I have to admit I did not know that they would be so coarse. I was expecting, I suppose, some sort of sophistication.'

'And now he has invited them to his quarters. Just whose palace does he think he is inhabiting?'

Henry sighed. 'All right, calm down. I will make sure it does not happen again.'

To my horror, I found out the next day from pages and churls who served Becket in his quarters, that the boys who played the part of girls in the play remained dressed as girls. Many of the activities were not fit for my ears. That was it. I was no longer the innocent girl who thought a catamite belonged to a religious order. Becket had to leave. I went to Henry. Thomas Becket was gathered with our justiciars and scribes around a large table in the assembly hall. Becket was looking at Henry with adoring eyes. God's teeth, the scales fell from my eyes, was he in love with Henry? My stomach churned; I felt the blood drain from my face. Surely not! The room revolved.

***

I spent two days recovering. Henry cancelled his appointments. Matthias was summoned. Everyone

Chapter 5: Chancellor Becket

thought it was the child; perhaps I was miscarrying. I was in shock and could barely speak. Henry was gentle and attentive, holding the physic I was prescribed to my lips. When I regained strength, I clung to him in desperation, begging him not to leave me. I told him I had to confide in him most urgently. I believed he thought I had lost my wits, that I feared I had lost my baby. It took a little time to reassure him, to convince him I was concerned about him. I had no idea of how to broach the subject, so I called for the pages and churls who had attended Thomas Becket on the night he invited the mummers to his chambers. I could see Henry was still worried about my health. Tim, Fulk, Robin, and Peter entered. They were shy, not used to seeing their queen in bed looking wild-eyed and propped up on pillows.

I thanked them for attending. Henry was sceptical. I asked them to tell their Lord King what they had witnessed.

The boys looked at each other, their faces reddening. None of them dared to open their mouths.

'Come on, boys,' I coaxed. 'Lord Henry does not bite. Tell him what you saw.'

Peter nudged Robin who blurted, 'The boys dressed as girls stayed in their gowns.'

Peter then whispered, 'They had rouge on their faces and that black stuff around their eyes, did they not, Fulk?'

'Aye, my Liege and Master Becket was hugging them to him, and we had to serve them wine.'

'Some of the older mummers put their hands up their dresses.'

Henry looked at me and said, 'Was there any other odd behaviour that you noticed?'

'We are not sure. We had served all the wine and had to go for more. But we decided not to go back even if we got into trouble. As I was shutting the door, one man kissed one of the young girls/boys. They were getting drunk, even Master Becket.'

'Now, lads, I hope you are not making this up.'

The boys shook their heads vigorously.

'No, Sire,' Tim blurted, 'I swear to God we were shocked. I – we – did not know about such things. That is why we did not go back with more wine. We were frightened.'

Henry said naught, mulling over what he heard. With a heavy sigh he at last replied, 'All right boys, I believe you. But I do not want you to mention this incident to anyone. I thank you for being so forthright. We will take care of everything from now on. Off you go to your duties.'

The boys nodded their heads and backed from our presence almost falling over each other in their haste to leave the room.

Henry paced. I slipped out of bed, stopping him mid-stride.

I had to know. 'Henry, Becket is in love with you. Has he ever, have you ever done what it is that catamites do?'

I think Henry was amazed I knew of such things. 'God in heaven, Eleanor! No, a thousand times no! What are you thinking?'

'I have seen how he looks at you, and of late you have spent so much time with him. He manipulates you for God knows what purpose except for his own advancement or to perhaps compromise you in some manner.'

'No, Eleanor, if anything it has been my purpose to manipulate him. I am aware he has designs above his station, though his proclivities I did not suspect. He is a bit effeminate, but I thought naught of it. This may now shock you, but I want him to be the next Archbishop of Canterbury. Theodore is getting on in years. I need someone in that post who will do my bidding regarding the application and division of Civil and Canon Law. I have been grooming Thomas Becket to be that person. Now, believe it or not, he will be more likely to do my bidding if he thinks his secret might be discovered.'

Chapter 5: Chancellor Becket

I was dumb struck. The thought of Thomas Becket becoming Archbishop of Canterbury was anathema to me. A popinjay, a catamite, how was he to be trusted to follow Henry's will. He might be clever, he might be deeply versed in the Lord God's rule, but was he not committing a sin? Some time ago, Becket vowed to be celibate: no women were to sully his life. But does celibacy exclude men? I knew, however, that no matter how much I protested, Henry had made up his mind. My only consolation was that Henry knew what he was doing, and he had no interest in this commoner except to make him his man. I knew Henry wanted to put down opposition to his laws. Many of the church's hierarchy were obstructionist over the trials of lay clerics who had committed a criminal act. They argued, instead, that these offenders would be justly tried under Canon Law even if, for God's sake, they committed murder. Mostly they were set free. Certain members of the clergy insisted these unordained men be tried under the church's ruling, which forbade them to be retried under common law because the sentencing was more severe. It was an ongoing frustration.

Henry persuaded me to allow Becket to remain under our roof for the time being. I had to acknowledge that to have his own man as the most powerful prelate in England would be an advantage.

I had to endure, but I used my own methods to prove to this obnoxious man that Henry preferred me, his wife. Except in private, I did not initiate my desire. Now I made a point of arousing Henry. After a few ales or games of chess or backgammon, I would sidle up to Henry as if to whisper in his ear, but instead, I would nibble his earlobes, something I knew that drove him mad. If we were sitting side by side, I would rub my hand up and down his leg, getting closer to his groin. My tactics were always successful. Henry was easily stimulated, his resistance, weak. Becket, I could see, was green with envy. There was nothing he could do. No matter what tactics he tried, another game of chess or a discussion, nothing was going to interfere with Henry's desire for his wife.

***

Richard's first birthday was approaching. I managed to persuade Henry not to take young Geoffrey to York until after the small celebration I was planning. He was to be taken under the wing of Archbishop Roger for schooling and entry into the church. His birthday was soon also; he would be eight years old. I thought he was too young to be sent so far from home. He had settled in with my children, who adored him. Richard loved his big brother, squealing with delight when he came to play with them. Geoffrey was very patient with Richard, who could be quite a handful at times. He was by far the most determined of the three. Perhaps he felt a little isolated. Hal and Matilda were so close in age they were almost like twins. They played happily together, not appreciating Richard rampaging through their games like a wild boar. God help them when he can walk.

Richard snatched one of Hal's wooden soldiers one morning. There was much screaming and yelling. Everyone dropped what they were doing to rush to see what the fuss was about. Hal was furious because Richard would not give it back. I tried to explain he was too young to understand he must share. Matilda pulled Richard's hair, which did not help matters. The nursery was in uproar, so much so that Henry was disturbed from his breakfast.

Henry stormed into the nursery. Of course, both Hal and Matilda petitioned their father to take the soldier from Richard. This was not going to be pleasant. Richard clung to it; his baby face darkened into an obstinate pout, Plantagenet jaw jutting out. I tried to calm Henry, who was determined not to be outdone by his eleven-month-old son. I said I would sort it out, and that he should go back to his repast.

'Eleanor, you have spoiled that boy. He needs a jolly good spanking.'

'You touch one hair on that baby's head, and you will be never allowed in my bed again.'

'Richard, give Papa that soldier – NOW!'

With that, Henry wrenched the damned toy out of Richard's hand, sending him into a volume of screaming that could have shattered glass in Constantinople. Richard held his breath and turned purple, terrifying everyone till he was forced to breathe.

'As Queen of England,' Henry thundered. 'I would have thought you could control your own brood so a man can enjoy his morning in peace!'

'That is not helpful, Henry.'

He stomped back to his breakfast. I was having difficulty picking up the kicking, writhing boy. Agatha ran to my aid. Peace was eventually restored.

'Where that streak of determination comes from, I know not,' said Amaris as she handed me my tisane, wryly raising an eyebrow.

***

Richard's first birthday was a success. I had asked one of our carpenters to whittle some toy soldiers for Richard so he would have his own. He was so excited. We had all the children's favourite sweetmeats, lots of songs, games, and a juggler to entertain. The only sadness was the imminent departure of young Geoffrey to York. We were all going on progress, Henry with Geoffrey to York, and I, to Mother Joan near Lincoln. We travelled together for part of the way, staying with the nuns in various abbeys where we were trying to establish refuges for women in dire poverty and their children. The monies from the Aquitaine treasury were being distributed. Word soon filtered through the towns and villages across the countryside that succour was at hand at various religious houses. I was overwhelmed at the response. But it was also sad to realise just how much suffering there was still throughout the land after the civil war.

After I settled with Mother Joan, Henry left for York. I was feeling dejected having to say good-bye to young Geoffrey. I wished him every success in his studies and emphasised that knowledge was the greatest gift God could bestow, and to never stop learning. As I hugged him, I told him he would be in my prayers. I hoped he could visit us as often as possible. For enlightenment, I gave him books by Homer – the *Iliad,* and the *Odyssey,* in Latin. I said one day I hoped he would know Greek, so he could read them in the language in which they were written. I made Henry promise Geoffrey would be with us at Christmastide. I kissed Henry. I would miss him.

***

My trip was a success. It was inspiring to see my plans implemented but I was concerned that abbeys and convents were being stretched to house the needy as they seemed to be pouring out of every crevasse in the country. Mother Joan's building program was already overextended. More must be done. I promised to apply to Henry and Uncle Ralph for more funds.

By mid-October with winter nipping around the corners of woods and draughty monasteries, it was time for me to return to London. Although not as bulky as I had been with Richard, I needed to be on my way. I still rode, much to Henry's and my maid's consternation. It was a slow plod or a canter at most.

The weather turned against us. Sudden squalls of rain impeded our movement. River fords became deep and dangerous, forcing us to continue by different routes. Henry was affected, too. We diverted to Coventry where Henry caught up with us on his return from York. We decided to ride to Warwick Castle which was closer, and the roads passable.

Chapter 5: Chancellor Becket

At last, we were dry, warm, and out of the saddle. The Avon was flooding so we were forced to stay at Warwick. The castle is large and rambling, but our quarters were comfortable, if a little primitive when it comes to heating. One day, I would have fireplaces installed throughout the land. Braziers are all very well, but, unless the wood is bone dry, they smoke, and this is most unpleasant, permeating everything from one's clothes to one's hair.

Henry was like a caged bear. We were stuck in Warwick with rain pouring down in sheets. Even the moat was threatening to overflow its contents. It was becoming nauseatingly smelly. The dry wood was threatening to run out. The churls and woodsmen were doing their best to keep the braziers going, but the dry wood had to be mixed with the damp. We were all enveloped in furs. The roof leaked in places, so we were cramped together for warmth and to keep dry. We could all end up in the kitchens, which were the warmest corners of the castle. My maids were concerned I might have to remain here with my confinement getting closer. That would be the last straw.

God be praised, sunshine at last and the end I hoped of the Autumn rains. Henry had a smile on his face at last and had stopped his irritable pacing. During our painful incarceration, he had to play chess with me, which did nothing to improve his humour. Dear God, we were a competitive pair. Robert had to become referee. Henry kicked over the board when I started to thrash him. He deigned to accuse me of cheating. Well, that started a war. I do not cheat! I screamed at him, and he screamed at me, till Robert, Lucille and Celeste said enough was enough when chess pieces flew like iron balls from a catapult. Robert announced he was never going allow Henry and me to play chess against each other again.

We were finally packed. Everyone thought I should be able to survive the trip to at least Woodstock without giving birth on the way. Henry agreed to accompany me but insisted I ride in a carriage. I was not happy, but for once gave up protesting. Everyone was against me mounting Rebel. Amaris, I suppose was correct when she said Rebel could become fidgety, but also my normal good balance was becoming compromised by my bulge.

It was time to leave. I placed my quills, ink, and parchment in their travelling chest always my duty. No-one touches my journal. The weather looked beautiful, praise God. We crossed the Avon at Evesham, a pretty market town surrounded by orchards with a fine old abbey. The carriage was the only pall in my journey. How I would have loved to have been on Rebel, enjoying the sun, with the breeze ruffling my veil, instead of being cooped up in stuffy surroundings with Henry rubbing in my discomfort by describing the birds, butterflies, and pretty scenery from his destriere. Woodstock was a joy to behold when I could finally alight to take in gulps of fresh air.

I had a wonderful time with Hal, Matilda, and Richard. Richard was beginning to talk, though his favourite word was *NO!* He could also run like a hare. He was a strapping handsome little boy. The other two were learning to be more patient with him, but sadly father and son still clashed, both being stubborn. The three children latched onto one of the gardeners who had the patience of a saint allowing them to 'help'. It was so reminiscent of Nilla and me and our tolerant gardeners at L'Ombrière and Poitiers.

As I scribbled away in this corner of my chamber, I found concentration difficult. The baby was imminent, I was sure. I had a backache on and off for most of the day. Last night I kept Henry awake and told him to go to his own bed, but he was determined to stay regardless of my restlessness. I could not sit with any comfort; it was time to lurch towards my chamber.

***

Chapter 5: Chancellor Becket

Another boy arrived. This one managed to be punctual on the 23rd day of our Lord, September 1158. God be praised he was not an elephant like Richard, though he spent longer getting here much to his mother's roaring dismay. He was put into my arms, and we stared at each other. Is it possible for a new-born babe to be able to read one's mind like a prophet? His eyes seemed to bore into the depths of my psyche, calculating.

When Henry arrived, he looked at us both, uttering, 'Dear God, Eleanor! He looks exactly like you right down to the shape of his eyes. What is the colour of his hair? He seems to have naught.'

I looked at my *duplici* muttering,

'Not the nose, I hope.

'Eleanor, I do not understand why you keep complaining about your nose. It is neither hooked nor bent, just straight. It gives you an aristocratic bearing. I know not why you are so obsessed about it.'

I was too exhausted to argue that I always wished for a turned-up button like Nilla.

We had to name this boy. The other children had names decided for them before they arrived, but this little fellow not so. When his brothers and sister came to see him, I asked for their help to choose. Hal announced he should be called Geoffrey, after big Geoffrey. Henry agreed, but for his father, of course, the one name I was trying to avoid. This I said could be awkward, with two half-brothers called Geoffrey. How to differentiate? But no, the two Henrys had made up their minds. So, he was christened Geoffrey. Hal thought he was all right, Matilda had another dolly and Richard went straight for his beautiful large eyes. By now, I was too tired to care. Birth does not get any easier.

Henry was strutting like a peacock, boasting how his wife was so clever! 'Look at me, she has given me another son!'

There were times I felt like a brood mare.

I took my time after Geoffrey's birth. I was usually active, with plenty of tasks to keep me occupied, hounding Henry for more administrative duties, but this birth slowed me down. Nevertheless, I was ready to return to the bustle of London, tired or not, because Henry had evicted Thomas Becket from Westminster. Much to my disgust, however, he set him up right royally on the Surrey side of the river on a small estate. I was happy he was not near my boys, though, no matter how clever he was. He could attend when he was ordered, so long as he kept out of my sight.

***

We had been in London for several weeks. I had been too ill to do anything. After two weeks of settling in with baby Geoffrey and the other children, Henry dashed off to Winchester for treasury discussions. One morning I awoke feeling most odd. I knew I could not be pregnant. This was not morning sickness. When I arose from my bed the room revolved in circles, and I was forced to sit down. I felt clammy and flushed. Again, I attempted to rise to begin my morning ablutions, but remembered little else. It was fortunate Amaris appeared with a bowl of water because I had collapsed to the floor. My legs would not hold me. She helped me back to bed and told me not to move while she summoned Matthias, who discovered I was covered in a rash and had a fever. I was isolated from the children, especially Geoffrey. Cecilia, his wet nurse, had to take over suckling him day and night.

At first, they thought it was measles, but I survived an epidemic in childhood when all the children of Poitiers were afflicted. Matthias diagnosed scarlet fever. Along with the malaise, my throat was so sore I could not swallow, my tongue felt it was encased in sand and soon the rash had spread in nasty weals all over my body.

Where I had been infected was a puzzle. Recently, Henry and I had distributed alms to the poor throughout

Chapter 5: Chancellor Becket

the London streets. It was a cold damp, typical London day as we approached Christmas. We moved among the people, stopping, distributing alms, and talking as part of our tradition to help the needy. Dressed in inadequate clothing, the poor were so grateful for a few coins. Many clutched at us with outstretched hands, holding often snotty-nosed children to be blessed. Henry and I spent hours in this manner, not noticing the bone wracking cold until we returned to the warmth of the palace. I must have been in contact with some poor soul with the illness.

I remembered little of the days and weeks I was struck down. My fever rose. Henry told me he could have boiled mutton on my face and forehead. He had been summoned back from Winchester. My recollection was vague, and I was too ill to care. They tell me I rambled in a variety of languages, even in long-forgotten Aramaic which, Amaris said, was a good thing no-one understood. With a wry look, she told me later the poem I recited in Aramaic was 'not from the *Songs of Solomon*'. Oh dear. That poem of love and desire, penned by my first lover, darling Abraham, was secreted away in a chest in Poitiers. Amaris saved my life when I was accused by the French court of adultery after the poem had fallen into the wrong hands. None of Louis's court spoke Aramaic, but Amaris did. She was forced to translate but her clever recitation came from the *Songs of Solomon* of the old bible instead of Abraham's verse.

***

The whole of England was praying for me. Henry did not leave my side regardless of me possibly spreading the disease to him. He helped to sponge my face with cool water steeped in lavender. The children, too, were frightened. Their Maman was usually robust. Matthias explained the infection occurred probably because I was still recovering from the last birth. I think that was a hint for Henry to show some restraint without thinking his wife might need to cool her ardour as well.

Prayers and remarkable physics eventually had some effect. Matthias said because I had a healthy constitution, this held me in good stead. After the fever broke, I started to return to the real world instead of some nether place in the weird regions of my mind. Once my sore throat eased, I could sip a little broth with some bread soaked in it. But my skin was left rough and scaly. Amaris, Marion, and my other maids must have rubbed enough oil and lanolin into it to grease a slippery pig at a town fair. When I was out of danger, Henry returned to his duties and the children were permitted to visit. Poor little Geoffrey, he had to get to know me again. I felt bereft, I could not suckle him. My milk had gone with my fever. He was bonny, thriving at Cecilia's breast. She loved him, too, which was a little heart-wrenching, but I cannot be too envious. Her baby had died, which was why she was with us.

When the weather was pleasant and not too cold, I was able to venture into one of the courtyards with the children, though Amaris flustered too much, hovering hawk-like and insisting I was bundled in a warm cloak. Nevertheless, I could not be ungrateful, because she and the others had been dedicated nurses, daily easing me back to health with devotion, love, and infinite patience. I would have liked to join Henry at Winchester, but he had to travel on to Normandy. Louis was being a bother again and so were a group of rebellious nobles and clerics, and just about anyone who could clank around in armour or mount a horse on the Angevin-Poitivin border.

Henry made me regent in his absence. My quill would be needed. Some of the provincial justiciars needed to be convinced I could read and write. I would be lonely without Henry. I prayed to God for his safe return.

I had no sooner settled into my role when an argument regarding woodlands was brought to my attention. It involved the Abbot of St Albans and his neighbour, a

Chapter 5: Chancellor Becket

powerful baron. As it happened, this land dispute should have been resolved by the Earl of Aylesbury, who was appointed by Henry to judge local disagreements, but he failed to issue a writ protecting the abbey's property. The baron trespassed and cut down trees in the woodland and intimidated the monks. I was angered this had taken place. I managed to prevent further losses to the abbey, which feared their powerful neighbour. I also reprimanded the Earl of Aylesbury for not being more diligent in his duties. He did not like that one jot.

It was a salutary lesson for representatives on all judiciary panels, however. They learned I expected them to carry out their duties with care and responsibility. They should know by now I am no fool and I read all documents from beginning to end; nor do I attach my signature and seal to any piece of parchment or velum until I am certain what is scribed is correct.

My copying of the *Common Laws of England* held me in good stead. It was appalling what some sheriffs did to avoid their duties. Laws were devised and written for a purpose and, as far I was concerned, they must be obeyed. Henry's jest about finding an honest sheriff would be funny if not true. They were supposed to collect the taxes for the exchequer, not accumulate the geld for their own coffers. I had to be mightily strict with several, especially the sheriffs of London and Suffolk. Complaints were made and their activities brought to my attention. They had become adept at twisting the law for their personal benefits. Bribery was common and incorrect revenues were arriving at Winchester.

When I met with the two men in question, they tried every sneaky trick they could, winking at each other that they could fool a woman, because heaven forbid, what would she know, queen or not? After I read them the laws they had ignored, quoted others, pointed to the anomalies in their calculations of monies owed to the king, they realised they were in trouble. No amount of grovelling was going save them from punishment. The men of England were discovering I was as forceful as my husband the king if they disobeyed the laws of the land. Word was spreading. I was as knowledgeable as the best advocates.

Most of my other duties involved signing charters that granted land or privileges to nobles for exemplary services to the king. Writs demanding my signature needed more scrutiny for evidence of land tenure or boundaries, especially if they had been distributed during Stephen's reign. There were the usual clerics or others wanting permission to leave the kingdom to travel abroad and suchlike. Alms requested were distributed to worthy abbeys and monasteries. It had always given me great pleasure to aid God's work.

Henry was away longer than we thought he would be, but I had at last received missives from Barfleur. He was getting ready to embark. I would miss being regent. I had enjoyed being 'in charge'. It gave me pride to have handled my duties better than the men around me expected. I was, little by little, gaining respect.

Chapter 6. An Awkward Talisman

A bulky package arrived by courier for my attention. The seal was unknown to me. It was so beautiful I was reluctant to break it. I teased it open to find a small, quite plain box of oak. Inside, wrapped in soft cloth, was an unusual object which could be made of bone. It was oval and fitted into the palm of my hand and carved with words I did not understand. Delicate gold leaf was pressed into the letters, highlighting them. There was a hole drilled through the top where a soft leather thong was looped, long enough to wear around one's neck. It was beautiful in its simplicity. It could be pagan. I had seen something similar in northern France of Celtic origins. I was charmed by it. Tied in leather also was a velum scroll.

I unrolled it and read a well scribed note in English:

To Lady Eleanor, Warrior Queen of the Wood Sprites,

It has been brought to our attention that a pestilence recently laid thee low. Please accept this ancient talisman to protect thee, ever-more.

- A Druid

I knew not what to think. It was obvious who it was from, but how he found out about my fever was a puzzle. I had been well now for some time and London was a long way from Wales. I lived in a world of spies.

Should I show it to Henry? What will he think? I was mightily flattered and honoured, but Henry was no admirer of anything pagan, nor would he approve of me receiving gifts from another man. While I was admiring it, Cecilia brought Geoffrey to me. I showed the gift to her without telling her who sent it. She told me she thought the bone was from a whale. I thought how apt, a play on words. She also told me the strange script looked as if it was Welsh or ancient British, maybe Celtic. When I asked her if she had learnt the language, she said no, but she had seen similar inscriptions on stones in the far west of the country in Cornwell. I asked if the words or the whale bone had healing properties? She shook her head, but she said the ancient Druids believed many things, and some of the Welsh still did.

I let it dangle in my hand. As it swung, Geoffrey reached out trying to grasp it, gurgling, and grinning with delight. Cecilia laughed and changed the subject. Geoffrey, she said even smiled like me. He caught the bauble and put it in his mouth and gave it a good suck. After he lost interest, I wiped away his dribble and hung it around my neck. In my glass, I admired it. I was curious to know more about its design and what it said.

I decided to consult Jerome. He was one member of the clergy who would not throw a fit about the talisman if it had pagan origins. Like me he was intrigued by its simple beauty. When I told him it was gifted from King Owain of Wales his eyebrows shot up to his hairline, aware of a possible conflict with my lord. He asked me if I was going to show it to the king. I told him I was not sure. Jerome thought I should, but not the note which he read with disapproval. He knew Henry and I had met with the Welsh king at Shrewsbury, but not the steaming rage that sent me off at a gallop to the unexpected encounter. Jerome copied the inscription, saying he would speak with some monks who had early British ancestry, and who might be able to translate the inscription. I thanked him and burnt the note!

In the meantime, rather than wear the talisman around my neck, I decided to tie it to the belt that held my scabbard. Like my blade it would be concealed in the folds of my gown. If it was supposed to protect me, I thought why not see if it does. To be honest I was sceptical but touched King Owain showed concern for my wellbeing. If he had regard for me, as Henry had used for his advantage, I could not see why I should not make use of his charm. It

Chapter 6: An Awkward Talisman

was interesting to note, since our unusual encounter, that peace on our border continued without the treaty I had wished was officially signed.

***

I sorely missed being able to suckle Geoffrey so instead I spent a lot of time playing with him. This annoyed Richard who was jealous of the attention I was paying his baby brother. I would end up on the floor with him climbing all over me. Sometimes it became impossible because Hal and Matilda, not to be outdone, joined in the fun. What our vassals would think of the Queen of England flat on the floor with her four children using her as a palliasse, I knew not. My children gave me unbelievable joy. Hal now had a pony which he was learning to ride. He took his lessons with his groom very seriously. Matilda wanted a pony too, but she must wait another year until she was three.

Henry had returned and was somewhat taciturn. He would not enlighten me why. Instead of spending his first evening with me as he would normally, he went into a closet with Becket. I was mightily annoyed and curious as to why he needed to consult with him. I wanted to spend the evening together. There was much to discuss about the affairs of state which took place during my Regency. I ended up listening to our minstrels and playing backgammon with my maids.

At bedtime there was still no sign of Henry. I awoke, in the night and he was not by my side. This was more than odd. He usually could wait to lay with me after a long absence. Apart from when he had been on progress or away, he had spent his nights with me. Even when I was heavy with child, he liked to be in my bed. By morning I went to his chamber. He was not there. I sent for Robert; he too did not know where Henry was. I became distressed. His guards told me Becket and Henry had gone out. They were dismissed and not needed. Why, I asked? They did not know.

I was about to order them to search for their king when he appeared in my chamber.

'Thank God!' I cried. 'Where on earth have you been? I have been more than worried.'

'Indeed! My whereabouts, Eleanor, are immaterial.'

'Henry, your whereabouts to me are more than immaterial, especially as you have only just arrived home from Normandy. I wanted to be with you.'

'You amaze me, Eleanor. If you wanted me to be with me, how come you are receiving baubles from strange men.'

How in God's name did he know about my talisman? Jerome knew about it as did my maids, but they would never have said a word to Henry. It was none of their business. I was puzzled. Somebody who knew, told Henry.

'Do you mean my good luck charm?'

'By Satan's arse, I do not give a damn what you call it. Where did you get it and from whom?'

'King Owain Pendragon, as if you did not know.'

The colour drained from Henry's face. 'Then perhaps you would like to explain why the Welsh king is sending you gifts?'

My heart was thundering, and fury was dancing on my lips. 'He heard I had been ill and sent me this talisman, as a good luck charm to keep me safe in the future.'

Henry bristled, 'So, you believe that pagan rubbish?'

'Of course not. I just thought it was a bit of fun.'

'Then why are you hiding it on your belt.'

'Henry, I am not hiding it. I did not want to wear it around my neck, so I tied it to my belt.'

'Well, the first thing you are going to do, Eleanor, is send it back. Do you understand?'

'Henry, I am not your serf to be ordered around. And sending it back could be misconstrued as an insult

Chapter 6: An Awkward Talisman

regarding a kind intention. Why would you want to jeopardise England's peace with Wales over a mere trifle?'

Henry's menacing voice sent a shiver down my spine. 'In Shrewsbury you wrongly accused me of adultery, rode off endangering your life, terrifying me as to what had become of you, and placing our children in danger, only to end up in some liaison with Pendragon.'

'I had no liaison with the Welsh king, as well you know. I did not know who he was. He helped me remount Rebel and showed me the way to the trail by the Severn because I was unsure of my bearings.'

By now I had had enough of his jealous rage. Henry was behaving like a mad bull. My good intentions failed. 'And may I ask where were you tonight? Out carousing with your catamite friend with his little boys painted and dressed as girls?'

Louis hit me once and it stung my cheek, but Henry's blow knocked me to the ground. There was a ringing in my ears like cathedral bells. I tried to stand but could not. Blood trickled from my nose. Henry dragged me to my feet, but I was seeing two of everything. My knees buckled.

Henry engulfed me in his arms, carried me to my bed then kissed my forehead. He was sobbing, 'Oh, Eleanor, darling! What have I done? I cannot bear the thought of another man being attracted to you. I love you too much. Forgive me?'

I recalled little else, or my reactions, I was too stupefied. I did not think I cried out or wept.

***

I was now a walking puppet. I went through the motions of being Queen of England. I reported all that transpired during my Regency. I was back to my usual duties; I smiled, I was the charming hostess, I laughed at the jesters and applauded the musicians. I accepted the fawning and the flattery; I dressed in my most exquisite gowns and heard the gasps when I entered a room. Occasionally, I was asked my opinion on some rule of law or encouraged to distribute alms, I said my prayers and I prayed on saint's days. I appeared dutiful, attended to my children. And I was pregnant again. I might as well be a stud mare. Again, I feared the birth. Henry would not let me out of his sight. Depression was swallowing me up. I wished I could go home to my kin.

Henry now insisted I travelled with him always, something I had wanted, requested over the years of our marriage. He did not like my subjugation any more than I did. I must find the energy and desire to be Eleanor the tigress again, to re-discover my passion. Where was the girl Papa encouraged to speak her mind? Could I relight the flame to emulate my feisty grandmother Dangerosa who shocked courts and households but never allowed herself to be intimidated or subdued?

Yes, I could flirt and play coy if needs be, yes, I could be the coquette, but I calculated the response. With Henry, I have had no need to push the boundaries because I fell in love with him, not immediately, but, when the realisation hit me, I just knew he would be as portended, the *love of my life*. Maybe the shine had tarnished. I knew not.

***

We moved to the Palace of Winchester. I brought every bauble in my possession, so I looked 'appropriate'. This morning after prayers, I returned to my chamber. I dismissed my maids from my presence to go about their usual activities – stitching, weaving or whatever.

I found myself daydreaming, dawdling through my jewellery. I spread bits and pieces out on a large chest and picked up my mother's dainty amethyst and pearl coronet. I wondered what she looked like, my mother. Nilla was supposed to resemble her. I was supposed to be more like Dangerosa, my mother's mother. Even as an older woman she was said to be eye-catching. I could only remember her through a child's eyes. She always had time for Nilla and me. She told us stories, listened to our prattle. She was tall and elegant and wore beautiful gowns. I had her favourite diadem studded with golden topaz and pearls and other pieces she wore.

I stared at the trio of regal crowns, the Aquitaine, Normandy, and England. Necklaces, earrings, the Briolette diamond, bracelets, particularly William's lion, I spread across the chest. I lined up the lockets for each child that held a snippet of their hair with their names and dates of birth engraved on the back. I picked up and gently kissed the one holding William's sweet curl. I have not had the courage to have the date of his death put on the back. I was terrified I would forget what he looked like. He was so like Henry in many ways. When I hold little Geoffrey, though unlike in looks, he reminded me of William, the baby smell, the milky odour. Melancholy swamped me; his death haunted me still as I laid the locket back at the head of the line. Not a day went by when I did not grieve.

Amidst all these gems and gold was the simple oak box that held the inscribed whalebone. Jerome was told the engraving on it was a Celtic prayer which said something about protecting the owner from all things *"governed by earth, fire and water and the heavens and stars."* So sad when something so simple, so beautiful can cause such ugliness. I refused to send it back to Owain Pendragon but agreed I would not wear it. The carved chest from Antioch had not been opened for years. As I raised its decorative lid, I breathed in the sandalwood perfume. The Knot of Hercules glittered and gleamed in the sunshine streaming through my windows, its rubies and pearls tantalising. The knot had never been untied. After our coronation, it was eased back over my head. It had not been worn since. I lifted it from its nest of silk still amazed at its weight. I draped it over my arms. Visions of Judith, Abraham and Prince Hamid Abdullah flashed before me. I wondered where they were now. Were they still alive and well? As I pondered, the door opened. It was Henry.

He asked what I was doing. It was too late to cover the talisman. So, to distract him I reminded him of when and where I wore the exotic girdle. He looked at it, again wanting to know its history. I told him, as before it was gifted to me in Antioch during the Second Crusade when I was the young Queen of France. But he would never know of its true background or how I was singled out or by whom. He took it from my arms, noting its weight.

'Wear it for tonight's banquet. I want to ask about the arrangements.'

'Everything is in order unless there are any last-minute instructions from you.'

'What gown will you be wearing? There are some barons, knights, and eminent clergy we need to impress.'

'Maybe I'll just wear just the girdle,' I quipped.

He gave me a look, 'Do so for me, anytime you like.'

That made me feel like property. He noticed my sigh as I started to return my jewellery to rightful boxes and velvet bags. He said nothing about the whalebone charm. Perhaps he had not noticed it after all midst all the other gems. William's bracelet he picked up. A cloud passed his face and hoarseness caught his throat.

'You never wear it.'

'I cannot. The ache is too much.'

He picked up the diamond pendant. It swung, catching the light, flashing, and sparkling. I watched.

His eyes were mesmerised. 'You never wear this either.'

'No.'

Its ninety carats could buy England, Normandy, and half of Europe. Henry had no idea of its worth. I caught it as it swung and returned it to its specially crafted strongbox lined with black velvet. I felt I was more its guardian than its owner, as if it needed my protection.

Henry picked up the simple cross studded in rubies he had given me, hanging on its black ribbon.

'Wear this, too, tonight.'

Chapter 6: An Awkward Talisman

Piece by piece he examined my collection. Then out of the blue, he recollected when he first saw me in the garden at L'Ombrière. I was unaware his memory was so clear.

'I remember when I first set eyes on you.'

His smile was nostalgic. 'You wore a light blue gown, no jewellery, but flowers had been wound in your hair which was plaited, falling down your back. All your maids had flowers twisted into wreaths, you were all laughing about something. Renée made up some story about being unable to introduce you all because none of you were veiled. You had difficulty standing. I think you had hurt your knee. You turned your head and caught my eye. That penetrating look I will never forget. I believe my heart jumped out of my chest.'

Yes, I had hurt my knee and needed a stick to help me walk. My recall was that he would see a cripple. Apparently not.

'It was the night of the banquet when I realised who you were. I thought I had died and gone to heaven. Never had I seen such beauty, such glamour, such sophistication, and something else – power. That is the only time I remember you wearing that diamond pendant.'

Henry paused, his eyes misty.

'You came towards me sparkling like a sky full of stars. At that moment, I fell in love. I had to make you mine.'

Henry knelt wrapping his arms around me. Again, his thickened voice, begged me to forgive him for being a brute. I was, to begin with, unresponsive, then I threaded my fingers through his curly mop. His shoulders shuddered. Some grey strands were among the auburn. His face had become craggier, more weather-beaten. Except for his hair colour, he had become his father. My heart lurched at the memory of the man who through fate could never be mine. Like Abraham.

Only pride stood between me and forgiveness of Henry. I knew he had a temper and was easily enraged, so why did I taunt him the day after he returned from Normandy? Then he knew me, too, that my tongue could lacerate, utter venom in the heat of the moment. Both of us juggled for domination. We had screamed and ranted at each other since we met, but we had always settled our differences in a passionate embrace. When asked on that nasty day about the bruising to my face, I told my maids I had tripped on my hem and hit my face on the side of my table. Amaris was suspicious.

I wore the black velvet gown with sleeves lined in scarlet silk and edged in pearls. The Knot of Hercules fitted better because this child was not as advanced. I was seven nearly, eight moons with Hal when I was crowned Queen of England wearing that mighty girdle. The rubies danced in the candlelight catching the simple cross as well. The décolletage enhanced my neck. My rounding breasts were pushed high by hidden binding. I was not veiled because of England's crown. As usual, the assembled guests gasped as Henry escorted me to our thrones. Fecund, rich, and ornamental, possessed by *"enri Plantagenet-a."*

***

I had refused to allow Becket to accompany us to Winchester. Henry recognised the fire was not completely dampened, so agreed. I wanted to become privy to the new laws on which he was working with Henry. They were developing a principle to establish royal courts to try criminal cases and those involving ownership of freehold property. Under Stephen, and presently, these cases were examined by local lords who depending on the personality and morality of the baron, could be manipulated or be open to bribery or suiting the lord's interests. Some people had been unjustly treated. Henry wished to stop this practice. Barons would still be responsible for minor cases and continue to deal with their serfs.

Henry surprised me by allowing me to join his justiciars

Chapter 6: An Awkward Talisman

so I could become familiar with their deliberations. I arrived early in the audience chamber. As I entered, the assembled justiciars stood. While we awaited Henry, I read the scroll rolled out on the table. My frowning alerted them that something was amiss. I was not expecting perfection, but I was surprised there were so many errors. I could spot bad or misspelt Latin from across a moat, and some of the wording was so poorly couched that the meaning was distorted. I had to read it through twice before I could interpret the new laws correctly. A clever advocate, someone like Becket for instance, could argue uncertainty in the law; therefore, a criminal could receive a lighter sentence or none because the inaccuracies made the ruling unclear. Also, how could the new jurists make impartial judgements if those defending or prosecuting cases could twist the legality to suit themselves? Clarity, as far as I was concerned, was mandatory.

I said nothing till Henry entered. I insisted on a word in private. I did not wish to dispute my observations in front of the panel. Henry grunted but accompanied me back outside the chamber to the gallery.

'Henry, the Latin scribed in that document is poorly executed. There are errors everywhere from spelling to grammar. How can future panels of jurists correctly interpret the new laws when the document is full of mistakes?'

'It is early days, Eleanor. All will be correct in time.'

'If the Latin is accurate and precise to begin with, you will not be wasting your precious time or the scribe's who can then be more gainfully employed.'

'Dear God, you are so bloody pedantic. The main purpose is to have the new laws put in place to improve the ruling of this kingdom. This is not a lesson in Latin grammar.'

'Pedantic I may be, but I believe a legal document should be written correctly in the first place. I do not want the writing of the document protracted because of clumsy Latin.'

'May I suggest you not interfere.'

'I am not interfering, I am advising. For God's sake, Henry, make it clear from the start, then it will not have to be re-written.'

'Eleanor, you are being finicky. Leave those versed in jurisprudence to renew and develop England's laws. How many times do I have to repeat, that these things take time?'

'The longer it takes, the more it costs. Just remember whose treasury is paying and whose treasury has dragged and continues to drag your little kingdom out of the mire.'

Insulted to be treated thus, to be humoured like a brainless idiot, I stormed off. Henry followed like a bristling mastiff. At the top of the grand staircase, he caught up with me and grabbed me by the arm. I pulled away, lost my balance, and ended in a heap on the landing, with blood pouring down my face and gown from where my front teeth had bitten through my lip. I had winded myself, so could not stand. My nose was bleeding too, and I had a lump forming on my forehead. There was blood everywhere. Henry was beside me yelling for me not to move. Hearing the commotion, my maids rushed to my side as pages and churls ran from every corner of the palace. Matthias, Jerome, and Robert arrived on the scene. Henry wiped the blood from my face, relieved it was only my lip and nose. It was a relief I had broken no bones, though my left shoulder and hip were tender. I must have fallen to that side as I rolled to the landing.

They carried me on a litter to my bed, no matter how much I protested I could walk. My tongue tasted as if I had licked iron. My lip was swollen.

I was cleaned up and told to rest. Amaris brought me a soothing drink though I had difficulty sipping. Matthias said I had been lucky. My heavy gown had cushioned my fall. I was feeling sore and a little unwell. Matthias said it was the shock. Henry hovered in the background. I could have said something sarcastic, like 'have you not some Latin to correct,' but I did not have the energy. I do not remember much after that. I went into labour.

***

I gave birth to another little boy on June 2nd, in the Year of Our Lord, 1159. He died an hour later, so tiny he could have fitted into the palm of Henry's hand, but perfect in every way. Before he took his last breath, he was baptised by Jerome. We called him Phillip. I felt numb, too shocked for grief. Henry was distraught. Regardless of the protestations, I rose from my bed and insisted the tiny baby be bathed. He was wrapped in one of my silken veils. I emptied out one of my ornate chests that held jewellery. We buried him in the chapel rose garden. The children stood around crying. My little family Hal, Matilda, Richard, and baby Geoffrey.

Geoffrey was nine months old. He would have been as close to Phillip as Hal was to Matilda. I still had not wept. Everyone was praising me for my strength and courage, but I felt nothing, no pain, no grief. My milk, I was surprised to discover seeped from my breasts a day later. I called for Geoffrey to be brought to me, insisting he be left with me alone. At first, he had no idea why he was being offered this strange breast. He only recalled Cecilia. I rubbed my nipple across his lips. He licked his lips with me encouraging him, his large duplici eyes staring into mine.

'Read my mind Geoffrey,' I whispered, 'I know you are my little Merlin, suck.'

At first, he stiffened, but then he relaxed. I was Maman after all. I think as well as milk, he recognised my perfume: jasmine and roses. Henry insisted I wear it more often now. Geoffrey's suckling was strong and regular. His eyes never left mine. One pudgy fist entwined in my loosened hair. How sensual it felt. Tears at last fell and I could weep for my loss combined with relief I had milk for the baby I had been unable to suckle for long after his birth. I would deal with Cecilia in time. I hoped she would understand.

Cecilia hugged me, saying she was pleased and relieved because her milk was drying, and she feared having to wean him. Now Geoffrey had a ready supply. Henry, as I expected, was not happy. He did not wish to be reminded of the child that did not survive. I knew he blamed himself. I told him the accident was as much my fault as his as I was the one who lost balance. It was my temper that made me pull away from him. He was afraid my fall would harm my fertility, for God's sake. I told him that was unlikely, but I would have to heal, just as if the child had been born at full time. To be honest, I was tiring of his uneasy temperament. He seemed to be often irritable and more and more possessive.

Chapter 7. The Disgruntled Lion

Henry was unwell. The last two jousts ended badly for him. I rarely watched these days. It terrified me; the thundering horses, the screeching of lance on armour, the sickening, crashing thud as beaten iron with its frail human enclosed hit the ground. Then with pounding heart the wait in fear till the jouster rose on unsteady legs, often to collapse again. Henry tried to keep up with younger knights and squires who had no fear and were so lightweight they seemed to bounce if knocked off their steeds. Henry had suffered too many falls. Twice he had been knocked out when his head hit the hard ground after his helmet dislodged. For now, Henry had kept his wits, but he was often wracked with headaches. His hip ached; so did his right shoulder where the lance rested. Not only did he resemble his father as he grew older, but I also had visions of him with similar jousting scars. I hoped I never uttered the wrong name in moments of passion.

The last headache he endured had him grinding his teeth and growling at everyone in his court and mine. The children were becoming wary of his moods. One minute he wanted to follow tradition and crown Hal as the young king, next he was yelling he could not ride his pony with any skill. Richard was like a small cannonball, defiant, sticking out his bottom lip, and refusing to do what his father bade him. I was forced to keep the peace. Then Henry accused me of spoiling them, heaven forbid. Matilda, bless her, was even-tempered. She could charm her way around her brothers and was quite the little coquette with her Papa.

I begged Henry to rest. Matthias and the apothecary prescribed a physic that helped him once we convinced him to swallow it. The fuss and to-do were a jest to watch. One would think we were poisoning him. I sat with him and massaged his temples with lavender oil. He appreciated that. Robert confided in me that Henry was worried he was losing his potency as king because a few nobles had baulked at his strict land tax and the revised laws. Even laws that had been drafted by his grandfather were being questioned. Henry insisted they must be obeyed to the letter, and I agreed. Henry should be meeting with the obstinate nobles to explain that to keep stability within the kingdom the rule of law must be followed. Instead, he wanted to leap on his horse, have siege engines and battering rams fly at the speed of comets, and storm their castle walls. Barons were afraid of his wrath, but he feared they had heard his physical prowess was compromised by his jousting injuries, but would he stop jousting? No! I hoped this attitude was just a result of his fall and would blow over.

***

Henry was up and around and much better. While we were sipping wine by the fire, he grumbled and whinged he was getting old. I nearly choked.

'Do you think *I* am old then?' I pouted.

Henry turned and stared. His eyes like augers drilled through me. I felt diminished. Why did I not control my tongue? I held my breath.

'Damnation, Eleanor! No, you are not. Not one strand of grey hair, no lines or wrinkles crease your face, your skin is like cream. Happy now?'

Henry sounded petulant, muttering that it was not fair. Even so, I worried about my age. When I was no longer able to conceive, to carry a child, Henry would still be potent, regardless of his greying hair and weather-beaten face.

I was silent for once. Then Henry demanded I stop nursing Geoffrey, saying it was folly. For whom, I thought, Geoffrey or me? It was more likely Henry wanted another child and soon. Frustration was rising in my breast. How could I tell Henry I was tired of producing baby after baby? There was a slim hope I would not have another while my milk still flowed. I could not keep, nor wished to keep, Henry from my bed. I hated to admit it, but I almost hoped the rebel barons would force him around the country. If only I could come by those little waxy, herbal pellets used in the harems of Antioch. Henry would not allow me to douche. No, my best option was for Henry to ride to the Scottish border.

***

It was the New Year. Henry shocked me this morning by announcing he was returning to Normandy. I had seen little of him since he arrived back from his last visit. He had barely related what happened then, as he dashed hither and yon. He was on edge. From Robert I gleaned Henry imagined his vast empire was fracturing. This annoyed me because most of it was mine. Like Louis before him, he only ruled below the Anjou border because of my name. His head was full of conspiracies that the various dominions were either warring against each other or plotting his downfall. At times he behaved like a raving tyrant. Some of his vassals, I knew, needed strict rule, but only a few required a warlike approach. Diplomacy usually brought the majority to their senses. Particularly in the Aquitaine where the laws were more conciliatory than the Anglo-Norman. My people did not appreciate being bullied.

'By the way I am fulfilling a promise I think will end our long-drawn-out dispute with Louis.'

'Well?'

'Louis and I have agreed on a betrothal between Hal and his daughter, Margaret.'

'YOU HAVE WHAT? Why have I not been consulted?' To say I exploded like a Sicilian volcano was an understatement.

'God's teeth, Henry! How dare you! Never! Never! Never will I allow a child of mine to be swallowed into that genuflecting garderobe of piety, that moat of ignorance and pestilence that is Île de France. To think you would even dream of allowing Hal into the household of that lily livered bastard Louis Capet when you know how I was treated. Have you lost your senses?'

I spewed vitriol, I ranted, I raged, I threw a goblet at Henry drowning him in wine. He threw it back. I ducked. It bounced against the wall.

'Will you damn well calm down?' he yelled. 'I am tired of your tantrums, Eleanor!'

As he stepped towards me, I pushed him away with all my strength. But he came back, fuming. Now in fear, I raised my hands to protect my head and face. He shook me like one of Matilda's rag dolls. I collapsed in his arms hysterical.

'Please, Henry, please. I beg you. Do not do this.'

***

So much for me keeping Henry out of my bed. As always, our terrible fight ended in a passionate embrace. Henry smelt of wine and lust. Wearing only my perfume, I conceived another child.

I could not influence Henry to change his mind. He said the betrothal of Hal and little Princess Margaret would be an alliance with the French, and that Hal would eventually rule both kingdoms because Louis was only capable of fathering daughters. His last child with Constance was another girl. I was saddened to hear Constance did not survive the birth. It was hard for me to feel sorry for Louis, but his poor young wife was in my prayers. Louis, I heard had already remarried, with little love I would imagine but insisted upon by the carping clergy in his court and the Pope.

I eventually calmed down. There was some logic behind Hal and Margaret's betrothal. Margaret would bring the

Chapter 7: The Disgruntled Lion

Vexin as her dower, and I would be more than proud as well as avenged if my son became king of France and England. But it was the Vexin that swayed me, aware of how important that tiny slither of land was to Normandy. Although Henry was travelling to Rouen and beyond, much to my disgust he had decided to send Becket to Paris to finalise the betrothal agreements. I could just see Becket prancing and preening, like a peacock. Perhaps he would fall in love with Louis. He might have more luck there. Louis, I was sure, preferred men to women. I had never told Henry of my suspicions about him. Catamite or religious fanatic, or both. Who knew? Perhaps I should goad Becket into batting his eyelids at Louis? Was I being spiteful? Never!

Henry appointed me his regent again. I would have to organise my days for the next few weeks to accommodate my morning sickness. I had not told Henry I was with child. Also, I did not want him to consider my condition unsuitable to rule. *Ce qu'il ne savait pas ne lui ferait pas de mal*. What he did not know would not hurt him. He would leave at week's end. I would return to London after farewelling him.

I threatened Becket with exposure of his proclivities to Archbishop Theodore if I heard one breath of him trying to seduce Henry. I still have a few friendships within Louis's court and beyond. Brother Joachim was but one. I would know exactly what Becket was doing, even before Henry was informed.

***

Henry left more quietly than usual, which was most odd. I accompanied him from Winchester to Portsmouth where it was a bitter-sweet farewell. He was distracted. Before embarking, he turned to me, his eyes haunted.

He pressed me to him, then, cupping my face in his hands and stared intensely into my eyes, he whispered, 'You are so beautiful.'

'Please take care, my darling.'
'I love you, Eleanor.'
'I will keep you informed, Henry. I will write often.'

Henry was not, as I had come to expect, eager to be off. Instead he had a catch in his voice, as if he was regretting something. God knew what. I asked Robert to look after him.

We waited on the dock while Henry's pile of baggage was being loaded onto his galley. I watched him limp up the gangplank with a lump in my throat. The anchor was weighed. A gust of wind clacked and snapped the sails as they were hauled up the mast. The galley caught the stiff breeze as it blew back the hood of my cape. My veil billowed across my face. Tears flowed down my cheeks. I waved till I could no longer see him. But my heart was heavy. Henry was turning into someone I no longer understood. The jealous rages and violence one minute, and the tenderness like now before he boarded his galley, all had me perplexed. Judith's prophesy hovered: *you will marry the love of your life; your life will be tumultuous…* Eh bien.

***

I pushed Henry's and my farewell to one side as duty called. I was excited and invigorated. I was ready to take up the reins of leadership as regent, to make decisions on behalf of our people. It was rewarding to follow my destiny. Of course, there were all the usual justiciars to aid my duties. Archbishop Theodore was always a sensible mentor whose good council I appreciated. He had never attempted to intimidate me like that parliament of crows on Île de France.

As there were treasury matters to attend to, I stayed for two weeks in Winchester before returning with the children to London for the Pentecost.

My maids were flapping around like excited doves, hauling out gowns for me to choose for the Pentecost banquet. I reminded them to keep my appearance simple. Without Henry at my side, I did not want to be thought the 'gaudy' queen. Why, after all this time, my so-called torrid reputation was still uppermost in the minds of some, I knew not. The Bishop of Worcester was one who forgot his place. My epistles went unanswered. He was tardy acknowledging a request I made about the appointment of a new archdeacon to his parish. One of my clerks, Brother Solomon, was qualified and suitable for the post. Henry and I agreed on this before he left. I knew the bishop did not approve of me and I knew Archbishop Theodore had chided him for his sour remarks. It appeared he could not abide clever women or the female sex in general, not odd among some clergy. The Abbess of Amesbury, an erudite and cultured woman, had riled him too. He claimed, without proof, she had some cleric dismissed from his church without due process of Canon Law. One would think she had committed murder, the fuss the wretched man caused. I did not see an early end to these disputes. To be honest, there were more pressing concerns to which I had to attend. The pile of letters on my desk were of more importance.

The first I opened had an unfamiliar seal. It was a most pathetic and begging letter from Lady Grenvale. She requested we return Aeled. I had no love for this evil woman, and, what was more, Aeled had settled into our court, was receiving an education and, although not cosseted, he was better housed than with his parents.

She pleaded in appalling Latin for her son, citing her husband was in poor health because of Aeled being held hostage. She feared for Lord Grenvale's life. I had little sympathy for her husband either, but something niggled at my heart. I had the conscience of a mother deep in my psyche, but I knew Henry would not consider releasing the boy. Whether Lord Grenvale's poor health was being used as a ploy, I knew not. But I did have a convenient spy just over the border. Could a letter to Owain Pendragon answer the question? Henry would have a jealous fit if I attempted to contact the Welsh king. I must think very carefully on that. If Aeled's father was so ill he could be called to God, the boy should be beside his father as Henry was with his. Later today I will speak with Archbishop Theodore because it will take too long to send a letter to Henry and wait for a reply, should the man be dying. What a dilemma.

Henry and I had argued over Aeled's fate when we arrived back in London after the Shrewsbury incident. Henry wanted to throw the poor child into the nearest dungeon, he was so furious by the betrayal of his parents. But, as king and queen, I believed we were above simple revenge if revenge was simple. So, I put it to Henry that we treated the boy with decency and educated him. I argued it would encourage him to respect us, and to pay us the homage we expected from his parents.

Henry was bored with the boy by then, so he told me to do whatever I liked, except let him loose. I arranged for Aeled to have simple but warm quarters. I found tutors for him, so he would know his letters and Latin. Over time, I had not seen much of him. By now he would be about twelve years. Jerome and my confessor Peter told me he was likeable. I should make more of an effort to acquaint myself with him.

***

Celeste was knocking on my door for me to inspect gowns for the banquet. There was no escaping my diligent maids when it came to being decked out like a maypole I must obey and return to my epistles and writing later.

I chose an indigo samite gown, a simple design though the fabric was extravagant. A modest veil, I felt was necessary, without Henry there to be 'possessive'. I found one of pale blue silk. Archbishop Theodore had proclaimed I was duty bound to wear my crown. I thought he was being a little high handed. I was only too aware of my role.

Chapter 7: The Disgruntled Lion

After I had made my choice of a robe for the banquet, I shared a simple lunch with Archbishop Theodore when I brought up the subject of Lady Grenvale's letter. Theodore believed I should find out more about Aeled's father's health before letting the boy go home and would contact clerics in Shrewsbury on my behalf. I must wait in the meantime.

***

The banquet exceeded my expectations. I was greeted with Vivat Regina after the usual regal fanfare. I felt an overwhelming pride in my position, though I missed Henry's arm on which to rest my hand, and his little glances of adoration, even if I often felt like a prized possession. My choice of gown was successful. My maids picked up compliments from some unexpected quarters and not too many grunts of disapproval from those who still regarded me as an adulterous *putain*. Maybe I was at last being accepted for my intellect and efficiency.

The food, wine and entertainment were of a high standard. One plus of not having Henry at my side, I was not being nagged to eat more. I knew I tended to nibble, but I was happy with a little of what I liked rather than having my plate piled high. Also, unlike Henry who would eat anything with four legs including, I think, a table, I preferred poultry or fish. There was some delicious quail, some pheasant, and divine trout from nearby streams. Dried fruit, sweetmeats and cheeses finished the repast. The wine recently from Bordeaux was rich and mellow.

On the Sunday after the banquet, a beautiful service was held in the Abbey. Since our coronation, repairs had been made to the old building. Now its sandstone walls gleamed in the spring sunshine, and the stained-glass windows were ablaze with colour, enriching its soaring architecture – so uplifting! It was such an honour to serve God in a building of beauty where one's earthly thoughts could rise to a higher place. Careful, Eleanor, you could be sounding pompously pious.

***

There was still no news regarding the health of Lord Grenvale. Theodore had returned to Canterbury when another begging epistle arrived from Aeled's wretched mother. I must travel soon to Warwick now I have passed the morning queasiness. I could take Aeled with me should I decide for him to be with his father. Shrewsbury was not too many leagues further.

Common sense in the end prevailed. I did not trust Margaret Grenvale and I knew Henry would be against any decision to return the boy. It could jeopardise future regencies, which I did not want to lose.

As I ploughed through my correspondence, another more important missive arrived from a tired courier, which was far more intriguing. It carried the familiar, beautiful seal of the Welsh king. I eased it open.

Greetings, oh, Beautiful Sprite,

I hear you are now both king and queen, that your firebrand and most jealous husband is guarding his territory across the sea.

I rolled my eyes at the lack of formality.

King Owain went on to state he would be travelling into British territory, that soon he would be in the vicinity of Shrewsbury and was informed of my duties in Warwick. His damn spy network again. I would love to discover who his informants were. He continued,

There is a treaty I believe we need to sign
between our two kingdoms, do we not?

I found my heart was pounding in a most immodest manner. It would be quite a feat for me to achieve what Henry had so far not accomplished or bothered about for that matter. The sticking point was whether Henry would condone me meeting with King Owain. I could be surrounded by my entourage and the palace guard, but Henry would still be suspicious of me having any contact

Chapter 7: The Disgruntled Lion

with a man he thought more interested in me other than as Queen of England. I suspected Henry also sensed I found the Welsh king attractive.

I did not answer Owain's missive. I burned his piece of parchment in my grate, almost choking myself with excessive smoke. The beautiful seal ended as an unrecognisable lump to be thrown out with the ash.

***

I set off to Warwick with my excited little children and long winding retinue. We moved at a sedate pace through the countryside from manor to manor, with visits to some monasteries to distribute alms. I must be becoming more benign as I get older because I gave alms to a convent to include the soul of poor little Queen Constance of France in their prayers. I think they were mightily surprised at my gesture. Nonetheless, I did not include the king of France.

We reached Warwick mid-morning two weeks after leaving London. Henry would have tried to reach Warwick in a day. After establishing my little ones and household, I set about meeting with the castle constable and stewards and introduced myself to the various barons who made up the justiciars of the district. Several writs and charters were brought to my notice. I surprised the barons as usual by insisting on reading every scroll before attaching my signature. Most of what was presented to me was straightforward. There was a dispute between two barons over a tract of hunting ground, which I would need to delve into before speaking to the antagonists.

I asked for appropriate documents so I could make a clear judgement on the case. Yellowed velum scribed in faded ink was produced. The land was part of one earl's sister's dower. Back in Henry's grandfather's rule, a charter had been granted by Henry Beauclerc, Henry I, to her family for loyalty and service to the king which was nothing unusual. In time, part of the estate was given as

Lady Catherine de Goulet's dowry. She was now deceased, and the family wanted it back. Her husband believed the land was his. Dowries cause a multitude of problems. The patience and wisdom of Solomon were required but then I have had plenty of practice over similar disputes in the Aquitaine.

To clear my head regarding the contested dowry, I decided on a quiet ride. I was accompanied by Antoine, Simeon, Jerome, and Lucille. Lucille and I were not veiled as we were amongst those, I consider family. We ambled along beside the Avon, surrounded in bird song, the weather sunny. When I think of the cold, rain and flooding we experienced the last time we were here, the contrast was a joy to behold. I was dawdling behind the others deep in thought when Rebel propped at something, her ears pricked, and nostrils flared. I came out of my trance to look up to see what had spooked my mare. In the shadows of a dark oak was a figure in white. There was no guessing as to who it was – Owain Pendragon – who had appeared like the wizard Merlin out of thin air. The others, I knew, would soon miss me and return. He tilted his head to one side, uttering in a throaty lilt how wonderful it was to be reacquainted with the mighty Queen of the Wood Sprites. What in God's Name was he doing so far into English territory?

'The letter I sent, ye did not answer.'

'No.'

'And why would that be?'

I knew. It had nothing to do with treaties – I did not trust myself or him for that matter. 'I must consult with King Henry. It is he who must make this important decision between our two kingdoms.'

It was a lame excuse. As he stepped out of the shadows, I tightened my grip on Rebel's reins, ready to gallop. She side-stepped in flighty anticipation.

'I believe you not, my beauty.'

Before I could move, he had my reins and was purring

Chapter 7: The Disgruntled Lion

sweet nothings to Rebel and stroking her velvety nose while provocatively staring up at me. My heart was aflutter. I did not fear him, but I did not trust myself. God be praised I was about twelve weeks with child, but, even so, Owain aroused me in ways I only felt for Henry, and worse, I think he guessed.

Out of self-preservation, I said, 'I will sign the treaty if you bring it to the castle where it can be witnessed by my justiciars.'

'Mayhap.'

Then I heard the others coming back no doubt wondering where I was. Owain heard them too, chuckled and blew a kiss. He vanished into the darkness of the oaks.

As Jerome, Antoine and Lucille came into view, I called out that I wanted to return. I turned Rebel's head and whipped the innocent animal into a gallop. The others had to keep up as best they could.

Back at the castle, I pondered on my encounter and wondered how Owain had tracked my movements. I questioned too why I found this man attractive when I loved Henry. In the future, I determined I would never again put myself in a position of temptation, nor would I ride anywhere, or dawdle behind, where I might be discovered by Owain Pendragon, alone!

***

A strange woman arrived unexpectedly in my household. Like the whalebone talisman, she said she was sent to protect me. She had a bearing of grace but was not of my nobility.

I tried dismissing her, but as if mesmerised my children fell in love with her. My whole household fell in love with her. I had this uncanny feeling I could not rationally explain. There was something ethereal, mystical about her. Her lilting accent placed her across the Welsh border.

'Well, you have certainly impressed my children and my court. What is your name?'

'It is Brynn, Milady.'
'Brynn. Welsh, I presume.'
'*Oes*, it is. I have come to protect you.'
'To protect me. From what might I ask?'
'Death, Lady Eleanor.'

A shiver ran through my body.

'Brynn, only God can protect me from that inevitability and if he calls me to him, nobody in this world can prevent it.'

'There are many things one needs protection from, other than death.'

'Really. You must forgive my suspicious nature, but do I presume you were sent here by Lord King Owain?'

Brynn smiled.

'You are not his spy I hope.'

Brynn laughed, 'No definitely not. I am here only for your protection as I have said.'

'Hmm!'

I discovered she had an uncanny knack with herbs. Her knowledge of apothecary was as great as or even more so, than Renée's or Clotilde's. She like baby Geoffrey could read my mind, or so it seemed. Brynn materialised when I appeared to think of something. I found this disconcerting.

***

I had completed my duties in Warwick. The warring earls I threatened with the confiscation of their hunting rights, so they agreed to make use of the woods and forests jointly. The agreement stated that on the death of Lady Catherine de Goulet the lands were to be shared equally between her husband's and brother's houses. If they had taken the time to practise their Latin, I would not have had to intervene. My justiciars at Warwick were impressed. Furthermore, they realised I was as capable as the king in solving a dispute, except I did not threaten to run them through with a broadsword.

We travelled back to London via Worcester where I

visited the newly appointed bishop, an improvement on the last sour old man. It was not a formal meeting, more a gentle progress to promote my Regency. We stayed a few days. Letters from Henry, which were following me around, reached me. Becket had impressed Louis. He would be bringing little Margaret to Normandy.

But I was mortified, furious. Louis forbade the child to enter my household. Did not Henry let him know, I was rearing four children, and would continue with others we conceived? That Louis still had the capacity to enrage me was frustrating beyond belief. The thump of my fist on my desk upset the ink, blotted the page of my journal, and ruined my gown. I should demand Louis, Becket and Henry replace the garment.

I stared at the ink stain on my rounding stomach reminding myself I had yet to tell Henry about this child and I was getting close to six moons. To add to my temper, Henry informed me he must travel to Angers. His vassals were restless and causing problems with the Poitivins. On opening another epistle, I read the Poitivins were objecting to Henry's Anglo-Norman heavy-handed methods of governing. I told him often enough he needed to adopt a subtler approach rather than tearing down their castle walls in retribution. One day he was going to rue his aggressive military solutions.

I needed to ride back to London to hand over the Regency to Archbishop Theodore before he arrived and I was waddling like a duck and looking like a whale.

***

Everyone suffered on the return journey. I believed no good was going to come out of what was occurring on the Anjou/Poitivin border. I travelled under my own thunderstorm. Jerome complained, 'Elly, you are pricklier than a hedgehog.'

'Mind your place, Jerome.'

I regretted the moment I spat the words from my mouth but could not bring myself to apologise. My children were the only ones not to undergo the full force of my wrath because they were kept at a distance. I played with them in the mornings before we set out and read to them in the evenings, so they missed my ugly humour.

Now, back at Westminster, I have calmed a little. I was missing Henry. But I was furious with him over Princess Margaret of France and what he was doing to my Poitivin people. Why will he not listen to me? He trusts me here as regent but ignores my knowledge or advice regarding the population of my County of Poitou. I wrote telling him of my pregnancy then tore up the epistle because it was full of abuse regarding my County and his belligerence.

It was now obvious I was having another child. My justiciars and Theodore were kind, delighted and supportive. They wanted me to rest, putting down my moodiness to my condition and probably being a woman in general. Jerome, who was not holding judgement on my foul temper, offered to write to Henry on my behalf.

My hair rose on end, and I yelled at him, 'Do not you dare.'

Then I burst into tears of rage as much as self-pity. Jerome wrapped me in his brotherly arms. For the first time in his life, he received a kicking from the unborn child. Poor Jerome was nonplussed and jumped away, not knowing what to think. I laughed for the first time in weeks. The incumbent broke Maman's nasty mood.

'What was that?'

'My baby.'

'Do babies do that?'

'One only feels them when they are about six moons and beyond. They can be quite vigorous.'

'God's teeth!'

'I will write to Henry. I will try to be kind.'

'Lord be praised, Elly. You have been snakier than Medusa.'

Chapter 7: The Disgruntled Lion

Baby did a few rounds of my belly for good measure, so I took Jerome's hands and placed them on the bulge. Poor man went pink with pride and embarrassment.

'Jerome, I am worried about this business on the Anjou/Poitivin border. If something should happen to Henry, he might never know this child.'

'Elly, Lord Henry is a seasoned campaigner and knows what he is doing.'

'Well, when he is about to face my Poitivin vassals, I am not so sure.'

Some of my tension abated. Then the thought of Louis and Henry conniving over Hal's future without consulting me, plunged me back into impotent fury. Louis forbidding me any contact with his daughter was as exasperating as it was humiliating. I could hear his high whining voice lisping around in my head, 'any acquaintance with Eleanor, and no betrothal.' I went to find Hal.

'Hal, darling, I must talk to you.' I sat beside him interrupting a game he was playing with his soldiers.

'What do you want, Maman? I am in the middle of my campaign against the Saracens!'

I sighed and ruffled his hair. 'It will not take long.'

'You look serious.'

'Papa has arranged a betrothal for you.'

'Why?'

'Well, because one day you are going to be king.'

Hal was looking bereft, 'Why? Is Papa going to die?'

'No, darling he is not, but, because you are his heir, we have to plan these things in advance.'

'Why?'

'It is important for many reasons, but mostly because it will seal a treaty between King Louis of France and our kingdom. Papa wants you to marry King Louis' daughter, Princess Margaret.'

'Maman, I do not understand. Is she not a baby? I do not think I should have to marry a baby, they wet themselves and they smell.'

I had to smile.

'Darling, you do not have to marry till you are older. By then, Margaret will have grown.'

'Well, I have decided I do not want to get married, so there. I do not want to have fights like you and Papa.'

'Hal, Papa and I love you very much and although Maman and Papa sometimes yell does not mean we do not love each other.'

I gave him a hug. Poor little boy he was only five himself. He and little Margaret were pawns in a far greater game played by their fathers.

The door opened and Agatha, Millicent, Agnes, and Cecelia arrived with the others. I left them playing happily. But it was a consolatory lesson. I needed to have a hard look at myself, and Henry.

***

I was given time away from my duties to relax, to prepare for this next baby. Henry's letters arrived in which he said he regretted he was unable to return to England as planned and I should look after myself. Archbishop Theodore, Jerome and anyone who could hold a quill had reassured Henry I was in safe hands.

In my letter, I told him I had a new addition to my court – Brynn – an exceptional apothecary. She was also a midwife, something I discovered when I was relating my usual fear of giving birth, even though this was my eighth child, not counting poor wee Phillip. She was as reassuring as Renée and calmed my anxious nerves. Brynn said I was one of the healthiest, strongest, individuals ever to cross her path, one of those lucky women to whom birth came naturally. Regardless of this, I wished I felt more confident.

***

Henry, as I knew he would, had a hard time trying to achieve peace between the Angevins and Poitivins. My vassals loathed Anglo-Norman interference in their

Chapter 7: The Disgruntled Lion

governance at any time. Henry's attacks flattened castle walls and left their lands torched, achieving nothing. Revenge would be sitting 'like patience on a monument'. But by now Henry, in Henry fashion, had galloped on to other ventures. I received a letter asking me to join him as soon as possible, probably to douse the flames of discontent brewing after his actions in Poitou. I was too close to giving birth to leave England, so I replied I would sail to Normandy as soon possible after the baby arrived. He also said he wanted to regain control of Toulouse. Very noble indeed, and I would love to have my inheritance from Grandmother Phillipa restored, but it would not be an easy campaign. The latest ruler, Raymond V, was a nasty, wily, clever tactician, and I feared Henry would be tested.

***

Henry's desired campaign to retake Toulouse was received with a mixed response in the Aquitaine according to Uncle Ralph. Henry had made an ally in Raymond-Berengar. He was Count of Catalonia and Aragon. I imagined he had his eyes on Gascony. That would ruffle a few feathers. He was expanding his influence along my southern borders and into Provence.

Henry asked (a blessed miracle) what I thought about betrothing Richard to Raymond-Berengar's daughter. What was Henry thinking? I felt like all my children were being played off on a gigantic chess board. I knew I should accept the status quo. After all, that was what I was there for, was it not? To bear Henry's brood so he could shore up his empire with abiding treaties all over Europe. But I felt saddened all the same, for I knew they must grow up. All of them had destined pathways. I knew only too well from bitter experience what was likely to happen if they were not promised to someone, especially Matilda. She could be abducted or end up as I did in an unsuitable, incompatible alliance. Would not it be heaven sent if they could do as Nilla did and fall in love and marry the person of their choice? But that was not what life had ordained for my beloved children.

Was I odd that I loved and wanted my children nearby? Did Papa set the standard so high by keeping Nilla and me close to his bosom that I believed I must do the same? We knew only the joys of being within our family circle. Papa refused to send us off to a convent when our mother died. Papa's love for us, his care for us, was all important, more than betrothals into strange households even if his tardiness undid me in the end. To whom, if he had been able, would he have promised me? Not to Louis Capet, I was sure. I did not believe he thought beyond my personal safety when on his death bed he put me under the guardianship of Louis's father. Surely, he did not expect the old king to marry me off to his pathetic son.

After my divorce from Louis, Henry's father sent him to woo me, which I resented with all my heart. I was slow to fall in love with him, but I did, and, like Judith's prediction, a stormy relationship resulted. Sometimes I thought I hated Henry as much as I loved him. There were times I had an overwhelming feeling of dread, with no idea why. My usual fear of birth most likely. I heaved myself out of my chair and blew out the flickering candles.

'Come on, baby, cannot you stir yourself? Maman is mightily uncomfortable. I want you in the world, not in my belly.'

On my slow shuffle back towards my chamber, Brynn scared me as she appeared out of the shadows.

'God's teeth, why are you not in your bed?' I said.

'I could ask the same of you, Milady.'

'I have discomfort. It is difficult to get to sleep.'

'Try putting a pillow under your belly. It will give your stomach more support and take some weight off your back.'

'How much longer do you think, Brynn?'

'By your shape, not long. The baby is low in the birth position. Now I will accompany you to your bed.'

Chapter 7: The Disgruntled Lion

Amaris was asleep on the trundle at the foot of my bed. Without disturbing her, I managed to heave myself onto my feather mattress. Brynn arranged a pillow under the bulge, then tiptoed out. Whether it was the comfort or my absolute exhaustion, I fell into a deep sleep. Towards morn I awoke in a wet bed as the first pains shot across my lower abdomen. My moans disturbed Amaris, who rallied Brynn and my attendants.

Just after the noonday bells, on the day of our Lord, October 13th, 1161, I gave birth to another daughter. She was named after me on Henry's insistence. Everyone said she looked like me, another little *duplici*. I checked the nose I think before the sex.

The bells of Westminster hailed the birth, ringing out with joy. As Eleanor II snuggled into my breast suckling steadily, I wondered about her fate. It was silly, I knew, but I was weepy. I wished Henry were with us. Eventually, Hal, Matilda, Richard, and Geoffrey were permitted to meet their new sister. Matilda was overjoyed there was another little girl in the family. They all crowded on my bed peering at baby Eleanor, then fought over who was going to have the first cuddle. To save a war, I said we would start at the eldest and move down, to which Matilda pouted it was not fair, because as she was a girl, she should be first. I was exhausted, not in the mood for a family dispute, so I demanded they follow my order, or they could leave.

'You sound like Papa!' cried Richard.

'Do not be cheeky,' I sighed.

But I was tired and struggling with my emotions. I did not want my brood squabbling on my bed. Geoffrey, reading the situation though he was only two, and far more articulate than any of the others at the same age, said he was happy to be last and could they get on with it. Baby Eleanor, like a game of pass the parcel, was rotated, and jiggled from hand to hand.

Geoffrey, never to be outdone, knew being last gave him a longer cuddle. He stared at her little face and said, 'She looks like us, Maman.'

The others crowded around jostling the bundle till she decided enough was enough and let out a lusty howl. Brynn came to the rescue, shooing them all off the bed. I told them they could come back later after Maman had rested.

***

I had regained my strength, so prepared for Normandy. The children were as excited to see their Papa as I was. But I needed to get to the Aquitaine with all haste. The reports on my desk did not bode well. Henry's recent foray into Poitou had angered everyone. I knew I would have to quell the eruptions breaking out throughout the duchy, not just in Poitou.

We arrived at Barfleur after a gentle crossing. For the children's sake, I was grateful. Henry was met with squeals of delight from his happy clan. He took Eleanor II from my arms. She looked at him, luckily giving him a gooey smile. She could be a little clingy at times. Henry remarked on her likeness to me and that she would be a great beauty before handing her back. He noted how the others had grown but showed little interest in them otherwise. My heavy sigh alerted him to my disappointment. I told him they were so excited to be seeing him after so long, he could make more of a fuss over them. His efforts improved but I sensed they were half-hearted.

To be honest, he was distant. I started to panic. Was it my age? Did I look worn and tired from the baby's birth? Henry looked haggard. His father was only a few years older when he died. It was as if a fist was squeezing my heart. That night, after the children had been taken to their beds by their nurses, I waited for Henry's advances. I had dressed to allure, to be provocative, with the bodice of my gown laced down the front, my breasts rounded with milk were pushed up, my hair was unveiled and tumbled in waves to below my waist. Once, he would have already taken me to bed, but, today, he was aloof. I stood and took his empty goblet, filled it with wine and as I returned it to him, I leant close, so my breasts brushed against his hand. I was wearing his favourite perfume. I had shooed everyone from the chamber – what was wrong with him?

'I have missed you so very much, Henry. My bed is lonely without you.'

He seemed to come out of his trance. 'I ache all over sometimes, Eleanor, longing for you.'

I knelt, burying my head in his lap. He pulled me upright. We kissed. Passion was aroused at last and later fulfilled, though he was not as vigorous as usual.

***

On the morrow we exchanged reports from our respective activities over the year we had been apart.

'Henry, you will be pleased to know that before my departure, our nobility and clergy are behaving themselves, but I am worried about Archbishop Theodore. He is becoming more stooped, and I am concerned about his health.'

'I suppose he is getting on.'

'Yes. He developed a nasty cough during the winter. I had decent fireplaces built in his palace. Mind you, it took some persuading. But his braziers were doing little to warm him, and the smoke was making his cough worse.'

'He said, in his missives, that he appreciated your kindness, and that you have become quite a daughter to him in his old age.'

'Oh, that is good of him. I suppose we have grown close. His Grace has defended me when poisonous remarks about my past have come to his ears for which I am more than grateful. And he loves our children. They call him 'Uncle Archbishop'. He often joins in their games when he is at Westminster.'

Henry did not comment, so I hoped he would pay more attention to his offspring now we were a family again. I changed the subject to the fate of Aeled. I had written to Henry about his mother's pitiful letters, but felt it was up to him to decide if they should be reunited. He said he would think about it. It was obvious Aeled's fate was not a high priority. To be honest neither it should be. There were far more pressing concerns on our agenda.

'By the way, Owain Pendragon wrote to me wanting me to sign a peace treaty between our two kingdoms.'

'He wanted you to sign it?'

'I refused. I informed the Welsh king it was up to you to put your name to a document of such import. Do you not agree?'

'Damned opportunist.'

Henry harrumphed but said no more. I thanked God I followed my instinct on that one.

We now approached the prickly discussion I did not want to have about his forays into my territory. He would know I would be contacted by a multitude of disgruntled Poitivins as well as Uncle Ralph and my justiciars in the Aquitaine. But there would be some informants who would surprise him, from Île de France, for instance. Also, before I left England, Owain Pendragon and Malcolm of Scotland couriered reams of parchment into my hands. They warned me they had *'heard'* Henry had been far too heavy handed in this dispute. I thought their network of spies was knowledgeable indeed, no doubt some burrowing away in the French kingdom, so the two kings had a foot in both camps. Whether Henry was aware of Malcolm and Owain's activities, I knew not.

I decided there was no point in avoiding the subject. I suppose it was only fair to hear his account of the campaign.

I asked casually, 'By the way, Henry, are you going to tell me about Poitou?'

'I do not want to talk about it. No doubt you have already been given a biased version of events. Your mind will be made up in advance of anything I might say.'

Henry's reaction almost undid my good intentions

Chapter 7: The Disgruntled Lion

and had my eyes narrowing, *'You mean, as you play chess, wildly, without a thought, until you are out of your depth with no tactics in mind to avoid a checkmate?'*

Instead, I agreed it was better to be left unspoken – for now.

'When will we be riding to Poitiers.'

'I have decided we will go by sea to Bordeaux, more comfortable for you and the children.'

Yes, but I suspected his true motive was so I could not see the devastation of his battles.

I let him win that round.

'That will be pleasant. Now before your baby daughter screams Normandy down, I had better attend to her.'

I excused myself to give the baby my breast. Robert was hovering,

'For God's sake, Robert, take Henry hawking. He needs some exercise to clear his head. We are a bit on edge. I am going to be distracted and I do not wish to leave him simmering.'

***

Our trip to Bordeaux eased tensions. Henry and I were both able to relax. The children loved the experience, though we had to watch them like hawks for being too adventurous. Richard climbed up a rope ladder alongside one of the masts and almost stopped my heart. He had to be retrieved by a sailor. I scolded him in no uncertain manner. I think Henry approved of his dare-devilry. Men!

I promised Henry I would wean Eleanor. We were calling her Lenore to avoid confusion. Not that I wished to conceive another child but, at L'Ombrière, I had other means to prevent that eventuality. We would see. I was so looking forward to seeing Renée, who, although now an old woman, was, from all reports, well and sprightly.

The dock at Bordeaux brought back so many memories from my childhood and of my first meeting with Henry at L'Ombrière a league away. Memories were triggered for Henry, too.

The Lion and the Tigress

As the barque dropped sail and we glided to our mooring, he took my hand and whispered, 'This is where it all began.'

Nostalgia, I thought was quite an aphrodisiac. 'We must revisit the folly.'

Henry squeezed my hand. 'I still have your red cape.'

I kissed his cheek. 'You may wear it this time.'

'I brought it especially.'

I was surprised by his sentimentality.

There were moments when Henry's tenderness overwhelmed me, but then there was the other side that filled me with dread and fear. God help anyone who did not bend to his increasingly irrational, callous will.

From my firsthand experience of war during the Second Crusade, I knew brutality in battle was needed for survival; one life pitted against another. But during my Regencies in England, except for a few belligerent characters, most hostilities could be quelled by discussion and careful argument. By applying the laws of the land, and making pig-headed men acknowledge these laws, bloodshed could be prevented. When faced by the pros and cons of their actions, most combatants agree to settle their arguments through peaceful means. Henry, after his early fiery rampages in England, used appeasement too, but now... The only other person I knew who bolted in where angels feared to tread, ignoring all advice, was foolish Louis. But Henry's intelligence was far greater than Louis's, so I wondered what had changed. I blamed his jousting accidents, pains in his hip, and his headaches. I noticed when he was in pain his judgement was challenged, and he was more short tempered, if that was possible.

But this was not the time or place to mull over my husband's problems. I was home, surrounded by all who loved and valued me, with my precious children. L'Ombrière opened its welcoming arms, enveloped us in its bosom. I ran into Renée's embrace. Either I was

Chapter 7: The Disgruntled Lion

growing taller, or she had stooped a little, but I found myself on my knees in front of her. We laughed, we cried, we babbled in Langue d'Oc. The children thought I had lost my wits. Renée looked so well. Clotilde was looking after her. I was so happy she was now living a peaceful, simple existence, no longer having to placate my flighty disposition, worry about my numerous pregnancies, or put up with Henry's and my disagreements.

After our welcome, we made ourselves comfortable in our quarters. A delicious but simple meal was served. I had decided to avoid talking about anything regarding politics. After our repast, I wanted to wander in the gardens. Renée had nodded off in her chair. Henry had raided the library for a book, so I decided to take a quiet walk. Clotilde herded the children to the back of the palace where there were swings attached to trees, some tough leather balls for the boys to kick around and other games to keep them occupied. Their nurses went with them to referee disputes. Hal and Richard can, at times, get out of hand with the occasional kick or punch being thrown.

The garden was as I remembered from my last visit – a tumble of flowers spilling down the old rocky walls and over trellises, forming peaceful arbours abuzz with bees. I found myself at the herbarium and perfumery. I poked my head in the door, but everyone was sleeping off their repast or at other tasks. I sat on the stoop at peace, musing on my surroundings, when my attention was drawn to the infamous bed of *silphium*. I had planted it from seeds brought from Antioch what seemed like a lifetime ago. There were now several large vigorous plants, and their clusters of yellow flowers nodded in the sun. No-one was nearby. My mind was racing. I do not want more babies. Could I grind the seeds and mix them with bee's wax to make those tiny pellets to push high into my woman's parts to try to prevent a man's seed from taking? I could but try. It took no time at all to collect the heart-shaped seeds. I chose the driest, remembering Abraham saying that the unripened ones caused severe cramps and sometimes were used to get rid of unwanted babies.

Inside the herbarium, after I shut the door, I found a pestle and mortar. It took only minutes to grind the seeds into a fine powder. It had a pungent odour. All I needed now was the bee's wax. I searched, but there was none that I could see, then I remembered our old parfumier when I was young, used to make scented candles. The heady bouquets of my childhood flooded my nostrils as I pushed open the door to the adjoining room, along with the poignant memory of my first love making with Abraham in that faraway perfumery in Uncle Raymond's gardens in Antioch.

Stacked on a shelf was a collection of bee's wax candles. The medium-sized were destined for the chapel, the larger ones for the cathedral. I hoped God would forgive my theft. I dared not think what God would make of my intentions, however. Amongst the candles were some tapers that I thought would be easier to soften. I took two then peeped around the herbarium door to check if anyone was about. All was quiet. The warm sun made it easy to soften the wax in my fingers. It was easier than I expected. Soon I had plenty of small round pellets of blended, ground seeds and bee's wax. I placed them in the small pouch on my belt where I kept my favourite thimble and other little trinkets as well as coins. But I knew I would need a more permanent storage place, one that was not going to get hot, or all the work would be undone.

My next dilemma was how I was going to push one in place. In the past it was Abraham who performed what he considered a delightful duty prior to lovemaking. Henry's father Geoffrey had insisted I douche. But Henry I knew would go berserk if he found out. Tonight, would be the first test. Henry was itching to revisit the folly – and I was as well.

***

Chapter 7: The Disgruntled Lion

I was as nervous as a virgin. I drank too much wine and ate little. Renée was frowning, as was Amaris. I said it was just the excitement of being home. I whispered to Henry; I would meet him after I had changed from my gown. He gave me a look dripping with lust. I hurried to my chamber. My maids did not have to be scholars to work out Henry and I wanted to be alone. I undressed then donned a fine silk lace-trimmed chemise. I wore my red chamois slippers but no hose. Another miniver cape lay across a nearby chair. I shooed all my maids and attendants from my presence. Taking a pellet from their hiding place, I gave myself a quick talking to, to stop being squeamish and get on with it. Squatting, I did just that. It did not fall out.

The sunset behind the Aphrodite temple was heaven sent. Henry sang a heart wrenching love song while strumming his lute. He wore nothing but my old red, miniver-lined cloak. Unlike our first encounter, we took our time. Neither of us were the physical beauties we used to be but that meant naught because now we knew what gave the other the maximum pleasure. My rampant lion might not be as "rampant" throughout the night, but we relieved our recent marital tensions as I stroked his hardened manhood till, he moaned for entry. The silken cave awaited with the same eager longing. Ecstasy took over as the old Roman couch was strained to its limits.

The days spent at L'Ombrière were full of poetry, music, laughter, and joy. Even the arguments about Greek philosophy were debated with good cheer. The Duchess of Aquitaine was spoiled, allowed to be herself. The children, except for baby Lenore, joined in the fun and were whisked off to their cots only after the cathedral bells rang nine hours after noon. Geoffrey fought drowsiness for as long as he could, falling asleep often in mine or Cecilia's arms. Often, I had to juggle him and Richard as both fought for position in my lap. Hal and Matilda were being taught to dance. Hal leapt about with wild enthusiasm; Matilda made each step a serious endeavour. Their efforts made me smile. But Henry's lack of enthusiasm for his children disappointed me. I think he saw his sons as competition. God knows what will happen when they were grown. He mentioned again his desire to crown Hal the Young King as was his tradition. Lord be praised, Hal was still too young.

***

All good things must end, and we must away to Poitiers where I knew fun and frivolity would end. The piles of sealed parchment I left till the last minute to read were on my desk. I opened them with reluctance. They did not carry good news. Henry was not going to receive a welcome reception from the Poitivins. Uncle Ralph was ready to string him up by the part of his anatomy that would be most unpleasant.

As if reading my thoughts, Henry told me he would instead ride with his men to Blaye to meet with Raymond-Berengar to finalise their assault on Toulouse. I was disappointed to learn he had sent out an edict to all the nobles throughout the Duchy to prepare to besiege the city. It stuck in my gut I was not consulted. Regardless that the County of Toulouse should be part of the Aquitaine, my justiciars reiterated earlier information I had received. They were wary and feared the outcome could be a disaster. My uncle continued to beg me to talk some sense into Henry. They heard that Louis, who was now married to Raymond V of Toulouse's sister-in-law Adela, was aiding him. So much for his recent friendly discussions with Henry. Louis was not to be trusted. He would do anything for revenge. And to think Henry had betrothed Hal to his daughter, Princess Margaret.

Chapter 8. Rebellion Looms

All my hope and good will towards Henry that sparkled in L'Ombrière spluttered out like a gutted candle. My heart was heavy. Did I love him? Yes, but I felt more often I was living with a stranger, and was searching for the enthusiastic, eager, funny, and adorable Henry through an impenetrable fog, seeking a man who had appeared to have lost his way. Toulouse hung like the Sword of Damocles.

Henry rode off after kissing me tenderly, and probably wondering why I was wooden. As my horse and I plodded towards Poitiers, my mind was in a turmoil of torn loyalties – loyalty to my husband and his Anglo-Norman empire as his queen, and loyalty to my people as Duchess of Aquitaine and Countess of Poitou. It was as if someone told me I had to choose one of my children over the others.

When I reached Poitiers, I was greeted well enough, but there were gathering storm clouds. Henry's rampage into Poitou hovered in unsaid words from Uncle Ralph downwards. The chaos in my head was ready to erupt into frustrated rage. I felt I could not cope with affairs of state until I had worked through the problems before me, so I locked myself in Papa's library. I warned I was not to be disturbed by anyone unless it was an emergency with the children. Behind the locked door, I hoped to clear my mind. Instead, my troubles overwhelmed me. I stuffed the hem of my gown in my mouth and bawled in muffled despair and sorrow as I curled up on the floor like a newborn babe.

How long I was like that I knew not. I must have wept myself to sleep on the Byzantium rug. I was woken by light knocking on the door. Someone was asking if I was all right. When I got my bearings, the rage returned. A carved figurine of the Virgin ricocheting off the door and left chards of pottery across Grandfather William's exquisite carpet. Now I would truly rot in Hell. The knocking stopped.

Later, thirst dragged me out of the library. I was dryer than a mistral wind. It was dark. I knew not what hour it was. Asleep in chairs outside the door were two slumped figures, Peter and Jerome. One would be fearing for my mortal soul, the other there to give me comfort. I managed to tip-toe past both and leave the building. In the courtyard, I guzzled from a water-butt not caring if it was full of wrigglers. The fresh night air cooled my face. Hunger drove me down to the kitchens where I terrified a group of snoozing churls, family retainers from my childhood. They must have thought I was some sort of apparition. Empty tankards indicated they had been drinking ale. After they realised who I was, they sprang to attention, grinning a welcome. I asked if there was any ale left?

The oldest, Jacque, bobbed and nodded. I asked him to pour me a cup. I sat on a stool and helped myself to some leftover cheese from a board. A large leather tankard was placed within my reach. I downed it in one gulp impressing the churls no end and held it out for another. After about three, or maybe five, I lost count. I think by then I had drunk them dry. The room circled my head. My tongue was stuck to the roof of my mouth; it would not articulate anything of sense. Nor when I stood to leave would my legs work. I think I sat again. The whole kitchen was moving as if I were on board a ship in a storm. Everything was sideways no matter where I tried to put my feet. The number of churls had quadrupled. Some of them joined in song. Everyone in the Aquitaine seemed to know Grandfather William's dirty ditties.

The next day, I think it was the next day, I woke in my bed. Never had I felt so ill. My head had at least twenty armourers inside it hammering for the next crusade. My mouth felt like it had been stuffed with wool. I vomited worse than any morning sickness. But my dear loyal churls had placed me on a pedestal, giving me hero status. Everyone else in my household either joined the churls or were disgusted. The children proudly announced to everyone, including the bishop, that Maman got roaring drunk.

Amaris gave me a filthy look, suggesting I bathe. I rose from my bed and took a tentative step. Again, the room rotated. With no sympathy whatsoever, Amaris did little to support me to the tub. I lowered my shivery, goosepimply body into the water. Amaris poured a full ewer of water over my head.

I gasped, spluttering, 'Are you trying to drown me?'

'No,' she harrumphed. 'But I will pray for your debauched soul.'

Lord in heaven, what had I done?

After my bath, I felt more normal. Lucille was now helping. She could not keep a straight face, much to Amaris' disgust, and was finding it difficult not to convulse into laughter. Amaris gave me a physic that almost had me vomiting again, but the threatening look on her face said, if that happened, I would be cleaning up after myself. She rubbed my hair with such vigour, I thought my head was going to fly off my shoulders. I moaned that I wanted to die. Getting dressed was torture. Lucille departed, giving me a naughty wink.

Amaris left me slumped in a chair. Warm sunlight streamed through the window to dry my hair. There was a tap on the door that sounded like my epitaph was being hammered in stone. Jerome peeped around the door and asked if he could enter. By now if the devil himself had appeared, I would not have cared. He tiptoed across the parquet. At least he was showing some sympathy for my plight. By the wicked grin on his face, I gathered he was on the side of the churls.

'Elly, you look terrible.'

'Thank you for the compliment.'
'Is there anything I can get you?'
'An axe, so I can behead myself.'
'Oh, dear. That bad, is it?'
'If I could remember what happened, it would be useful.'
'You do not recall?'
'Not a thing.'

Jerome pulled up a stool and gleefully elaborated, 'You drank the churls' ale, all of it, and sang every naughty song you know, much to their amusement. It took the five of them to get you up the kitchen stairs. By then you had awoken everyone in the palace.'

'You jest?'

'No,' Jerome said, grinning. 'At that stage, what you called your two husbands was unprintable. Your description of Louis' expertise in bed was most enlightening. Henry got better marks.'

I went pale, if I could turn any paler, hoping dear Lord I did not reveal Henry's father or Abraham. Jerome smiled knowingly, as I looked horrified.

'Do not panic. You did not mention anyone else. By the time the churls hauled you close to your chamber, your maids and others joined in and carried you across the threshold. By then you had passed out.'

'Amaris said I was sick.'

'Yes. That too, but I think that was after they got you to bed. Peter is suggesting penance.'

'Oh dear.'

***

It took me several days to get up the courage to face my justiciars. Uncle Ralph was not on the side of the churls. After a few black looks,

'Eleanor, presuming you are now up to it, you are going to have to ride to Blaye to speak to Lord Henry. The consequences of his actions in Poitou can no longer be ignored and there is this stupidity over Toulouse.'

'Yes, Uncle, I will do my best.'

'I sincerely hope so. And may I suggest in the future you remember who you are and act with some decorum.'

'Yes, Uncle Ralph.'

But I believed nothing was going to alter Henry's thinking. Like Louis before him, the recapture of Toulouse was as much for his ego as it was for my inheritance.

The County of Toulouse was a sore subject. Grandfather William's infamy in leaving his wife Philippa to battle for her inheritance while he abandoned himself in Dangerosa's arms left many in my Chatellerault family with a loyalty dilemma. Worse, the County was lost, usurped by Alphonso Jordan, and passed down to his heirs.

My pride had a lot to do with the Aquitaine people's valiant hopes, but I was beginning to doubt whether it was worth the sacrifice of the lives of the men who were to go into battle. Most of my people wanted a victory for me, but I was not so sure they wanted it on Henry's behalf.

I left the children safely in Poitiers and rode with haste to Blaye through the devastated countryside of my County of Poitou. I could not believe my eyes. How could he! What could I say? No wonder Uncle Ralph insisted I ride to Blaye. Words cannot describe the destruction: the burnt out villages, destroyed crops, castles and manors devastated, not to mention the rape and pillaging that took place. My next encounter with Henry would not be a happy one.

As for Toulouse, would Henry heed my concerns? I doubted it. I could plead for him to show restraint, to take care but little else. Then, after I arrived at the castle, already down-hearted, I was dumb-foundered to find Henry had gone ahead betrothing Richard to Raymond-Berengar's baby daughter without further consultation with me. It was too much, and I raved like a lunatic.

'Will you ever consult me on the fate of our children?'

'I thought you saw the merit and had agreed.'

'No, Henry. You mentioned it and that was all. And how can I see the merit when I know not what it is? As you well know, Richard is my heir. I would have thought his betrothal should be my decision at least in part. What is more, he is only a little boy.'

'Well, it is not binding considering their age, but it will make Gascony more secure as well as help protect the future of our kingdoms.'

'I am sure *my* vassals in *my* Duchy of Gascony will be absolutely delighted.'

Henry ignored my sarcasm.

'Eleanor, you are too emotionally involved with the children. You need to be more objective.'

'After nine months of carrying them within my womb, going through the hell of giving birth, then watching them grow daily before my eyes, why would I not want the best for them? Our children are not possessions, Henry, who you can parcel off on a whim for some ephemeral alliance, so you can expand territory, which is my dowry may I remind you.'

'You never let me forget that, do you? Jesus, Mary, and Joseph. You, and your bloody dowry. Why in God's name did I marry you?'

'Because you would have had nothing if you had not. Nothing! No wealth, no treasury, and furthermore, no England or children to use as pawns.'

I turned on my heel leaving him fuming and kicking the furniture.

That night, I bolted my door. I planned to return to England. I had received letters that there were eruptions and pockets of discontent. I was, after all, still regent. Of course, Henry could cancel it, but, because he was so angry, I knew he had not given it a thought – another chess tactic ignored by storming ahead, taking pieces willy-nilly then being checkmated.

Never in our marriage had I prepared to leave without

Chapter 8: Rebellion Looms

saying goodbye to Henry. I felt I could not face him, regardless of his plans to recapture my stolen inheritance. As I was about to mount my horse, he stormed into the bailey of the Castle of Blaye.

'Where in Satan's name do you think you are going?'

'Back to Poitiers, thence to England.'

'No, Eleanor. Not yet.'

Henry's voice was menacing, his eyes wild.

Antoine and my Praetorian guard were like cats, ready to spring to my defence against their king. I held up my hand; they retreated but were still on their toes. I had to think quickly to dampen the fuming rage that was about to erupt. I knew if he touched me, one of my men could run him through causing an event of monumental consequences. Henry's fists were clenched as hard as iron knockers. There was nothing I could do but swallow my pride, turn, and put my arms around him. He was like a post. I lay my head on his shoulder, glaring at Antoine and his cohorts to back away. They got the message but only retreated as far as their horses.

I could think of nothing to say, so I rubbed my hands up and down his back and arms as if he was one of the children who was hurt or frightened. He began to relax. My emotions were all over the place.

'I do not have to leave yet, if you do not wish, but I was not feeling very welcome.'

'Stay. I insist.'

I wanted to snap *is that an order* but kept my mouth shut.

'I am feeling cold, Henry. Can we go to your chamber?'

With a tilt of my head, my guards relaxed a little. Henry turned. I followed. In his chamber he prowled. His pacing was irritating as usual, but now was not the time to ask him to be still. Instead, I buried my head in my hands fighting to keep my impatience in check. I was trying to think of something to say when Henry blurted, 'Why are you leaving?'

'I feel unwelcome, and I have duties to perform as your regent in England also as Duchess of Aquitaine.'

'You locked me out of your chamber last night.'
'I felt you did not want to be in my bed.'
'Then why lock your door?'
'Maybe I did not want you there, either.'

This was getting us nowhere. There was no point in avoiding our issues. So, before he could set sail on another tack, as gently as possible, I said, 'We appear to be drifting apart, and, moreover, I am deeply worried about your health. You seem troubled.'

'It is your over-vivid imagination. There is nothing wrong with me.'

Now what should I say? I had avoided discussing the plundering and destruction of Poitou for too long. I had to face Henry whether I liked it or not.

'I believe your attack on my County of Poitou was excessive. You have gone too far this time. All you have succeeded in doing is alienating the Poitivins further. I am being accused of betraying my county and my duchy to the Anglo-Normans. I cannot speak to my justiciars who have become hostile. It is going to take every tactic of diplomacy I can muster to get them just to listen to me. Nor am I relishing them tearing my husband to strips in front of me.'

Henry thundered, 'The only action your vassals understand is a display of force.'

'There is force and then there is downright cruelty, the action of a tyrant. The burning, looting and destruction of towns and villages full of innocent peasantry, women, and children is not equal to knocking down castle walls that hold the perpetrators of the revolt. Like Louis's maniacal attack on Vitry-sur-Marne all those years ago. That nearly destroyed him.'

'How dare you compare me to that fool!'

'Then stop behaving like him! You are trying my people to their limits. You are going to need every scrap of cooperation you can glean from my vassals if you want to take Toulouse. Many have no desire to join your army. Most are only doing so out of loyalty to me.'

'Well, they had better start showing some loyalty to their king!'

That will be the day, I thought. 'I presume you know Louis is supporting Raymond V and is already snug and warm behind his walls.'

I could see by the look on Henry's face it was the first he had heard of this. I also guessed why he had not been informed. The courier I surmised got no further than the Palace of Poitiers. Revenge from the justiciars of the Aquitaine I would think. It stung. By hurting Henry, they hurt me. Somehow, I had to win back their trust and respect. That encounter could be unpleasant.

'So, you knew I was being lured into a trap.'

'God's teeth, no, Henry! I am amazed you did not receive this information. When I found out, I was furious. I want Hal to have nothing to do with the House of Capet. You know my feelings on that, Vexin or no Vexin. I want Hal's betrothal to Louis' bloody daughter declared null and void.'

'That, Eleanor, is impossible. Regardless of Louis's treachery, Hal could be king of France.'

I threw up my hands. Now it was my turn to pace, trying to keep my anger and frustration under control. Although it humiliated me, I emphasised,

'Henry, I do not need Toulouse. I have done without it all my life. It has only been the pride of desire that has inflamed me from time to time. Let it go. It is not worth more death. I am sorry, but I have to leave.'

Nevertheless, there was no stopping him. There was no way he was going to let Louis get the better of *'enri Plantagenet-a*. I could see I was not going to change his mind; he was more determined than ever. My guards, horses and the rest of my entourage were cooling their heels in the bailey. I could not keep them waiting any longer. Besides, we would be running into darkness before we reached our first accommodation for the night unless we left now.

Henry begged me to stay until the morrow, but I could not. I wanted to visit Nilla on her estate for a few days before I returned to Poitiers. She was not keeping good health these days, so I needed to spend a short time with her. I wished Henry God speed. I told him he would be daily in my prayers. I entreated him to take care of himself. He crushed me to him. He needed a good haircut and his beard trimming. I ran my fingers through his curly locks now streaked with grey. I told him I loved him regardless of our disagreements and kissed him goodbye. I would see him when he arrived in Poitiers.

***

We had to make haste to make up for lost time. I left the more cumbersome wagons of my retinue to leave the next day at cockcrow, which meant most of my maids as well. Lucille was the only one to accompany me. We kept pace with the men. Shear willpower kept me on my horse regardless of the lump of lead in my heart which wanted me to gallop back to Henry.

We spent the night at a monastery where we had hospitality before. The monks were kind. I requested them to pray for the safety of my beloved husband, Lord Henry, King of England, and his men as they prepared for war to regain Toulouse.

Lucille and I shared a cell wrapped in our furs for warmth. The daytime temperatures were balmy, but without heating the heavy, old, stone abbey was chill at night. Lucille was tired and fell asleep like a baby. I lay awake staring at a patch of starry sky through the slit of a window as tears coursed silently down my face. I prayed silently, *'Please God, Mother Mary look after Henry, keep him safe. Placate what ails his angry mind.'*

Sleep or exhaustion caught up with me, for the next moment I remembered was Lucille gently waking me to join the monks for a simple breakfast in their refectory. When we were ready to depart, the Abbot, Father Paul,

Chapter 8: Rebellion Looms

said their community would include Henry and his men in their prayers for which I was more than grateful. As soon as I reached Poitiers, I told them, I would arrange with my almoners to distribute funds for their coffers.

***

We arrived at Nilla's picturesque chateau late in the day. She was waiting to welcome me. We hugged, and she led me indoors where she had arranged for me to bathe and change from my travelling attire to a fresh, more suitable gown. Clean and settled with a goblet of fine wine from her estates, I was able to assess her physically. I was shocked. She had lost weight and had aged. She looked more like someone of Renée's vintage. She had a sharp cough which I did not like the sound of and I could see she was a little short of breath. But she was prattling away, wanting to know all about my children, especially the latest addition. Her children were now young adults. Ralph was wed and running the estate with his older stepbrother. Eloise was betrothed to a young noble from Limoges and was happy in his family household. They would wed when she turned fourteen. I did not wish to concern her, but in fury I told Nilla about Hal and Richard's betrothals, fuming that they were too young and cursing Hal's predicament. I ranted that we were all pawns, possessions of the Plantagenet dynasty. So much for my urge to ride back to Henry. What a muddle.

The floodgates opened.

'Nilla, Henry is becoming more and more irrational. He sees conspiracies amongst his barons where there are none. He is alienating his own people as well as mine. His barbaric foray into Poitou was devastating. It will take years to return the County to prosperity, to repair the damage. Our vassals will never trust him again and I am torn between my loyalty to the Anglo-Norman empire and to the Aquitaine.'

'Yes, it must be difficult. I know about Poitou. It has been 'discussed' in detail on my estate and others. Poor young Ralph has had to try to be neutral.'

'I am so sorry Nilla that Henry's actions have come so close to home.'

'It has been awkward.'

'I can imagine. On top of this are his jealous moods. We are always arguing, the quarrels are getting worse and personal. He is so pigheaded.'

'I do not suppose that "the pot is calling the kettle black" by any chance?'

'What do you mean?'

'Darling Sis, you were always headstrong even when we were little.'

'I was not.'

'Yes, you were, and you had Papa wrapped around your little finger. You forever got your own way.'

'I did not, you are exaggerating.'

'Noo!'

'You, Jerome, and Clotilde were allowed out to play, while I was stuck in the school-room learning the bloody laws of the Aquitaine off by heart.'

'Renée spoiled you too.''

'Oh, come on Nilla, that is not true. I often got a damn good slap round the ears.'

'Mostly for swearing I seem to remember.'

'Look I did not come here to have an argument about our childhood. And talking of children, Nilla, I am tired of constantly being pregnant.'

My sister raised an eyebrow.

'But you still want Henry in your bed.'

The rising colour in my face answered that statement. I gulped down my wine and poured another. If I were not careful, I would be turning into a sot.

'I have a confession to make. I got drunk trying to drown my sorrows over all of this.'

'You mean the churl incident?' Nilla gave a hearty

guffaw and laughed so much that it brought on a coughing fit I thought would choke her as she gasped and spluttered for breath. She regained control and wiped her eyes.

'Jerome told me in his last letter. He said you were hilarious, very entertaining though not particularly regal.'

'Nilla, you might think it funny, but Uncle Ralph is hardly speaking to me, let alone the justiciars. Furthermore, their disapproval of Henry's heavy-handed treatment of my Poitivin vassals I have yet to face.'

We were both quiet while she mulled over my outburst, and I chewed my lip. Why was my life so complicated? 'I have never told you this, but I was given a prophesy in the Holy Land.'

She gave me a penetrating look. 'Well?'

I told her about Judith's pronouncement, how it had worried me and how I dismissed it as foolery – even heresy.

'The "tumultuous" part has obviously come true. So has the prediction about *marrying the love of my life, and having many sons*, but I cannot foretell of being *a great queen*. That is too frightening to comprehend. Does it mean as Henry's wife, or as his regent, if something should happen to him before Hal is grown?'

'Elea, you have a brilliant mind. Dear God, I remember you would read a page of the scriptures and then recite it back word for word. Whatever happens, your intelligence will see you prevail just like when you play chess. Also, I have observed the way you perform your duties; sometimes, you actually sound wise.'

I was not sure whether she was joshing me but, noting the twinkle in her eye, I laughed in spite of myself, 'Including my foul temper, impatience, and stubborn streak.'

'Mm, like I said... but no-one is perfect.' Nilla smiled then continued, 'Maybe the prophesy refers to what you are now. Maybe it is what you must continue to be if, as you say, Henry is becoming more impetuous.'

'Nilla, I find it terrifying. No wonder I got so sozzled. I just wanted to obliterate what is constantly racing round my mind.'

'The prophesy?'

'No. The responsibility.'

'It is your duty. It is what Papa trained you for.'

I sighed. 'Yes, indeed.'

A page entered to inform us it was time to dine. My sister and I walked arm in arm to the table prepared for us. Darling Nilla was as picky as me, not usual for her. As all the talk had revolved around me and my problems, I felt ashamed. I had not asked about her cough and loss of weight. She brushed it off as just a lingering cold that had put her off her appetite. She would not enlighten me further.

After our meal, we were joined by her son Ralph and his pretty young wife Magdalene. Both were shy, a little nervous about being in my company. I suspected I was a bit of a towering presence. Before Nilla could intervene, I hoped I quelled their apprehension by rising and kissing Ralph on both cheeks and asking him to introduce his wife to Tante Eleanor. The kisses reddened his ear tips, but he relaxed and introduced Magdalene, who gave me a little curtsy.

We then got down to family chatter, which was a lot more fun, allowing them to forget titles, and more pleasant than being surrounded by fawning, grovelling hoards who were charming to my face then derided me behind my back.

By now Amaris and the rest of my train caught up with me. I think we stretched Nilla's accommodation to its limits. I spent as much time alone with her as I could. I knew she was putting on a brave face for me, but I could see at times she was struggling with her health. Her apothecary and physician were doing their best to control the symptoms causing her cough. Young Ralph feared how the coming winter would affect her. I asked him to keep me informed; I would send her more warm garments as soon as I returned to Poitiers.

Today was time to leave. I was packed ready to farewell my sister. Except when she first met Raoul, and her life was uncertain, she had been happy and contented, so why must she, the younger be afflicted and I strong. All I could do was pray God would look after her. I knew she was loved and in good hands for which I was grateful, but with the distances between us, I feared this could be our last meeting. Last night Nilla said she would pray I prevailed, that Henry was only suffering some temporary affliction. Dear God and all the saints, I hoped so.

***

On the journey back to Poitiers, I saw more of the damage caused by Henry's rampage through Poitou. I was so conflicted. I tried to make sense of his actions and was not relishing my confrontation with the panel. My justiciars had every reason not to support his campaign to reclaim Toulouse, which I knew would test their loyalties. What a predicament. Although I was not comfortable regarding Toulouse, I must support Henry: it would be disloyal not to, even treasonable. I must convince my good men to follow their Duchess.

But I had the joy of my reunion with my children to look forward to, especially my baby girl, whose baby smell and chuckles I had missed over the past few weeks.

As I rode back through the streets of Poitiers with my winding entourage, the good burghers, artisans, and ordinary folk gave me a rousing welcome. Grooms awaited in the palace courtyard to tend to tired horses after we dismounted. I hitched my riding-cloak and gown over my arm and wearily made my way to my quarters. There was a warm fire in my grate with enough wood stacked on the hearth to last a siege. Tied in a piece of twine next to the wood was a pretty bunch of lavender which had me puzzled. As Amaris and Celeste were removing my cape, there was a gentle tap on the door. I nodded to Celeste to allow whoever to enter. Five shy, grinning churls shuffled in begging to know if there was anything I needed. I thanked them and said I had everything for the moment, then realised they were responsible for the stack of wood, likewise the sweet gift of lavender. One scuttled to my table depositing a large jug of ale.

'Just in case, Milady, you should want some refreshment after your long journey.'

Then bobbing and bowing, they backed out the door. My drinking companions no less. I glared at my smirking maids daring them to utter one word, though I could not help but smile, if a little sheepishly.

No sooner had I removed my cape when the door burst open and there were my boys and Matilda, with Lenore in her nurse's arms. They flung themselves into mine, jostling like puppies for my attention. Soon they had me flat on the floor swarming over me with tickles, hugs, kisses, and squeals of glee. Their nurses had no control no matter how much they protested that Maman was being squashed. Overwhelmed by the din, Lenore wailed in protest, and only then was I able to scramble to my feet. I took her in my arms as two fat tears ran down her chubby cheeks, but they were soon replaced by a happy grin. The only sad note was Hal wanting to know where was Papa? Coming soon, I told them.

Surrounded by my happy boisterous clan enabled me to forget my troubles and to praise God for their being, their unquestioning love, as rowdy as it might be, and the overwhelming happiness they gave me.

Chapter 9. Duchess Or Queen?

I had to concentrate on meeting with my panel of justiciars. Procrastination was going to prolong the inevitable, so I summoned them to attend me in two days' time. I took myself back to the library, this time not to avoid the issue, but to consider how to address them. I wrote notes, screwed them into balls, or scratched words out. Finally, I knew what I had to say.

On the morning of my reception with the panel, I prayed my speech would be accepted. I chose a sober gown for such a serious audience and wore the English crown. Above all my illustrious titles, I was now first and foremost Queen of England, King Henry's wife.

As I entered the audience chamber, they stood bowing their heads in homage – Guile, Uncle Ralph, Saldebreuil, Guillaume and three Poitivins representatives, as well as the Bishops of Poitiers and Perigueux. The latter, although representing the west of the Aquitaine, I presumed were there as referees. I indicated for them to sit while I remained standing.

Without wasting time, I addressed them. Their faces were as expressionless as statues, but I was no longer nervous, nor was I going to be intimidated regardless of the stony reception.

'Gentlemen, do the Nobles of Poitou consider to whom they owe their allegiance? Through my marriage, they are beholden to the rule of law of the Anglo-Norman Empire. Should they rebel against these laws we, Lord King Henry and I, Queen Eleanor, are obliged to put down the rebellion. The Poitivins must know, must understand surely, that when they defy Lord King Henry of England, their actions affect me also.

'You may ask, to whom do I, Eleanor, owe allegiance? By inheritance, I am Duchess of Aquitaine and Gascony and Countess of Poitou. By marriage, I am firstly Queen of England, then Duchess of Normandy and Countess of Anjou, among other titles.

'Therefore, put yourselves in my position.

'My loyalties have always been to my people, so where are their loyalties to me when they revolt against my husband, who is also their Duke and whom I love.

'If the Nobles of Poitou or the Aquitaine have grievances, they can be brought here to this panel of justiciars, to this table. Their grievances can then be discussed before developing to the point where a mark is overstepped, resulting in conflict.

'I admit the consequences of this rebellion have been dire. I cannot make excuses for these facts. Reparation will be made to the innocent caught up in the dispute. But I make no apologies to those who took the law into their own hands. I find no justification for their actions in placing me, as Countess of Poitou, in this invidious situation of having to choose between loyalty to my husband or to the perpetrators of rebellion against my husband. I pray you will in future respect my position.

'Furthermore, gentlemen, may I ask where were you when trouble was simmering in Poitou? I am certain not one of you sitting here in front of me did not know what was stirring not so many leagues away. May I remind you, you are my representatives. When I or my husband, Lord King Henry, are not residing within this Duchy or in the County of Poitou, you have the responsibility of implementing the laws of the land. Lord Ralph de Faye, you are my regent just as I am regent in England when the king is absent. I take my duties seriously; I would like to think you do also.

'The rebellion that was fermenting among the Poitivin Nobles could have been curtailed with judicious discussion. If you were not aware of the discontent to our north, you should have been, either that or you were negligent in your duties.

Chapter 9: Duchess Or Queen?

'From what I can ascertain, little was done to calm the situation which brought down the wrath of King Henry on the insurgents, resulting in the devastation inflicted across Poitou, and sadly its people.

'I am aware many of you blame me for not counselling King Henry to take alternative action, which was difficult seeing I was doing my duty as regent in England before and during the rebellion. But you, my panel of justiciars, were here, entrusted with the rule of law of my lands and its governance.

'Finally, when you search your consciences, I hope you will dwell on my words and remember, "He that is without sin among you, let him cast the first stone."

'I thank you for your time.'

There was shuffling on chairs and clearing of throats as I left the room.

I returned to my quarters pleased with my speech. I wanted my words to have an effect. I hoped they made them think. Their accusations of my conduct hurt. Even if I had been at hand to influence Henry, I knew it would have had little effect on his ultimate decision. That the people I trusted to rule my lands did nothing to prevent the rebellion when the first spark of dissension ignited was unacceptable. Henry was not to be exonerated for his behaviour. He was responsible. He could have used diplomacy, met with the nobles of Poitou to discuss their grievances instead of raging through their countryside creating havoc. It would take years to undo the damage inflicted, both in the restoration of the countryside as well as physically for the people. Alms I can provide, which will help, but how can I restore trust in the Anglo-Norman empire or Henry?

When Henry reached Poitiers, I wanted to ordain Richard as my heir which would ease some of the tensions if the people could see continuity in the Aquitaine dynasty.

Henry was due to arrive with the army he had gathered to retake Toulouse. I arranged for his men to be accommodated in a large field two leagues from Poitiers. I did not want skirmishes or drunken brawls breaking out between my still disgruntled vassals and Henry's mostly Norman soldiers. Nor did I want them marauding through the taverns and the more bawdy establishments in some parts of the city.

In reply to my letter informing Henry of this plan, he agreed that he would settle the men there, and would arrive at the palace sometime after the midday bells with his elite guards and usual entourage.

I arranged for a tub to be ready for him as he had been on horseback for many days and would be tired and grimy. My eager churls, I knew, would produce a brimming jug of ale. The children were excited. I was a little worried, however. Henry would not want four of his bundles of joy bouncing around like excited puppies, yet I did not want to rein in their exuberance at seeing their father after so long. Nor did I want him grumbling at me or them, so I must have a word to keep them calm. A page knocked on the library door. He said it was heralded that the king was approaching at speed.

Henry dismounted from his lathered horse and hastened towards me as fast as his limp allowed. The sight of his children slowed him. Hal happily greeted Henry, Matilda squealed and giggled. Richard, as belligerent as only he can be, clung to one of my legs, and Geoffrey to the other, enveloped in my gown. Both were making it impossible for me to move. Lenore slept through the greetings. Nurses and maids hovered in the background. Henry's face expressed a thousand emotions. I knew the look; he wanted his wife, who was encumbered by his offspring. Lenore, I could hand to her nurse. I told Hal and Matilda to kiss Papa, that they would see him soon when we dined later. Richard and Geoffrey were not so easy to dislodge. Richard said 'no' and would not budge. Henry ground his teeth. Geoffrey, as usual, assessed the situation, and in perfect Latin queried why he should go

Chapter 9: Duchess Or Queen?

anywhere. As fast as I prized his grip from my leg and gown, he reapplied it like a vice. Hal came to my aid by hitting Richard in the ear. Richard howled and gave chase as Hal tore across the courtyard with Matilda joining in for good measure. Cecilia tried to extricate Geoffrey, who stuck his thumb in his mouth, his other fist anchoring him to my gown. Henry stormed off in a huff. By then I had lost my 'gentle' mother's temper and yelled at Geoffrey. My angry voice sent him into a high-pitched scream, so he ran to Cecelia who he decided was far nicer than Maman. I followed my irritated husband to his bed chamber where he was throwing his boots across the room. What a welcome! Bless the churls, at least; Henry's tub was full of steaming water.

I dismissed Henry's manservants from our presence and opened my arms for an embrace. He muttered he needed to bathe, because the best wash he had had in days was in a freezing river. I thought with a sigh that it had never stopped him in the past.

'Do you want me to leave?'

'No.'

Henry relaxed. I unlaced his travel-stained gown, and he removed his braies. He limped stiffly to the tub where he eased himself into the water and submerged himself. Coming up for air, he shook his curls, spraying water everywhere like a wet dog. Once I would have been in the tub with him. As if reading my mind, he complained he thought I was over-dressed. I said I would be back, exiting to my adjoining chamber where Amaris, Marion and my other maids were stitching, no doubt with ears pricked as to what might happen next door. I would have liked to undress myself, but this gown was laced down the back. At least I could not see their smirking faces, but I could guess what they were thinking. When they finished their task, I shooed them out the door. I inserted one of the little pellets secreted amongst my jewellery, and in my silk shift I returned to Henry who was blowing bubbles in the water.

The shift fell to the floor. I stepped in. There was only one way to fit, and Henry's manhood was going to pin me in that position. Water cascaded vigorously over the sides of the tub. I collapsed on his chest. Our breathing was heavy. Neither of us spoke. Love, or was it lust, does not need words.

Henry did not want to dine with the children; he wanted me to accompany him to his bed or mine, so we could continue what we had started. I told him I did not break promises to our children, and what was more, they wanted to spend time with him. Like it or no he had to comply. After all, we had the whole night after they had gone to bed. He grumbled but agreed.

Dinner with the children was not the riot I was half expecting. Their nurses and maids must have had a word in their collective ears. Richard for once did not rile his father. Much to my amusement, Geoffrey, who was nearly three, announced again in beautiful Latin that, when he had beaten Maman at chess, he would play Papa. Henry took that as a challenge, presuming I was letting Geoffrey win. The child had an incredible capacity to pick up learning as if he is soaking it up like a sea-sponge. Jerome told me I had been the same, reminding me for no good reason what a precocious, gifted brat, I was. Matilda batted her eyelids at Papa, reminiscent of Nilla. I would have to watch that one. Hal was shy, perhaps because the maids had done too good a job on him, so he retreated into himself. Lenore slept through the meal. Henry complained he had hardly seen her with her eyes open.

To please me, Henry played games with the children after dinner. I think, despite himself, he enjoyed having fun with them for once. I was so used to Geoffrey's curiosity, I did not find it odd, but Henry was nonplussed by his serious attention to the world around him while he still sucked his thumb. Geoffrey told Henry with the earnestness of a scholar that butterflies came out of armour, and babies came out of mothers, but he had yet to ascertain how they got in there in the first place. Henry told him it was something he would discover when he was older. By now, my face was scarlet.

After hugs and kisses, it was time for bed. Henry with a wicked twinkle suggested we should be doing something about putting babies into mothers. I reminded him we had a few matters to discuss before he met with our justiciars on the morrow. Also, I wanted to warn him about his likely reception after my address to them earlier today. But no, Henry's and my splash in the tub was only an entrée as far as he was concerned. Now he wanted the main course. I just hoped the tiny pellet was still viable. My serious conversation with Henry would have to wait till the morrow.

***

I rose early. I knew I had to interrupt his breakfast after his prayers, his quiet time. It was supposed to be sacrosanct.

While he was in his chapel, I quickly dealt with my ablutions, so I was dressed when he returned for his repast. His expression darkened as to why he could not have at least a small part of the day to himself. I drew up a chair to his table.

'You did not wish to talk last night, so I am afraid it will have to be now.'

Harrumphing, he grudgingly let me continue while he munched his bread and cheese with his ale.

'I intend to officially proclaim Richard as my heir. I have decided on a simple ceremony in the cathedral before you set out on your campaign to retake Toulouse. I hope it will do much to sooth the querulous rancour in some quarters of the duchy.'

I got no reply. 'Are you listening, Henry?'

'Yes, Eleanor.'

'If the justiciars and our people are assured of the continuous succession it will allay fears as to the fate of the Aquitaine after my death.'

Henry continued eating in silence. I was beginning to get annoyed, but I persisted,

'Yesterday I addressed our justiciars to try to dispel their displeasure regarding your foray into Poitou. I do not believe they would have been pleased having their loyalties questioned or being accused of doing nothing to quell the ripples of discord before they reached your ears causing you to react the way you did. I also promised reparation for the innocents caught up in the conflict.'

Henry pushed back his chair. His face was expressionless, but I knew his mind would be buzzing like a swarm of bees.

'Oh, and for good measure,' I went on. 'I more or less accused Uncle Ralph of not taking his duties seriously enough as regent.'

'Jesus, Mary and Joseph! I suppose expecting extra troops for Toulouse will now be out of the question?'

'I doubt that. They want Toulouse back as much as we do. Now I will leave you in peace.'

He called after me as I walked to the door. 'Following that revelation, you had better accompany me, seeing you have stirred Lord Ralph and the panel up like angry hornets. I do not wish to be stung.'

I quipped, 'Yesterday, I addressed them as Queen of England so who should I represent today?'

'Eleanor, as you are first and foremost my queen, we will present a united front.'

I hesitated. Should Uncle Ralph and the panel bring up the severity of Anglo-Norman laws, I would be obliged to agree to some extent. I had argued Henry's right to apply his laws as King of England and Duke of Normandy when Poitou rebelled, but in my heart, I believed consultation was preferable and force should only be used when all else failed. Henry did not try to confer with anyone. Instead, he galloped into Poitou with cannons roaring.

Anglo-Norman rulings were rigid compared with those of the Aquitaine and Poitou, whose laws had been adapted from old Roman influences, and had become more flexible over time encouraging greater consultation. Louis found them incomprehensible, mostly because they gave women more autonomy. My vassals felt that Anglo-Norman rulings were foreign and too severe.

In England, I could see the merit of the laws being strict, especially as Henry had to unify the country after a thousand schisms. It was the only way forward after years of civil war, but that method of governance was not necessary to keep order among my arguing vassals, who in most cases just bickered like children. If their grievances could be aired, they usually conformed, except for a handful of notorious nobles. To destroy the whole county in retaliation over a few dissidents had created resentment that would be long-lasting.

'All right, do not just stand there, Eleanor, with an expression like a bad smell has filled your nostrils. You have already interrupted my breakfast and invaded my peace and quiet, so spit out what is on your mind.'

'Well, you refused to talk last night and if you must know, I think there could be a dispute festering between the merits of Aquitainean law versus the merits of Anglo-Norman law.'

'And just who's side of the debate is Madame Cicero going to argue?'

My ire was rising at Henry's tone of voice. Once that quip would have been a jest, at the most a gibe, but now it had a nasty edge. 'I believe it will be best if I remain neutral. Now I will take my leave. You will find me in the library after I have said good morning to the children.'

His voice bounced off the closing door which I resisted slamming. 'I demand your loyalty, Eleanor!'

The word 'demand' fuelled the fire in my belly. I took a deep breath and made my way to the nursery. I entered to squeals and yells that alerted me there was some sort of game afoot. Matilda was attempting to feed Lenore some gruel. Not liking it, the baby sprayed it all over the little mother, which sent her brothers into stitches. A spitting competition ensued between the boys. The nursery was in uproar. Maids and nurses were trying to restore order, but my three sons could be handfuls if they set their minds to it. After Henry, I was not in the mood for frivolity, so I roared at everyone that, if they wanted to enjoy the rest of their day, they had better start behaving like Princes or the three of them would be shovelling in the stables. Geoffrey informed me he was too young to shovel horseshit. Rarely do I lay a hand on my boys, but he felt the full force of Maman's displeasure. I gave Cecelia, to whom he ran screaming, a look that said if she took his side, she would be joining them in the stables. Hal and Richard froze. Matilda and Lenore went out in sympathy with Geoffrey's bawling. I turned on my heels. The nursery door shook the palace to its foundations.

It took me a while to calm down. In my chair with my elbows on my desk and my head in my hands, I felt I could no longer fathom my husband, my children were turning into monsters, I had put my dear uncle offside, and I was warring with my justiciars. To confess my endless sins to Peter would take a decade. My maids were avoiding me except for their essential duties. The only person I had not offended was Jerome, whom nothing ruffles.

***

The day went from bad to worse. I was riled beyond sensibility. I stormed back to Henry's quarters where he was writing. Robert, Roger, and Martin took one look at me and bolted. Henry raised his eyes.

'How dare you presume you must DEMAND my loyalty! How dare you assume I will blindly agree with your Anglo-Norman rule of law if I do not believe it is suitable for my people who have lived by a set of principles put in place when Normandy was a pile of peasant dwellings and England a collection of primitive tribes!'

Chapter 9: Duchess Or Queen?

In one outraged sweep of my arm, I sent Henry's parchment, ink, and quills to the floor.

Henry was more stunned by the ink seeping into his white robe than my fury. His amazed look ricocheted from the stain to my thundering and back again. 'Calm down, Eleanor.'

His voice sounded even but as he stood and took a step towards me, my blade was in my hand. In basic Langue d'Oc and sounding like a raging fishwife I screamed at him. 'If you touch me, by Satan's balls, I will run you through, you Norman bastard.'

He kept his distance, letting me rant and rave till I ran out of invective and air to drive it through my lips. I felt an overwhelming desire to howl like Geoffrey and my daughters. I let the blade drop to the floor and followed it.

On my knees I pounded the carpet with my fists. *'Merde! Merde! Merde!'*

Henry hauled me upright and wrapped his arms around me, muttering that I had the filthiest temper of anyone he knew and could out-swear his roustiers and mercenaries.

'Not only that, the fierier your eyes are, the more beautiful you become.'

'How dare you patronise me!'

I squirmed in his arms as I tried to disentangle myself.

'I am telling the truth. Moreover, I take what you say seriously, indeed. And I do not want to be impaled.'

I broke free breathing like a grampus.

'This is not a jest *'enri Plantagenet-a.* You had better accept the differences between Anglo-Norman law and the laws of the Aquitaine and the rest of my lands with the significance they deserve, or you will never have the respect of my people. They consider your rule of law primitive, suitable for barbarians which my people are not. Until you get that into your head, they will rebel, and you will make no progress in regaining their homage, which as my husband you deserve.'

We stared at each other eyeball to eyeball.

'I can trace my ancestry to Charlemagne and to the Romans,' I went on. 'The Noble House of Aquitaine prides itself on its sophistication and learning, and the wealth that has come from it. It is galling for my people to have those who they consider uncouth upstarts impose a set of laws on them which are, at best, unrefined.' I smouldered like Vesuvius. 'Your attack on my county has proved what the nobles of Poitou think; that their neighbours know only barbarism. They were rebelling about the lack of consultation. Had you bothered to meet and to discuss their grievances, an understanding could have been reached without either side resorting to bloodshed.'

'Well, Eleanor of bloody Aquitaine, let me remind you of the fine education I received at Angers, and regardless of what your fancy poets and musicians may think, I come from an as illustrious house as you do. My Grandfather Fulk was King of Jerusalem while your grandfather was screwing your mother's mother in the Maubergeonne Tower.'

'Your father's father only became King of Jerusalem through his opportunistic second marriage to Queen Melisende whom I met with her son Baldwin during the Second Crusade. Furthermore, Fulk was never considered chivalrous by his peers, an upstart at best. As for my grandfather William IX of the Aquitaine, he gave his life during the First Crusade and Dangerosa might as well have been his widow, so do not insult either of my grandparents' love for each other.'

Henry, I think was shocked that I knew so much about his grandfather. It had slipped his mind that I had led an army to Jerusalem when I was still married to Louis and had learnt much about its politics.

But, not to be outdone, he yelled, 'And while you were being spoiled with excesses and the luxury of the House of Aquitaine, I was fighting alongside my mother to regain her sovereignty. And having won that hard-fought battle,

Chapter 9: Duchess Or Queen?

I am not about to lose it to vassals who do not like or wish to obey the laws of the land, which also applies to your poncy Poitivins.'

'So, *that* is where you learnt your brutality, your bullying tactics, at your mother's knee.'

Henry's punch missed me this time because I ducked as I threw myself to the floor to grab my finely honed knife. He flung himself on top of me to try to wrench it out of my hand. I clung onto it till he forced my grip open, and the blade flew across the floor. I grabbed a handful of his hair in one hand and raked my fingernails down his face with the other. He swore like a banshee trying to break free. We rolled over and over. Midst the struggle my gown was almost torn from me, but I was able to reach the knife.

At that point the door of the chamber flew open, and Roger and Robert wrestled Henry away as Jerome dragged me kicking and screaming from him. Henry's face was bleeding, but I staggered to my feet and kicked Henry's bad hip. Jerome wrenched the blade from my grip, almost breaking my wrist. I sagged to my knees, gasping for breath while Henry limped to a chair.

Uncle Ralph ordered everyone from the chamber. 'I cannot believe what I have just witnessed. You are both a disgrace to your nobility! Lady Eleanor, your father would be ashamed of you. Have you forgotten who you are? Have you forgotten all you were taught, your upbringing? As for you *Lord King* Henry, your behaviour is an insult to your parents. The late Duke Geoffrey Plantagenet was a gentleman of honour and your mother, the Lady Empress Matilda, is an admirable woman. I would have thought you would know better. Eleanor, stand up.'

I did with difficulty. If Henry hurt all over, so did I.

'I will leave you both to make amends,' Uncle Ralph went on. 'I will see you, Lord Henry, for our audience after the noonday bells.'

He left giving me a look that would have withered a healthy oak. He took our weapons with him for good measure.

I swallowed. My pride was smarting like my sore wrist. The air hung between us, a blanket of ice. Never was I going to apologise first. I did not move. In my peripheral vision, Henry was slumped with his head in his hands. I heard a sort of strangled choke which made me turn my head. Henry was weeping, trying not to let me hear or see. That was it, I rushed to him, my pride melting like frost in sunlight. I knelt in front of him, dragging his head down to my lips. He slid off the chair and we knelt rocking together. The floodgates opened. To think that last night we had made love enveloped in each other's arms. Who were we now? Brutes? Nothing more than animals? Was it vanity that drove us to attack each other because we could not get our own way? What sort of example were we setting as king and queen? Uncle Ralph was right; Papa would be ashamed of me.

It took some time before we could speak. We choked our apologies over the top of each then helped one another up. I went to the door to look for a churl. I needed some water to wash Henry's face, but the gallery was deserted. Everyone was keeping out of sight. Instead, I bathed it in wine left over from last night.

'I am sorry if it hurts,' I said

'Eleanor, you look like a sick tiger. You have kohl everywhere.'

'Thanks for the complement. You do not look so good yourself, Henry. I am sore all over. Can we lie down?'

We staggered to his bed and pulled the feather filled covers over ourselves. Fully clothed, we fell asleep in each other's arms.

After noon, Uncle Ralph sent a page for Henry. We were curled up together, so they let us be. I was awoken by bells, not knowing the time they rang out. The slanting light through our windows indicated sometime after

Chapter 9: Duchess Or Queen?

noon. For a few minutes, I thought what had happened was a nightmare, till I realised I was dressed. My sins, my arguments, my uncontrolled fury came rolling into my consciousness. Beside me, Henry was fast asleep, the scratches on his face visible. I eased my hair, my arms and body away from his embrace and swung my legs over the edge of the bed, marvelling for a moment I was wearing only one slipper. The other was on the other side of the room. Had I thrown it at Henry?

To say I hung my head in shame is an understatement. I slipped from the bed to my knees praying to God, the Blessed Virgin, the Saints and all the Heavenly Host to forgive me for my lack of control – though to be honest I expected nothing, and I deserved naught.

I had always valued my self-worth, but on this day, I despised myself with a loathing I could not describe. Could any good come out of my despicable behaviour? I could but hope.

I was so ashamed I did not wish to leave the chamber to show my face. My ripped gown was uncomfortable, so I started to undress after I kicked off my slipper and shed my hose which were around my knees, but the gown with its intricate lacings was impossible without help. I wept with frustration and woke Henry who, for a moment, was as disorientated as I had been, till it all came flooding back. I bawled like a child that I could not even unlace my gown as if it were the most important thing in the world. Without a thought, Henry helped as I howled, impotent that I could not look after myself. Henry wiped my face with the corner of the sheet like I was a little girl. I sobbed for my father. I said I was sorry about what I had said about his mother. At least he has a mother to remember. I said naught about his father. That was too close to the bone.

'Where have we gone wrong, Henry? How did we become so evil? Is it because many in the church see my marriage to you before God as adulterous?'

Henry reassured me, 'That is just foolish talk spread around by people who are jealous of my good fortune in having Christendom's most powerful, intelligent woman as my wife.'

Beauty was not mentioned, a poignant relief.

'I do not believe we are evil, Eleanor. Misguided from time to time in our human frailties maybe and driven by a determination to get our own way, but deep down we want to put the good of our people first. Nevertheless, our people are sometimes like sheep and need a good shepherd to round them up, to stop them endangering themselves by butting heads.'

A knock on the door forced us to emerge from our shame. Henry put my old red cape about me. I went next door to dress. Amaris hugged me. My dear maids dressed me again. Celeste tenderly washed my face and bathed my swollen eyes in cool lavender water.

Uncle Ralph summoned me to a personal conference. I felt like I was a child again having to confront Renée or one of my tutors for some naughty undertaking. In retrospect, Papa never scolded Nilla or me. With him, we could have got away with murder – well, almost.

I approached Uncle Ralph's quarters like a dog with its tail between its legs. He was waiting, looking sad. I started to babble out my apologies when he raised a hand to quieten me and ushered me to a chair. I sat twisting my rings around my fingers, staring at the rug expecting one mighty chiding. Instead, he told me how impressed he was by my address yesterday, how it had made him think. Yes, he and the panel could have done more to prevent the Poitivin rebellion. They could have taken measures to moderate tensions before they got out of hand and brought down Lord King Henry's wrath.

For five seconds, I thought I was safe till he exclaimed, 'Elea, what on earth created such a to-do, such an uproar between you and your husband whom you profess to love? Why in God's name did you come to blows?'

Chapter 9: Duchess Or Queen?

'Differences of opinion regarding Aquitaine and Anglo-Norman law.'

I could hardly mention Henry's reference to Uncle Ralph's mother, Dangerosa and grandfather William. That would have been too close to the bone.

He looked at me, stunned.

'Eleanor, I am horrified. It is incomprehensible hat you and Lord Henry could fight so vehemently over a subject that should have been debated by two intelligent people in a sane and sensible manner. Yester morn you put forward a disciplined, articulate argument about loyalty and duty. So how could you turn into a screaming fishwife and use language I am shocked could spew from your mouth?'

What could I say? Uncle Ralph was correct. How could I tell him I did not know why I behaved so badly? Was it because I was noticing Henry changing as he grew older; that I was observing him becoming obsessed his people must obey his rule without question or suffer the consequences? He had become distrustful, anxious, presuming his nobles from Scotland to Gascony were ready to rebel unless he was ruthless with troublemakers.

Taken to war as a young boy, he witnessed his mother's defeat and humiliation at Stephen's hands, saw men loyal to Empress Matilda change sides because they did not want to be ruled by a woman. When I married Henry, he was still fighting for what was rightfully hers and his as her heir. I knew how he had battled and worked to restore law and order in England, how he had dragged his ravaged kingdom back from anarchy and poverty. Not only that, on the day we wed, he gained responsibilities from Poitou to Gascony as well. And now, by God's teeth, he wanted to restore my province of Toulouse. Just as I worried my fertile days were numbered, Henry worried his virility as a ruler of men was in jeopardy as he aged, which was why he continued to joust.

I realised our stupid brawl this morning was more about me and Henry wanting to be what we were physically no longer, as much as trying to compete to get our own way. Whether we liked it or not, we had both drifted from each other. Henry wanted flattery and reassurance, and I was still fighting to be recognised for my talents, not just for my face and wealth or my ability to bear Henry's children. But how could I explain that to Uncle Ralph? He would think me odd indeed. So, I went to the library to try to make sense of myself and Henry, realising that I could have killed him.

***

My flaming quarrel with Henry took its toll on my conscience. I hid in the library for as long as I could. Then I slunk off to find Peter. He was in our chapel. With head bowed, I asked if I could speak with him. I told him this was not a confession I had come about, although I had sins aplenty, but rather confusion. He ushered me through to his little vestry behind the chapel.

I started by talking about little Geoffrey, asking if he noticed the boy's gifted intellect, to which he smiled and nodded. I said I was the same at his age. Like Geoffrey, I could read, though I remember no-one teaching me. Then Papa started the daily game with languages. Till the day he died, he was the driving force behind mine and Nilla's learning. Jerome joined our little schoolroom as did Clotilde, and at different times there were other children – Cousin Nannette and Papa's young brother, Uncle Raymond, though they were older.

By the time I was six, I knew the scriptures off by heart, but do not remember learning them. I soaked up the languages like bread in soup, I could also read and write in Latin. By the time I was eight I was fluent in Greek. Out of the three languages, I did not learn to write Greek properly till I was tutored in Antioch, but I absorbed it quickly and easily. Also, I was taught Hebrew and Aramaic though I no longer practised them. I had to teach myself Langue d'Oeil on Île de France, then English later. Apart from my accents, I understand both with ease.

I wanted Peter to enlighten me as to why Geoffrey's intelligence was admired and encouraged by everyone, when mine was considered the work of the devil, unwomanly. Peter was nonplussed. I continued to say he had no idea the pain this had caused me throughout my life. As Louis' wife I ran afoul of his deeply religious court every time I opened my mouth. And I was suppressed from further learning though I was surrounded in Paris by some of the greatest thinkers of the age, like Peter Abelard. Henry was more understanding, but often he too was condescending, or he frustrated me by ignoring my advice, which led to yesterday's eruption.

'I am fed up, Peter. I am sick to death of having to shut my mouth, suppress my thoughts, and to look beautiful so Henry, for God's sake, is admired, or of pushing into the world more sons so he is praised for his virility. What about my fertility?'

Peter let me rant.

'There are times when I feel I am nothing more than the walking treasury of the Aquitaine. When will I ever be judged for who I am? Instead of some stupid idea that I am inferior because I am a clever woman, a witch, even though I am Queen of England, Duchess of Aquitaine and every other damn title I have married or inherited.'

'Milady, it grieves me you feel so afflicted. To be honest this is not something I have ever been asked to judge. In the Bible, and particularly in the Old Testament, there are many brilliant and powerful women who were greatly admired and valued. I know you are revered and treasured in the Aquitaine, and I am sure it is because of your good governance and wisdom, more than, and as a priest I am not supposed to notice these things, your beautiful face.'

'Unless you are deaf and blind Peter, you would also know in England that I am called the French whore, more often amongst the clergy.'

'That is distressing, and I have taken many to task when I have heard such comments.'

Peter then went on to say something I appreciated. Instead of praying for me or asking me to get down on my knees to beg God for guidance, he told me, 'I will do my best to enlighten your court, justiciars, clerics and King Henry to look beyond the outward Lady Eleanor and to give credence to your intelligence, and to thank God you are so blessed. I will also point out that you are a grown-up Prince Geoffrey in female form.'

'Dear Peter, be careful there, because I have also been derided for trying to emulate men which, for a woman of my status is considered by critics a heinous crime.'

He smiled and promised to omit Geoffrey from his homily.

***

Henry had to go through his own humiliation, but, as the Bible permits him to chastise his wife, he was not criticised for his violence, another injustice against my sex. His meeting with my justiciars was straightforward, with them granting Aquitaine troops for his campaign. I hoped the men would obey his command because there was still resentment in some quarters.

Uncle Ralph gently reminded him about the differences between Aquitainean-Poitivin and Anglo-Norman laws, suggesting, in future, more consultation, should the Lord King, Duke of Normandy and Count of Anjou sense rebellion on his borders. He also told Henry that he, and the justiciars too, would be more vigilant to try to prevent all-out war should an uprising start to smoulder.

Henry had only a few weeks to gather his forces before marching on Toulouse. Shortly after his departure, I too would leave to return to my Regency. Sparks of discontent were waiting for a puff of wind to ignite them in England. I hoped I could quench the flames before they took hold. I would have to postpone Richard's investiture as the future Duke of Aquitaine for the time being.

Chapter 9: Duchess Or Queen?

Both Henry and I had administrative duties to attend. I wrote to Archbishop Theodore, the chancellor, constables, and stewards, and justiciars throughout the shires preparing them for my return to England. Except for dining together in the evening, Henry and I saw little of each other, which was probably a good thing. Peter, I knew, wanted to talk to Henry, but was having difficulty getting an audience as he dashed backwards and forwards between his encampment and the palace.

Then, just when Henry and I had stopped pussyfooting around each other, Becket arrived. His timing could not have been worse. He was to accompany Henry to Toulouse. I did not want him in the palace, but I did not want to have another screaming argument with Henry. I requested that Bishop Jean des Bellesmains of Poitiers meet with me. As subtly as possible, I asked him if Becket could be his guest, citing that the flurry of activity within the palace gave neither the king nor I time to entertain the chancellor. He agreed, so another dispute was averted. I offered a special dinner to welcome Becket, so everyone was appeased. A dinner was like a banquet in the Aquitaine, so I knew Thomas Becket would be impressed with the sophistication and elegance of the palace at Poitiers. He would also learn something of my background and come to better appreciate my heritage.

Our last days together I wanted to be a family affair with our close companions and nobles. I arranged a troubadour evening with the best of entertainers, mummers, poets, musicians, dancers, and jesters. Henry insisted I invite Becket.

'Why, Becket is neither kin nor of the Aquitaine,' I said.

'To show him how things should be done.'

Personally, I thought I had done that with the dinner, but when I thought of the tavern riff-raff Becket brought into Westminster, I could see Henry's point.

It was a dazzling night. My minstrels were outstanding. Within their group were musicians from as far and wide as Africa, Aragon, Sicily, and Outremer. They played many airs not heard before as well as old favourites like the Moresque. Women in colourful finery danced accompanied by lute, tabor, sackbut, and instruments too numerous to mention. I allowed the children to participate past their bedtime till one by one they fell asleep and were carried to their cots.

Jerome called for Henry and me to perform. Henry was a fine lute player. He also had a beautiful baritone voice. I may have the brains in my family, but I never felt I inherited my brilliant grandfather's musical skills. Henry and I have played and sung together in small gatherings, but in front of such a talented assembly I felt shy. When Henry noticed my reluctance, he said very loudly he had never known me to knock back a challenge.

Damn his eyes, he had reeled me in like some trout. Jerome handed me my mother's beautiful lute. They must have colluded because it was tuned to perfection. The great hall fell silent except for my pounding heart. Henry strummed his instrument and started the love song he sang by the Aphrodite temple at L'Ombrière. It could be sung as a duet. It was hauntingly beautiful. His voice soared through the Gothic arches of the hall, his eyes on mine. I joined in. How does he do it? Here was the Henry of old who could transport us both to a dimension beyond our world – my beautiful, once russet-haired lover. No one else in the room existed. Our voices blended, we sang of a love that was deeper than oceans, higher than mountains, vaster than the universe. Dear God in heaven, please let this be a reunion of our souls.

The minstrels took up the refrain. Then Henry took my hand, and they broke into a saltarello which, one by one, everyone joined. We danced out the door, disappearing into the night, leaving the revellers to continue.

In my chamber, words were not necessary. Naked in each other's arms, we whispered our love. I kissed

Chapter 9: Duchess Or Queen?

Henry's fluttering eyelids and I wondered why, oh why, we had to fight, why could we not just love each other?

***

The children and I farewelled Henry and his valiant men as they set off for Toulouse. I wished him God speed, to take care, that his life was too precious for me to find words to articulate. He kissed me goodbye, wishing us a safe voyage, poignantly telling Hal he was the man in charge while Papa was away, to look after his Maman and his brothers and sisters. Then with rearing prowess on his jet-black stallion, he was off pennants and banners streaming.

My silent little group of thumb-suckers waved their free hands, while I tried to keep my emotions controlled until I was alone.

We travelled across country to L'Ombrière; a quick visit with Renée and Clotilde, then on to Bordeaux where we boarded barques to Barfleur. From there we made our way to Rouen and Empress Matilda. She looked amazingly well although she said she was bothered by the bone ache. She had to be mellowing because she seemed pleased to see her rowdy grandchildren. Like me, she worried Henry was spreading himself too thinly throughout his empire, running himself ragged. I admitted to her I did not need Toulouse and thought it would be another burden to control. She had heard about dissension breaking out in some pockets in England. She was blunt, saying Henry should be spending his time governing his kingdom instead of chasing down his wife's vassals. That stung, but I had to agree. The difficulty was convincing Henry. I think I managed to reassure Matilda I could keep the English barons under control until Henry returned.

***

After a week, I was ready to move. Matilda might have mellowed, but her tongue was as acerbic as ever. She might accept me a smidgeon more, but by seven days we were getting on each other's nerves and the children were driving me insane by getting into as much mischief as they could.

Although much of my vast retinue in goods and necessities stayed in Barfleur to be loaded to sail directly to London via the Thames, I still had to get myself and my children, our maids and retainers from Rouen. My farewell to my mother-in-law was a relief as much for her as for me. The children were getting excited, ready to return to England, which to them was home.

We were destined to arrive at Portsmouth, then on to Winchester where I would take care of treasury matters and be brought up to date with the state of the country. Dear Archbishop Theodore's recent letters informed me he would be there to meet me with the usual justiciars and representatives of counties, shires, and estates. I was also prepared for the usual pile of petitions, and writs.

God, I hoped, would heed my prayers for a gentle channel crossing and a kindly breeze: arriving with green-tinged maids was not a pretty sight.

***

Winchester was a blur of administration compounded by the disquiet of niggling barons in what seemed like every county in the realm. Thanks to Archbishop Theodore, the grumbles remained just that, when they could have escalated into something akin to Stephen's disharmony. I had no choice but to take to my horse, to travel throughout the kingdom to find out what ailed these nobles and to restore law and order. Quite frankly, they had short memories. I was sure they did not want to return to the days of civil war where no-one could trust their neighbours, sometimes not even their own households.

We travelled to Westminster where I settled the children with their maids and nurses. The older ones now have tutors. They needed the continuity of their lessons, though I believe Geoffrey could teach his tutors. He had

Chapter 9: Duchess Or Queen?

taken to arguing anything and everything with me and anyone else. Even so, I was not enjoying the thought of not seeing them for some time, but I had little choice, duty was duty.

Before leaving I sat with Jerome who knows the children better than anyone. With their tutors, we discussed the children's abilities and their needs. Hal was good at working through tasks and liked to see solutions to problems. He was a practical boy, not unlike Henry. Matilda was smart and knows how to manipulate, but she had a sweet nature and was quite the little mother to her rowdy brothers and younger sister. I see so much of Nilla in her personality. Richard was going to be powerful. He was the most determined of them all, a natural leader, again like Henry. One could see why they clashed, but he did have a softer side too. He was talented musically and played his lute well. He loved poetry and song. Grandfather William's gift, I was pleased to say, had passed down to Richard. Geoffrey was just brilliant. There was little I could say about my little duplici, except he was a tad too smart and let everyone know it. He was a beautiful child with honey-coloured hair, large dark eyes fringed with lustrous eyelashes, as was Lenore. She, little angel, was the most placid of them all. She laughed and trundled around happily, and nothing ever seemed to fluster her. God only knows where she got her even temperament from – certainly not from her parents. Possibly Papa: I could not remember him ever losing his temper with Nilla or me, and I would have been enough to try a saint judging by Geoffrey's quick tongue.

With the children's needs taken care of and the rest of the palace running smoothly, I could turn my attention to my travels. I needed to attend to problems in Norfolk. Letters from the Abbot of Castle Acre Priory informed me that the Sheriff of Kings Lynn was lining his pockets with moneys from the sale of reeds used for thatching that should be paid to the priory, since the reeds grew in nearby fens and were part of their income. I was told the sheriff was quite a slippery character and this was not the first time he had acted unscrupulously. This man had to be brought to justice.

My visit to Norfolk would also give me the chance to meet Henry's half-brother, Hamelin Plantagenet, a little nerve-wracking as I knew only too well who Hamelin's father was. Hamelin was older than Henry, of course. I did not like to delve too deeply into that affair. Hamelin had married well, that too sounded familiar, and, through his wife Isabel, became Earl of Surrey. He had a castle in Norfolk as well as his wife's estates south of London.

I wrote telling him of my intended visit to the county and was invited to stay. I accepted their generous offer. They would also, I was sure, be able to give me further information about the sheriff. I was puzzled as to why Hamelin had not judged this man himself. Maybe it drifted into the king's jurisdiction.

**

The ride to Norfolk was restful with balmy weather. The undulating countryside was filled with bird song, relaxing everyone. The villagers I met along the way gave me humble pleasure. We were able to enjoy the hospitality of the simple monks and nuns who accommodated us, which helped me forget the concerns I left in Poitiers. By the time I reached the Earl of Surrey's estate I was in a much better frame of mind. My quarters were most comfortable, including a desk and writing material.

There was to be a formal gathering of nobles and clergy from nearby, including the Abbot of Castle Acre Priory on the evening of my arrival. I was welcomed by Hamlin and Isabel. I knew Henry's legitimate brothers, but I was nervous as well as intrigued about this encounter. I never saw Matilda as competition for Geoffrey's affection because I knew they loathed each other, but Hamelin's mother must have been loved by Henry's father. It made me a little jealous, silly considering how long ago was his

Chapter 9: Duchess Or Queen?

affair, and Geoffrey's and mine for that matter. Hamelin was sent away to England as a boy. I knew not what became of his mother, reputed to be Adelaide of Anjou who had died before I knew Geoffrey.

Amaris called me to ready myself for the banquet. As queen, I knew I must impress. Henry would expect me to be attractive.

I received an unexpected fanfare and cries of 'Vivat Regina'. Henry's queen was 'oo-ed' and 'ah-ed,' so I passed the glamour test. I was introduced to the line of dignitaries by Hamelin, who has the piercing blue Plantagenet eyes, a little disconcerting. I searched his face for Geoffrey, but he was not there except for the eyes. Hamelin's hair is dark, straighter than his father's or Henry's curly mop. His build was similar, but shorter than his half-brother. The evening went well. I liked Isabel. Hamelin, I found to be intelligent, with the Plantagenet wit.

There were times I felt like a seasoned mummer. I was practiced at being charming, winning my hosts, and my enemies, which of course was to my advantage. Sometimes I forget my real self. The assembly was mesmerised. However, the abbot, the least worldly-wise of the guests, needed to see more of Henry's regent other than beauty and charm. During my conversation with him, I think I allayed his fears I was not incapable of reining in the excesses of the sheriff. But I pointed out that this evening's welcome was not the place to discuss his concerns and arranged to meet with him on the morrow.

By the time all were feeling benign, I was wilting, tired from the long days in the saddle. I wanted my bed. Hamelin and Isabel heeded my request.

***

The abbot had organised for me to be escorted by some young monks to the River Nar where the reeds grew. I wanted to see how they were harvested, which meant a ride in a coracle. Now that was something to behold! I could see why the abbot said it was for younger souls.

I was hauled on board by two muscular monks who thankfully did not take into consideration one jot as to who I was. I ended up giggling like little Matilda.

I learnt much. The quality of the reeds differed depending on their use; the straighter and longer reeds were used for thatching houses and barns, the shorter and more twisted were destined for floors. They told me when cut, they graded them according to their value.

I survived my river transport then rode to my meeting with Abbot Timothy. I was greeted by a shy monk who escorted me to the abbot's modest sitting room where I was spoiled with freshly baked bread, cheese from their dairy, and a warming mulled wine.

'And how was your experience on the water, Milady?'

I beamed. 'Father, I have not had so much fun in years and my knowledge of your livelihood has been greatly expanded.'

Abbot Timothy smiled, then it was down to business regarding the sheriff.

'I am disappointed Sheriff Athel's misdeeds have not been curtailed by the appointed justiciars of the county.'

'Milady, Sheriff Athel is cunning. He plays one baron off against the other. It is said he keeps a tally of any infidelity or misdemeanour committed by those on the panel, no matter how old or how minor to blackmail these men.'

'I see.'

'Collecting hard evidence, though, is difficult. The sheriff is an expert at concealing his misdeeds.'

Abbot Timothy showed me the priory accounts. They were straightforward. Not a sou was hidden. I asked for further information.

'We have discovered that the bundles of reeds are not how they leave the abbey. Before we take them to the warehouse, owned incidentally by Sheriff Athel, we

Chapter 9: Duchess Or Queen?

divide them into sheaves depending on their value. The longer, straighter canes are tied together. The shorter and less perfect are bound separately.'

'And they are taxed accordingly as I see by your accounts, Father.'

'Yes, Milady. The best reeds are levied at a higher rate which our customers normally accept. But we are getting complaints. Our customers are not happy.'

'Can you elaborate, Father Timothy?'

'We believe the sheaves are being untied and reeds of different qualities are being mixed at the warehouse. The sheriff is then taxing the thatchers on what are supposed to be the superior canes, when what they receive are assorted.'

'You are certain about this?'

'Milady, our brothers have had suspicions for some time. Finding the proof though is hard. We know thatchers are not getting what they have ordered.'

'Is that so?'

'Yes. Not only that, the sheriff charges for warehouse storage and pays his men a pittance or uses slave labour.'

'So, Father Timothy, Athel is extorting the priory, the thatchers, manipulating taxes and his labourers, then using blackmail to have the justiciars turn a blind eye.'

'Lady Eleanor, I am afraid so. It is a sorry situation.'

'Thank you, Father Timothy, for your knowledge and your patience. You have given me valuable information.'

As he escorted me to my horse, he said, 'I must warn you, Milady, the sheriff has an unpleasant disposition and is most cunning, a short dark man who likes to strut around with delusions above his station.'

'Father, unfortunately I know the type only too well. And thanks to you I am forewarned.'

Abbot Timothy bowed his head. I mounted and was away.

***

Athel would know of my presence in the district by now. He would have heard that I was visiting my husband's half-brother, and this was a plausible reason for being in Norfolk. My visit to the priory would be considered courtesy, arranging alms or whatever, but if Athel had as much influence as Abbot Timothy suggests, he would soon know I was there on the king's business. Henry would probably burn the warehouse to the ground then throw Athel into a dungeon, but my methods were, I hoped, more subtle.

I had to find a way to obtain Athel's records, to prove his criminal activities. I wanted indisputable proof. Furthermore, I needed to retrieve the taxes he had wrongly charged the thatchers, repay them, return what had been extorted from the priory, then collect the correct duty that should be in our treasury. The panel of justiciars would need to be replaced as well.

Concern had me scrunching quills but not solving the problem. I needed to be as cunning as the snake with whom I was dealing. He would not freely hand over his accounts. Also, there was a mighty possibility they would be cleverly scribed to look legitimate. I needed to know more about Athel's personality and his business activities. I asked Hamelin if I could speak with him alone, hoping he was not one of the blackmailed. Because there was a cauldron of deception involving many men who were being compromised or in league with the sheriff, most of the detective work I would have to do on my own.

***

Hamelin and I went for a walk in his beautiful gardens where we discussed my morning activities.

'Hamelin, my visit to the priory was enlightening in more ways than one.'

'Father Timothy is an erudite man.'

'He is, and I learned a lot about reeds and thatching, but there also seems to be corruption going on under the

Chapter 9: Duchess Or Queen?

noses of your justiciars some of whom are turning a blind eye regarding the taxing of the priory's living.'

'Ah!'

'I want to visit the warehouse run by Sheriff Athel where the monks send their reeds. Can you arrange for me to do so?'

'Yes. That should not be a problem. When do you want to go?'

'The monks are sending off their final harvest for the season in two days' time, and I want to 'arrive' with it.'

Hamelin did not object or question me, so instinct told me he was not involved in the deceptions.

'What do you know about the shire taxes, Hamelin?'

'Well, Lady Eleanor, I think they are being manipulated. Our estate's land geld is higher than on previous years and I can see no reason for the rise. Do you know why?'

'No, but I am sure, the increase is not coming from our chancellor, nevertheless, I will look into it.'

'Thank you.'

As we continued our walk, I wondered if Athel was exploiting him, too?

***

On the morn of my visit to Athel's warehouse, I rode with a small number of guards to the priory. I informed Abbot Timothy of my plans. He grinned from ear to ear, wishing me luck with my detective work. Before we left, Brothers James and Thomas showed me the bundles already stacked on wagons. The best reeds were separated from their lowly cousins. Even I could see which were the longest and straightest. Each sheaf was tightly tied with sturdy twine.

I rode behind the creaking wagons. After a league, we arrived at a huge barn on the river. It was abuzz with activity. Reed bundles were being carried in from the front of the building. Others were being loaded onto river barges from the rear. The workmen were nonplussed to see a woman arrive with the monks. My armed, very tall, Praetorian guards gave me away as being of some status, so they stood and gaped. I said I was a curious purchaser. Brother Thomas told them to continue their work, to ignore my presence. From my horse, I could see all round the building, but to get a better idea of the activity I needed to dismount. Antoine assisted me. Of course, my six guards wanted to be close with hands on sword hilts, but I did not wish to be hemmed in. I ordered them to be vigilant but not overbearing.

So as not to impede the hustle and bustle, I stood aside and watched. Brother Thomas brought my attention to some activity on the far side of the building. Some bundles were being hastily retied. I nodded to my guards and sauntered towards the workmen.

I smiled with practised charm, remarked how hard they were working, and inquired if they could explain their occupation. One said they were retying bundles that had broken their bindings. I asked innocently if this often happened because the twines looked strong. The man muttered that sometimes the knots came undone. I had a feeling he was being evasive. So, I questioned if they had many mixed bundles, because even to my eyes the retied sheaves looked suspicious. Spilled around these men were a variety of canes of different straightness and length. Furthermore, these men seemed awkward, as if hiding something. But before he could answer, in the forecourt of the warehouse, a horse screeched to a stop, sparks flying from the animal's hooves. The man who leapt from the horse was small and swarthy. I guessed he was the infamous sheriff. My men stiffened. I moved to where some bundles of the top grade of reed were being stacked in neat rows.

Darkly robed and darkly tempered, the rider scuttled into the warehouse demanding to know what was afoot. I wondered what he had discovered. He peered in my direction, his eyes squinting as they adjusted from the

Chapter 9: Duchess Or Queen?

bright light of the forecourt to the dimness of the barn. At first, he could not discern who I was. I was as tall as Athel, which set him back a pace when he realised, I was a not a man. Antoine and my men were hovering, but he had not noticed them yet.

'You are a woman!'

'How clever of you to notice. And you are?'

'I am the sheriff. What business does a woman have here, may I ask?'

'I am interested in thatching and as I am visiting my brother-in-law, and the good Abbot of Castle Acre Priory, I thought I would take the opportunity to increase my knowledge of your activities.'

'I presume you have a name, if you would like to enlighten me.'

I do not believe any member of a minor office had addressed me so rudely since I left Île de France. In many ways, I found it amusing. 'Yes, I have a name, but firstly may I know yours? You could be any sheriff.'

'Sheriff Athel of Ramsey, from Kings Lynn,' puffed the bantam cock.

'Indeed. Well, I am Lady Eleanor, Queen of England. You may address me as Milady.'

A gasp escaped from his throat as I continued, 'I cannot say I am pleased to meet you. I am here on Lord King Henry's business as his regent. It has been brought to our attention there are anomalies in your tax accounts. My guards here will escort you to your office where you will hand over all scrolls and documents concerning this warehouse, along with your tax records.'

'I protest!'

'I should not object if I were you or try to conceal any of your activities.'

Athel made a move as if to flee only to be confronted by my towering knights. The sound of swords rasping from their scabbards as Antoine and his men surrounded the sheriff signalled it was futile to attempt to bolt. A sword in his back and one at his throat brooked no argument. His face registered shock and horror as he realised he could not escape his queen and her elite guard.

***

I excused myself from Isabel and Hamelin's company to peruse the documents removed from the sheriff's warehouse. His manor was also raided with every piece of parchment and velum confiscated. He was arrested, pending the investigation.

It was obvious I was going to need help to go through the evidence I had gathered, but who I could trust among the justiciars of the district? Many were in league with the sheriff, and I did not want to involve Hamelin. I appealed to Abbot Timothy, who said he had a young monk who was not only learned but was a genius with figures. So, Brother Bartholomew became my righthand man.

We burned many a candle down to its stub, but eventually a pattern emerged along with some most interesting foibles amongst the local barons and a few of their wives. In the end, we had more than enough proof to remove Sheriff Athel from his post. Bribery, extortion, blackmail, and tax avoidance were obvious crimes. The man's detailed bookkeeping was his undoing. He also kept every piece of parchment he had gathered reporting the adventures of local landowners, nobles, constables, and stewards, right down to their animals.

I demanded an audience with the justiciars of the county.

'Gentlemen, it has been brought to my attention that Sheriff Athel has been extorting many people in this district including the good monks of Castle Acre Priory. Sadly, I have also discovered that many sitting here before me are complicit in allowing him to get away with just about every crime in Christendom, except murder, so far the only offence he has not committed.'

Chapter 9: Duchess Or Queen?

There were glances between panel members as I continued, 'You are lucky not be accompanying the sheriff to the Tower. Instead, I order you to pay reparation to those whom you have exploited. As for the sins you have committed, adultery being the most common and for which most of you are being blackmailed, I suggest you confess.'

I overheard a muttered remark, 'The queen can talk.'

I replied, 'Milord, if you wish to believe all the rumours about my past, you will hear I have lain with every man in Christendom, including the Pope. Believe what you want but be careful you do not add slander to your list of misdemeanours.'

I disbanded their services. A new panel of justiciars was appointed, which took time. Some members of the previous council were fined heavily, others I stripped of their titles. The advice given by Hamelin and the good abbot was invaluable regarding suitable replacements. Although he was reluctant, I left Hamelin in charge.

I managed to clean out a lot of bad apples from the barrel. Let us hope it stays that way. I hear there was many a *mea culpa* between some barons and their ladies and *vice-versa*. Sheriff Athel was tried and sent to London in chains where he was now residing in the Tower, at the king's pleasure.

***

It had taken far more of my time than I had expected to bring justice to this part of Norfolk. I had to leave with great haste to continue my journey to York before autumn ended and the biting winds of winter engulfed us.

I found myself riding more like Henry. My long retinue trailed behind me. I would reach our next venue of hospitality way ahead of my changes of clothes, my maids and what I considered my necessities. Then I made myself unpopular by insisting they all rise early to be ahead of me before our next destination. By the time we reached Lincoln, my entourage was ready to rebel. A few words had them biting their tongues.

I decided to spend a few days with Mother Joan, who was delighted to be of assistance to my exhausted entourage. I also had great pleasure catching up with all her activities, learning about the success of our operation to look after homeless women and their children. Many had found employment as bondmaids with local barons. I was thrilled the venture was so successful. I also had time to pen a long missive to Henry about Norfolk as well as Mother Joan's good deeds.

There was no news from Toulouse, which I hoped would be awaiting me in York. I received however, some delightful letters from Hal, Richard, and Matilda, who were proudly showing off their squiggly writing skills. There was one from Geoffrey, dictated to Jerome, which had me laughing till I cried. He might be bright but so far could not manage a quill. He complained it was Greek day, but because Amaris and I were the only ones who could write in Greek letters, Jerome was forced to use Latin because neither of us were there. He told me Richard was naughty because he pulled the head off one of Matilda's dolls and made her cry. He said Lenore could run as fast as a hare now. He was practising his chess, but no-one would play with him because he won all the time. He asked when I would be home. Jerome added a note to say that Geoffrey was becoming more annoyingly like little Elly every day by questioning everything with a petulant 'WHY'. I was sure Jerome exaggerated.

***

The ride to York was picturesque, with trees crowned in golden, scarlet, and russet leaves. It was like riding through arbours of jewels. Even though we were surrounded by such beauty of nature, it was a relief to arrive where we could relax before heading south again. We were housed with Archbishop Roger in his palace. I was reunited with

Chapter 9: Duchess Or Queen?

the older Geoffrey, with whom I spent an enjoyable time chatting. His studies were progressing well. His Grace told me he was a studious young boy, worked hard at his lessons and was well liked. Henry would be delighted to hear this good report.

The archbishop gave me use of his library, providing me with a desk and writing implements. I had developed quite a reputation throughout the land regarding my needs, so it was rare I must ask these days for quills and ink, etcetera. Also piled on the desk were familiarly sealed epistles from Henry, my uncle, and young Ralph, Nilla's son. So many Ralphs – they were almost as confusing as those called Geoffrey! As Ralph had written to me rarely during his life, my heart was gripped with fear. I pushed it to one side, instead reading Henry's and Uncle Ralph's epistles first. They were similar. The siege of the city of Toulouse was accomplished, but as I read the later letters, was having little effect. Henry was thinking of abandoning the campaign as winter approached, having already purged the land of anything edible. Raymond and Louis were well supplied while Henry was struggling to feed his vast army. Some, particularly the mercenaries and roustiers, were deserting. I was not surprised.

My gut feeling before I left Poitier was that the retaking of Toulouse would be lucky to succeed. Raymond V was a wily fox. He would know he only had to sit behind his moat until the weather drove Henry's forces back across the border. Louis would have provided him with extra men and resources, but it would amount to little else, Louis being no tactician. Raymond would exploit him for the provisions he could supply, then sacrifice him if necessary. Raymond had no scruples.

I could not put off reading nephew Ralph's letter any longer. I called for Amaris to be with me as I slid the fine blade of my knife under the seal. Nilla was dead. I tried to stand but collapsed back into my chair. Amaris called

Brynn. Everyone came running, and I was taken to my bed chamber where I tried to come to terms with my loss.

***

I was numb with grief. Amaris and my maids were terrified for my health, knowing how I had reacted when William was taken by God. I spent the next few days in bed unable to function. Archbishop Roger and all his clerics with Peter were praying not only for Nilla's soul but for my well-being. Dear God, I needed Henry.

My maids managed to find me a white gown without adornment. I wondered if they packed for all eventualities, or maybe it was Brynn's foresight. The archbishop took my hands in his when I told him I must return to my duties, mourning or no. I explained there were barons and others who had resentments and concerns I must deal with when I turned towards London. He told Amaris I had a wild look in my eyes that worried him. When Amaris brought up the subject regarding my readiness to travel, I had to tell her I no longer had choices. Nilla would be furious with me if I did not continue with what Papa trained me to do. I must bring stability back to the counties that were threatening to rebel before Henry returned, because he would burn down their villages and create havoc in retaliation like he did in Poitou. Then there would be war again throughout the land.

I bade farewell to young Geoffrey and told him I would pray his studies continued well, and that I knew Henry would be proud of him. He said he would include my sister in his prayers.

***

Back in London, I was still finding it hard to believe Nilla was no longer. Although we did not see each other often, I already felt lonely without her. As children, we loved each other as fiercely as we squabbled. Heaven help anyone who tried to come between us. We joined forces,

Chapter 9: Duchess Or Queen?

we stuck by one another. On Île de France, I would never have survived those early miserable years without her naughty rebelliousness or her wicked sense of humour. I would miss her.

My flight across the country from York to one trouble spot to the other was now a blur. To say I was driven was an understatement.

I was sure Amaris and everyone thought I was too grieved to do anything sensible. To some extent they were right, but, like I said to Amaris, I had no choice. Like a battering ram, I pounded my way through the countryside. The first recalcitrant barons I encountered near Sheffield wondered what had struck them. I met with justiciars, listened to the complaints put before them, then laid down the law to the disgruntled and threatened, in some cases, to remove their royal charters. My oratory rang in their ears.

'Gentlemen, you have a choice; follow and obey the laws of the land and pay your dues or return to the chaos of the civil war you endured for years without stability for your heirs, or your carefully restored estates. If you find the taxes onerous, you should consider their use. Most go into the king's treasury so the country will prosper. Indeed, the king should not have to waste funds on unnecessary excursions, riding around the countryside urging barons to behave like adults instead of squabbling children. You may not know this, but to begin with when Lord Henry became king, it was my dowry that dragged you out of poverty. I find it mightily vexing that my Duchy of Aquitaine wasted its rich resources on the likes of you. Now, before I throw the lot of you into the nearest dungeon, abide by your obligations, stop bickering over tolls, levies, and land geld, and above all, uphold the laws handed down by King Henry's grandfather, the laws for which you fought and for which many of your brethren lost their lives. It galls me I must remind you that these decrees enable you to live in peace and prosperity under your present king.'

Yes, they received a tongue lashing they were not expecting. The charming beguiling Eleanor had turned into a virago. They were given no choice – obey or suffer the consequences. My towering guards, armed and menacing, would have had the first dissenter in irons should they say or do anything foolish. If there was not a fair but strict leader on the panel of justiciars, I appointed a respected baron to take their place, expecting him to keep Henry and I informed, and where possible to negotiate to prevent problems getting out of hand. Maybe my dress of mourning softened them a little, but I hoped it was my words that impressed.

On the road, I also penned some hurried letters. I wrote to Henry as well as Clotilde, though Ralph would have informed her and darling Renée about what had transpired. Tears welled up in my eyes when I thought of how the news would affect them. In my letter to Uncle Ralph, I asked him to contact Mother Isabella at Fontevrault to make sure alms were distributed for prayers for Lady Petronilla, Nannette also, who I hoped would put all rivalries and disagreements to one side to have prayers recited for her little cousin. I did not write to Jerome. I had no idea if Ralph in his grief would remember Jerome as part of the family. As I did not hear from him myself, I came to two conclusions; either he did not know, or he was waiting for us to be re-united in London. I had to break the news to the children.

My return letter to my nephew, Ralph, and one to niece Eloise, were soaked with my tears and were a blotchy mess, but I could not rewrite them no matter how they looked.

***

When I alighted from my horse, the children were dancing around my feet, including Lenore, who ran around trying to avoid Matilda's hand. They were boisterous, laughing, and full of happiness, so excited to see me after several months, so I let their happiness wash over me like sunshine,

Chapter 9: Duchess Or Queen?

listening to their exuberant babble as I accompanied them indoors. They were all vying for my attention. Regardless of my grief, I had to encompass their eager happiness which was as good as any physic. I had to calm them, so I could hear each tale, admire them, note how they had grown. I let them hang all over me, kiss me, hug me. I had little trinkets for all of them, which Amaris brought in from one of the wagons. Soon they were excitedly poring over their gifts, so I could escape to a tub of hot water and lather the grime of travel from my skin and hair.

Freshly clothed and scented, my hair clean and dry, always a drama as it is so long and copious, I made discreet enquiries as to Jerome's whereabouts. He was not with the children during their explosive welcome, which had me worried. Then I was told he had accompanied the Bishop of London on some errand down the Thames and had sent a courier apologising they had been delayed by the tide. This made me suspect he did not know about Nilla's death.

There were missives from Henry also for my attention, so I went to the library. I explained to the children I would eat with them anon. From Henry's missive, I found he had been informed of Nilla's death but had yet to receive my letter. His letter was full of endearments, lamenting he was not with me during my hours of sadness and distress. He wrote he would miss her very much as he knew I would. He said he would pray for Nilla's soul and have prayers said for her throughout the Aquitaine and the whole of our lands. By the time I finished reading his letter, I was a sobbing mess with my head on my arms on my desk, so I did not hear Jerome's knock and entry. He was beside me in seconds, begging to know what was upsetting me. I could not speak, so I pushed Henry's letter to where he could read it.

Heartbroken, we tried to comfort each other but to no avail. We ran out of tears.

'Why, Jerome? I am the older – it should have been me. Why does God hate the House of Aquitaine so much?'

'Do not say that, Elly. God does not hate you. You are chosen; you are ordained. Your life has only just begun, your duty is paramount to more than those around you.'

'What you say fills me with fear and dread.'

'Elly, you are a remarkable leader, many see that. I do not hold it against you that you did not inform me from York about little Nilla. To grieve alone waiting for your return would have been unbearable.'

'Thank you. I am not looking forward to telling the children, though only Hal and Matilda will remember her.'

I gave him a summary of my encounters with the various grumbling barons as well as Sheriff Athel's criminal activities, whom Jerome knew about because his arrival created a stir when he was escorted to the Tower. He was complaining loudly about being brought to justice by a woman, regardless of who she was, and questioned the legitimacy of me acting like a man. Much to his disgust he was put in his place by advocates, who informed him the Queen of England was better versed in British law than most men in the land.

***

Henry was due any day now. I took the children to Windsor for Christmas, which was not as jolly as usual. I was still mourning Nilla. Henry had to abandon Toulouse and was making his way back to England, which for now was calm. My threats to the disgruntled barons had them behaving. They knew they would be joining Sheriff Athel if they did not heed my words. I was sure when they thought about it, they knew they were better off with a stable kingdom than the one they had under Stephen.

I returned to London to await Henry. He arrived in not quite his usual flurry. When I met him, I was shocked by how haggard he appeared. All the tearing about from one

Chapter 9: Duchess Or Queen?

place to another was taking its toll. His limp was worse, his temper a lot to be desired. My tawny lion was becoming an old man, and he was only in his thirties. He had no patience for the children, who were so looking forward to seeing him. Worse, he had cropped his hair, which did not suit him and made him look older. Geoffrey, asking in a raucous voice if Papa had nits, did not help.

I made sure his quarters were warm, and all his needs were taken into consideration. I had our cooks prepare his favourite titbits. I dressed as beautifully as I could, even though I was still in mourning white. After he had bathed, I combed and dried what was left of his hair, which was greyer than his father's hair ever was. I must stop comparing the two. But, at times, I almost forgot which was which because of my love for both. After a simple meal together, Henry was so tired I suggested an early night. He warmed his freezing feet on me as usual and snuggled up, but he just fell asleep. When had *'enri Plantagenet-a* been too tired to be aroused to make love? Never!

***

Although I had written reports to Henry regarding my Regency, he wanted to know all the details of my journey up and down the country.

'As I said in my letters to you, gathering the evidence took a bit of detective work. Help from the Abbot of Castle Acre Priory and Hamelin was invaluable. Then it was just a matter of pouncing on the sheriff, quite amusing in some ways.'

'You did well. I do not know how Athel got away with his crimes for so long. Replacing the fools on the panel of justiciars should give us fewer problems in Norfolk too.'

'As I said, Athel was blackmailing most of them. I think they have learnt their lessons.'

'I appreciate the way you handled the other nuisances, too. Let us hope they now realise taxes and the law are there for a purpose and must be obeyed.'

'Henry, after learning of Nilla's death, I had no patience with those nobles who are now living in comfort and should be thanking God for their good fortune instead of grumbling over the new laws or taxes they must pay. I was in no mood to be tactful.'

'You are learning, Eleanor.'

'Perhaps'

As we sipped our brandy wine and Henry relaxed, I gently mentioned Toulouse.

'Toulouse was not quite the outcome you were hoping for Henry.'

'To be honest Eleanor, the fortifications would have taken a siege of a year or more to break through and with all due respect, I did not think your shaky inheritance was worth the struggle.'

I did not know whether to be relieved or insulted. I topped up Henry's goblet and kissed his forehead.

'It has been hard losing Nilla, Henry... me being the older.'

'Did you find out what caused her death?'

'She was unwell when I saw her before you left for Toulouse – a bad cough and she had lost weight. Her son suspected an ague at the onset of winter affected her chest, and she was too weak to fight it.'

'I am sorry, my darling.'

'Thank you. We had a wonderful childhood. Nilla could be quite wicked - she and her wretched monkey Simian. Jerome and I climbed a tree once trying to catch the little pest. He had stolen one of my necklaces and shot up an oak. I got it back in pieces after being bitten. I tore my smock too. Renée was not amused.'

I smiled at Henry. 'At times Matilda reminds me of Nilla. I think I will have to watch her. She can be quite flirtatious just like my little sister.'

Chapter 9: Duchess Or Queen?

Henry laughed. 'I envy your carefree childhood.'

'Yes, it was till Papa died...'

I knew how death could abruptly end a child's innocence, when at thirteen I lost my Papa and was married off to Louis Capet. Henry detected my melancholy. I suggested, as we were both tired, that we should retire. I started to nibble his earlobe, and soon we were kissing passionately.

Henry was more his old self the next day. Since his arrival back in London he had been irritable, short with everyone. His temperament was not helped by the failing health of Archbishop Theobald, who we heard was most unwell. It brought home the looming ascension of Becket. The thought of him becoming Archbishop of Canterbury concerned me deeply. But Henry believed he was his man and would do his bidding. On the contrary, I suspected Thomas Becket had only one loyalty and that was to Thomas Becket. Nonetheless, there was no point in me trying to persuade Henry otherwise; he had made up his mind and had already admonished me for thinking it a mistake. Robert told me that Empress Matilda agreed with me. She had her doubts too.

Chapter 10. Archbishop Becket

I was sprinkling the pounce over my parchment when I was summoned to the great hall. Henry looked distraught so I rushed to him.

'Archbishop Theodore has died, Eleanor.'

'Oh, dear God! Such a fine man. Here sit. Stop pacing.' I knelt before him and took his hands.

'Yes. He was much respected and much loved.' Henry wiped his eyes.

'We will miss him, the children, too. He was a great mentor. Where would we have been in those early difficult days without his council? England will grieve the death of such a good man and a revered Archbishop of Canterbury.'

Henry could only nod. I squeezed his hands as I fought back my own tears. Archbishop Theodore's wisdom, intelligence, and kindness, like a gentle parent's love, enveloped us in a cape of security as we made our way into our wretched and divided kingdom. During my regencies, he offered me a guiding hand when necessary. He crowned us and baptised some of our children, treating them all in a fatherly way when Henry was away. I appreciated that he never questioned my intellect or education and treated me with respect as Queen of England and as myself.

Without this great mentor, life would have been hard, not just for Henry and me but for the whole of England. Archbishop Theodore respected the laws and traditions. Like a good shepherd, he presided over his flock with gentle care, and was loved by the people as the leading cleric in the land. He would not be forgotten.

Archbishop Theodore backed and supported Henry. One sticking point had always been the judgement of lay clerks who broke the law. Should the offenders be tried by

Chapter 10: Archbishop Becket

Canon Law or the laws of the land? Theodore reinforced Henry's position that they must be tried as ordinary citizens in secular courts because these men, though employed by the church, were not ordained clergy. Many, from several bishops down, did not respect this law and wanted it changed. Henry believed Becket would support him which was why he was so intent on him taking the position. Archbishop Theodore too had been grooming him for this role. I could only hope he would follow in the late archbishop's footsteps. Nevertheless, I did not trust Becket. I never had women's intuition? Who knew?

I had to put my prejudices to one side, at least Thomas knew Henry's position on these matters. Furthermore, only recently he had helped revise some of the more antiquated laws of the kingdom and worked on the introduction of the new jury system. Henry trusted him and that was what counted.

***

His Grace, Archbishop Theodore's funeral was a grand affair, fitting for such an honoured man. Henry wore a hair shirt under his gown as penance. With the children, except for Lenore who was carried by her nurse, we followed the cortège on foot. Hal and Matilda were sad. Richard and Geoffrey being younger were bewildered as to why they would never see Uncle Archbishop again. Lenore was too young to understand the grandeur or our great sorrow. I warned Geoffrey to keep his eloquent mouth shut, terrified he could utter something inappropriate in a piercing, strident voice during the ceremony. Praise be to God, he said naught, clinging a little fearfully to me. I think he was overwhelmed for once. The streets were filled with our people wailing the loss of the great man. Becket had mighty shoes to fill.

Back in London, we were a sorry lot. I tried to return the children to their normal routines, but the overall gloom of our griefs was hard for them to comprehend, especially for Hal and Matilda, who best remembered Tante Nilla. Richard wanted to know if Archbishop Theodore would be in heaven with her. Of course, I said they would be chatting away to each other. Geoffrey, who had found his tongue again, wanted to know what they would be chatting about and why we could no longer see them, as if they had just gone on holiday. I had to try to explain to him that heaven was the place where all the good people went when they died.

'WHY!!! Why do they have to be put in a hole? Is Tante Nilla in a hole? What happens to the bad people?'

My youngest son's voice reverberated through my skull like a gong. Like a coward, I ran away to my library and locked the door, leaving the querulous questioner to his nurse, tutors and Jerome, whose collective patience was far greater than Maman's.

Henry was in consultation with Becket. He was to be ordained Archbishop of Canterbury in a planned opulent ceremony, which would no doubt suit his self-esteem. At least the children, except for poor Hal, would not have to endure the droning of his inauguration. Now, at seven, his education as Henry's heir was becoming serious. I was declared Papa's heir at six years old and was trained accordingly. I tried to protect Hal from the more onerous responsibilities life had ordained for him.

As Henry had shown little interest in the children's education until now, I was surprised when he came to me and said, 'Eleanor, it is time we discussed Hal's future.'

I was suspicious, to say the least.

'It is time he left your side to continue his education elsewhere.'

'And where would that be?'

'I have not finalised those details yet.'

'Henry, he is only seven. Too young to be separated from me or his brothers and sisters.'

'Oh, for God's sake, Eleanor. He is not a baby. I never lived under my mother's skirts.'

Chapter 10: Archbishop Becket

'No, you were farmed out to the de Lucys' till you were old enough...'

I had to bite my tongue, seething inwardly that his mother only wanted Henry to take to war when he was far too impressionable. His father had no say in the matter. In a detached manner, I knew Empress Matilda loved Henry and was proud of his accomplishments, but she never cared for her children when they were born. She never mothered them. Henry was closer to Maud in that respect, and Robert's family. He would rue the day he sent my sons away before I considered them old enough.

How lucky Nilla and I were. We might have lost our mother when we were small, but Renée more than compensated for her. Papa never allowed us to be taken from his care to be brought up by strangers.

Henry would not discuss his plans for Hal further and left me fuming. How I would live without Hal I knew not. In my throat there was a mighty lump. There were times I hated *'enri Plantagenet-a.*

***

After a suitable time of mourning, Thomas Becket was ordained Archbishop at Canterbury Cathedral in a ritual as old as the church in England. Within its mighty walls, soaring with plain song, chanting, and praying clergy, he was attended by his king and queen, and Prince Hal, as heir to the throne. Regardless of my personal thoughts the ceremony was uplifting.

Back in London, I was tired and glad it was over, but I was not expecting Henry's thunderbolt. 'I have discussed Hal's future with Archbishop Becket, and he has agreed to take Hal under his wing to further his education and prepare him for his responsibilities.'

'Not with that man.'

'Just listen for a moment, Eleanor.'

'Hal is only seven, for God's sake. To think that you are going to place our little boy under the care of that catamite is unbelievable.'

'You are being ridiculous Eleanor. Hal needs to grow up. He will soon be crowned the Young King. He needs to have his learning extended and that is not going to happen with you spoiling and mollycoddling him.'

'I do not *spoil* and *mollycoddle* him. I love our children. I help them learn, unlike you who merely fathers them then ignores them from the moment they are born.

'As usual, you exaggerate. I cannot spend my days playing silly games with them.

'So much for our nuptial agreement! You *promised* our children would not leave my household till I deemed them old enough to do so.'

'I have a kingdom from Scotland to Spain to rule if you had not noticed.'

'Most of which is mine but whose advice you ignore.'

'Vindictive witch, what would you know?'

Our raised voices brought a cordon. Jerome, Robert, and Roger, with Antoine for good measure, rushed into our quarters bravely accompanied by Amaris and Lucille. As they stood between us, we circled the protective moat of our retainers, but they prevailed. We were disarmed. Robert threatened to knock Henry senseless if he touched me, while Jerome told me to curb my tongue. Though he fought like a demon, the men managed to haul Henry into his bed chamber and lock the door. I threw an oak stool at the door, missing my loyal Antoine by a wood shaving. They could not manhandle me as they did Henry. But then my old playmate ignored chivalry.

'Let go of me, Jerome!'

'Elly, you need to calm down.'

'You are hurting my arm! You will regret this!'

With a final shove I ended up on my knees in the library. I heard the key turn.

'Leave Her Ladyship – if she deserves that title – in there till she comes to her senses, Amaris. Dear God, what a pair. So much for royal status!'

'Agreed, Jerome.'

Chapter 10: Archbishop Becket

Thumping my fists on the floor, I bawled myself dry like a two-year-old.

Later, I knew not how long, there was a knock along with the sound of a key turning. It was Henry. He had escaped. I was too exhausted to tell him to go away. I stayed on the floor. Henry looked like a scarecrow minus its stuffing. God, what did I look like? My hair was awry, my face felt blotchy. Kicking the door shut, Henry collapsed beside me, wincing because of his hip. Neither of us said a word. After a while, Henry, pulled himself to his feet, sagging into the chair at my desk. I stayed on the floor, head on my knees. On the desk was my journal. I heard a page turn.

'God's bones, Greek!'

'So unwelcome snoopers cannot read it.'

This received a harrumphing grunt. 'Have you any wine in here?'

'No. Only ink. There is some in my quarters. I can fetch it, or you can come with me.'

'I'll come with you if I can stagger that far. Robert and his cohorts nearly killed me.'

I dragged myself to my feet and wobbled to the door. Not a page or churl were in sight. The gallery was as quiet as a crypt.

With Henry using my shoulder as a crutch we lurched to my chamber. My maids skittishly formed a phalanx in case another Norman-Aquitaine war broke out. Amaris demanded to know how we had escaped. I told the lot of them that unless they wanted to find themselves begging on the streets of London, they could immediately remove themselves from our sight. Marion, Celeste, and Lucille nearly fell over each other to get through the door, but Amaris stood her ground.

'If I hear one raised voice, or things being thrown, I will send in the guards to manacle both of you.'

Henry growled, 'Out, Amaris! Leave us alone or I will be the one calling the guards.'

Amaris left snorting like a filly. Henry limped to the wine flask and gave me an almost over-flowing goblet while draining his. He then poured himself another. I held out my goblet for a refill. I became quite tipsy after a few goblets how many, I know not. The chamber rotated, and Henry multiplied before my eyes. I remember giggling a lot but little else.

We were disturbed by a shriek, a scuttled exit followed by a hastily slammed door. I discovered it was not my head that had fallen off, but all my clothes. The multiple Henrys were undressed also. Whatever the Henrys were doing was divinely pleasing.

***

Henry and I shared a hangover of mighty proportions. There were events in London celebrating Becket's ordination that we had to attend. We had organised a banquet at the palace. We were speaking to each other again but were prickly regardless of our night together. I told Becket, if he laid one finger on my son, I would emasculate him with a blunt knife.

Hal's household was to accompany him, so he was surrounded by Agnes, Millicent and his tutors, everyone with whom he was familiar, which did little to salve my sorrow. My farewell to Hal was hell. I had to put on a brave face for his benefit. His tears were almost my undoing. I reminded him he was not far away and that his father said we would visit often.

The night after Hal left for Canterbury, I was not the only one who was bereft by his departure. Poor little Matilda cried herself to sleep, and even Richard, with whom Hal used to fight, was missing his big brother.

Later, Geoffrey told Henry he was a cold-hearted tyrant, in perfect Latin of course. For days, Lenore kept calling his name, which was like water dripping. 'Where Hal, where Hal?'

***

The turmoil I experienced, was taking its toll, and I was pregnant again. I had no energy. Getting out of bed in the morning was almost impossible. Henry had slowed down as well because of his hip, and his headaches seemed to be more frequent.

He had to ride to Woodstock for meetings with justiciars and clerics. New appointments in Oxfordshire had to be made for some clerical positions since Becket's ordination. He left grinding his teeth, leaving me with a list of duties which I struggled to fulfil.

Time moved on. My morning sickness eventually subsided as my pregnancy progressed, but just dragging my quill across the bottom of charters and writs was draining. From Woodstock, Henry moved onto Oxford to speak to bishops where he was inexplicably delayed. I could find out little, but I suspected his hip was too sore for him to ride. Not that he would ever admit it. I would go to him if I were not so tired.

This baby did not move as vigorously as the others who frolicked around my womb as if dancing a jig. It was worrying me. Brynn said it was not unusual, and I should not compare. She said some babies were just quieter. Perhaps it was due to my lethargy.

***

I knew it. Becket went from peacock to drab sparrow. Worse, he was now siding with the unordained clerks, who should be answerable to the secular laws of the land as they were under Henry's grandfather. Now they demanded to be tried by Canon Law if they committed a crime, and Becket was acting holier than the Pope. Hal told me Becket had taken to wearing a hairshirt under his vestments. He always was one for drama.

After Henry returned to Westminster, he summoned the powers within the church to demand why they were not following the customs of the land. I heard that many were siding with Becket and would not budge. Of course, the unordained clerks were elated knowing any petty felony they committed would be given penance at the most.

I eventually found the reason Henry was delayed in Oxford was because of Becket. He had interfered with the local sheriffs' duties. This was followed by the excommunication of one of our royal tenants, who rejected a clerk's appointment made by the archbishop. It had always been our royal tenants' duty to make these appointments. This was overstepping the mark and interfering in the way we ruled our kingdom. His ordination as Archbishop of Canterbury had obviously gone to his head.

Henry was almost impossible to talk to with all the fuss Becket was causing. He was in a whirlwind of bias within the church hierarchy. As the year and my pregnancy crawled on, we had much on our minds hardly saw each other. Not that I was worth knowing. For the last grinding months, I fluctuated from being tired to totally exhausted. I missed Hal. I was short with the other children and with my maids. I burst into tears for no apparent reason. As usual, I lived in terror of the birth. Brynn was doing her best with Matthias to diagnose why I was so down. I just wanted the child out.

***

In the middle of the night of the 20th of October in the Year of Our Lord 1165, I got my wish. She was smaller than the others, but she could have been a little early, which was why she did not suckle well. Also, this time my milk supply was rather meagre. We called her Joanna. She was more like Henry, another redhead.

For a reason I knew not, I had difficulty relating to her. Was it because I was reaching a time when my fertile years were leaving me? In the past, I had not lacked energy,

Chapter 10: Archbishop Becket

I had been impatient to be involved in the workings of our kingdom to the point of frustration, but now I had little enthusiasm. At least Matilda and Lenore loved her. Richard and Geoffrey, too. Henry had hardly looked at her, or held her for that matter, muttering 'another one for which to find a dowry.' As if with my wealth she would ever want for one!

Henry was aging before my eyes, and I watched him panic as a result. This business with Becket promoting Canon Law, interfering with the sheriff, and excommunicating our tenant who rejected the clerk's appointment was disappointing him and grinding him down. It mattered not that I disapproved of Becket, but Henry must feel betrayed. It was hard not to say, *I told you so!*

I decided to hand Joanna over to her wet nurse. Brynn had found her. Like Brynn, she was Welsh. Her name was Megan, and we called her Meg.

***

Henry had another mighty quarrel with Becket over the laws of the land versus Canon Law. Henry accused him of breaking from the traditional English legal system – Common laws which Becket helped update as chancellor before he was ordained as Archbishop of Canterbury. Becket argued in favour of Canon Law to judge not only ordained members of the church, but lay clerics employed by the church as scribes. There was another meeting with the Ecclesiastical Council which ended in a stalemate, followed by the council refusing to observe English customs, and siding with Becket again. They continued to argue that Common Law conflicted with Canon Law when it came to judging lay clerks' crimes. Henry, unable to get his own way, removed Hal from Becket's custody. I was over-joyed. I would have my darling boy home again.

For the first time in weeks, a weight was lifted from my heart and mind. I must not allow my euphoria to rub salt into Henry's wounds, though. With all this bitterness over Becket hovering like smoke over a damp brazier, we had but few minutes together of late. As I was feeling better in myself, I asked Henry to dine with me. Hal would be arriving back in London on the morrow so now was the opportunity to devote some sympathy to Henry. I asked to have a simple meal served. My maids helped me choose a gown I thought Henry would like. He always liked me in blue, so blue it was, but simple, not bejewelled. I pinned a Plantagenet brooch in gold to the gown and wore the cross Henry gave me years ago. My hair was plaited and unadorned with a veil. I dabbed on Henry's favourite fragrance.

I waited some time, fearing he was not going to answer my request, preferring to drown his disappointments in ale with Robert and others in his retinue. I felt my eyes well up when I heard the bells of the abbey ring out. I feared I would end up with kohl smeared down my cheeks when the door eventually opened. I hoped I looked nonchalant with my book opened and a goblet beside me.

I greeted him and asked if he would like some wine. He took in the room, looking slightly suspicious. I panicked, thinking he suspected I had an ulterior motive.

'You seem to have gone to some trouble, my dear.'

'You have suffered much disappointment of late, especially the last few days, so I thought you needed spoiling... You look tired, Henry.'

'You look beautiful.'

I handed him a goblet of our favourite Bordeaux wine and we sat by the grate.

***

The evening went well. I deliberately did not bring anything into our conversation to remind Henry of his recent conflicts, which for me was a miracle. I managed to steer the conversation about the children without mentioning Hal except to say I was looking forward to

Chapter 10: Archbishop Becket

seeing him. I told him I had let Joanna go to Meg because I could not satisfy the baby.

We skirted around the Aquitaine and Normandy. His mother, who had been unwell – a cold – was now well and keeping the Norman vassals under control. The Aquitaine was peaceful. The only odd matter was that Henry, having pushed back his chair, had made no overtures of romance. I suppose I was expecting more to the evening than dinner and a chat.

So, when the churls and pages had cleared the table and we were alone, I asked, 'How is your hip, Henry?'

'It is a bit stiff – only hurts when I laugh.'

'Shall I massage it for you?'

'Mm!'

I desired him, but he was giving no indication he wanted to end the night in bed. So, I took matters into my own hands. I had some scented oil. I had no idea what curing properties it had for sore hips, but I knew it could be massaged into some interesting body parts.

I knelt in front of him and rolled back his tunic. He was not wearing braies or hose. God's teeth, he had been leading me on all the time. I paused, looking up at him. He had me like a poacher's trout with a look that said do not stop. His arousal was infectious.

Oh, Henry. When you love, you love. It had been so long since we had spent a night in each other's arms.

***

Becket continued to make Henry's life a misery. For many months now, Henry has been trying to find a diplomatic solution for the governance of the English Church. He had approached clerics on both sides of the channel, and many supported his views. With his supporters, he petitioned Pope Alexander, the latest to don the mantle of St Peter, but so had Becket. The Pope remained neutral, causing Henry to simmer in fury. The Pope would have known the laws of England were honoured by Archbishop Theodore, so why was he not insisting Becket do the same? It infuriated me the way Becket had betrayed Henry's friendship and trust. The man had lived under our roof, for God's sake! Henry entrusted our son to his care; and we had to put up with his shameful proclivities. Now he flouted the very laws that as chancellor he upheld. Who did he think he was?

We also heard Becket had petitioned Louis. There would be no doubt who Louis would support. He would do anything to hurt Henry, while continuing to take revenge against me. Useless man!

A great success for Henry was the signing of the Constitutions of Clarendon. This occurred before Joanna was born, taking weeks of negotiations, ending at Clarendon Palace with as many bishops and barons in attendance as were possible.

The Constitutions aimed to restore the judicial customs of Henry's grandfather, which were mostly ignored under Stephen, allowing the Church to take advantage of his weak authority. The Church was quick to introduce its own judgement on "criminous clerks". These men could commit murder and at the very most be punished by being demoted within the Church, even though they were never ordained in the first place. Any other person in the kingdom, if proven guilty, was executed for the crime; therefore, the negligible sentence meted out under Canon Law was unfair and unlawful under Common English Law. After all, murder is murder no matter who commits it.

Even then, with eminent members of the clergy and respected nobles in front of him, Becket at first refused to support the legal customs of the country. He ummed and hawed, frustrating everyone before finally agreeing to sign, then, at the last moment, asking for a postponement to consult with others. The delay had Henry white knuckled and fuming. Eventually, Becket put his name to the document. By the time Henry returned to Westminster,

Chapter 10: Archbishop Becket

he was exhausted and too tired to enjoy his hard-fought victory. It was fortunate Becket was not a castle, or he would have been stormed, sacked, and levelled to the ground.

No sooner had Henry relaxed, ready to perform his other duties, when he heard Becket was not fulfilling his oath to observe the Constitutions and had attempted to leave the country for France without royal permission, which was required by law even for an archbishop. Next, anomalies were found in Becket's accounting when he was still chancellor. Henry insisted he be tried. However, Becket's mighty ego would again not accept the law of the land, so he evaded judgement by bolting into sanctuary in Northampton. No wonder Henry was tearing his hair out.

***

All this business with Becket sent Henry from one end of England and Normandy to the other. Oxford and Woodstock had particularly demanded his time, so much so he seemed to spend more time there than in London.

A courier arrived today from Shrewsbury with a missive addressed to Henry. I recognised the Grenvale seal. I decided to open it, rather than it spend time on Henry's desk waiting for his return. I was shocked to read that Lady Margaret Grenvale had died. It was supposed to be Lord Grenvale who suffered ill health. He wished to have his son returned from our custody to help run the estate.

This time I believed it was time to return the boy because it was his mother who was the more conniving. Aeled, I was told, had done well with his education and was well disposed towards his king and queen. As far as I was concerned, he should be escorted back to his family estates. I wrote to Henry enclosing the epistle and suggested I either send Aeled to Woodstock for Henry to take him back to Shrewsbury or wait for his return to London so we could travel together.

Henry's reply surprised me. He asked me to take Aeled, agreeing the boy must return home. I was amazed Henry would allow me anywhere near the Welsh border without his supervision. He also wanted me to go via Worcestershire to thank the bishop for his support regarding Becket. Most odd. I would enjoy the journey and the responsibility entrusted on me though Henry was in England, except I had all the symptoms of another baby. Why do I have to be so fertile, still? God's teeth, I will be forty-four when this one is born. If I could make it to Worcester, by then I should be over the worst of my travail. I begged Brynn to find something to calm my twisting guts, though I do not think there was a physic in Christendom I had not tried.

Aeled, naturally, was sad his mother was no longer. I did my best to comfort him. I felt guilty we did not send him home sooner, but it was all very well thinking of these things in hindsight. It probably frustrated him that he had to accompany me to the Bishop of Worcester's See. I tried to make it up to him by making the journey as interesting and comfortable as possible. I gave him a fine animal to ride, which Aeled mightily enjoyed.

The bishop was delighted with my visit. I explained I had to go on to Shrewsbury but was not relishing having to spend time under the Grenvale's roof after escorting Aeled back to his father. I was delighted and relieved when the bishop recommended that I stay with his brother-in-law, Earl Reece of Ashwood, who lived a few leagues south of Shrewsbury, not far from Grenvale Castle. He told me his sister Imogen and Lord Reece were elderly but would be mightily honoured to have me stay. While I was enjoying his company, he sent a courier to the earl heralding my arrival in less than a week.

I decided to escort Aeled to the family castle by leaving at cockcrow, paying my respects, then riding back to the Ashwood's manor, which I calculated I could reach before nightfall. My Praetorian guard would accompany me. The rest of my retinue would travel directly to the Ashwood's estate to prepare for my arrival, so my kind hosts did not have to panic about preparing for the queen as their guest.

***

We travelled on swift horses. My retinue speared off to the Ashwood's domain, while I continued. The night before was spent at a monastery on the River Severn. I always enjoyed the simplicity of the lives of these good people. Mine was so full of opulence, pomp, and ceremony, that it was good for my soul to be welcomed into a humble existence from time to time.

My stomach was doing several lurches as we approached Aeled's home, and it was not my condition causing the problem. My mornings had calmed, praise God. Aeled had grown into a fine young boy, not the most handsome, looking a little too like his unfortunate mother, but he was intelligent and thoughtful.

'Milady, although not under the happiest circumstances to begin with, I enjoyed, in the end, being under the king's care. It gave me an education which I can now put to good use helping my father.'

'Thank you Aeled I am delighted to hear that.'

'My father, in the turmoil of King Stephen's reign, had his education cut short.'

'Learning, Aeled, is a gift for life. Make good use of it.'

We were met in the castle bailey by Lord Grenvale with several retainers. Aeled shyly greeted his father, who was overwhelmed by the sight of his son. I stood beside Rebel not wanting to interfere in Aeled's welcome. When Lord Grenvale approached, he acknowledged he was surprised I was not in attendance with the king, but would I accompany him for some refreshments. I had already notified him I would not be staying long, using the excuse it was better for him to re-acquaint himself with his son than having to fuss about my presence in the household. I was sure he preferred that I was not under his roof as much as I did not want to be there.

A simple repast had been prepared. I gave Grenvale Henry's and my condolences regarding the death of Lady Margaret. Though I did not play Eleanor to her imperious best, I had no compunction in reminding Lord Grenvale why Aeled was taken hostage in the first place, emphasising we would brook no further rebellion now the boy was returned. Should Grenvale revert to his old habits, I impressed retaliation by Lord King Henry would be swift and far more severe. He replied there was no necessity to bend the rule of law now that King Henry had stabilised the governance of the country, which under Stephen and Eustace meant survival often took on unsavoury necessities. And, I thought, a certain mentality to play one side off against the other.

***

I took my leave. Rebel and I left in a far statelier manner than my previous excursion across the Grenvale drawbridge all those years ago and Rebel was not the young filly she used to be.

My Praetorian guards and I were able to take a gentler pace back towards the Ashwood estates. We had crested a rise with a pretty view of the surrounding Severn valley, when we espied a large, well accommodated encampment settled on the far side of the river. We had approached by a different route in the morning, so this was our first sighting. My men and I paused, puzzled as to who it might be, followed by a sinking feeling when I recognised the fluttering pennants of the Welsh Dragon. What in God's name was Owain Pendragon doing across our border?

As we had not been travelling at speed, dust would not have announced our progress, but it was disconcerting all the same; we could be vulnerable because my guard was light. Not that I was afraid of Owain, but I wondered if he

Chapter 10: Archbishop Becket

was using Henry's pre-occupation with Becket to make incursions into England. That unsigned peace treaty hung like a rain cloud. I cursed how I had pussy-footed around it just to salve Henry's ego.

We stopped on the road where I thought we would not be observed. After consulting with Antoine and Simeon, we decided to wait and watch. There was little activity, which meant the inhabitants of the camp could be hunting in nearby woodlands. But, to continue, we had to ford the river within view of the camp, and my presence in the neighbourhood would probably have been known. Owain with his web of spies would have heard of my movements before I left London, let alone Worcester. Was he provoking me?

We decided to move on. My guards furled our banners. I was not conspicuously robed, but Rebel was no ordinary steed, nor was her fine harness that of a cart horse. My men closed ranks around me, swords loosened in their scabbards. We descended towards the ford. Luck seemed to be on our side, because once we crossed the river we would be obscured by a stand of trees. Simeon and Roger guided me across. Alert, Rebel picked her way carefully on the stony river bottom. Antoine took up the rear. I had twenty men with me who regrouped in a tight cordon once we were across. I gripped my stiletto once I did not have to use two hands to guide my mare.

As silently as was possible, keeping jingling harness to a minimum, we made our way along the line of trees, keeping in the shadows. Then, out of no-where, there he was in his white Druid's robe, Owain Pendragon, mounted on a black destrier. The abrasive friction of my men's swords drawn in unison from sheaths was reassuring. The warmth of the horses' bodies closed in against me, ears pricked, nostrils flared. My right fist tightened around the hilt of my honed blade, while my left held Rebel in a tight rein, her neck arched. Owain appeared to be alone. In Langue d'Oc, I requested my men to remain vigilant, but not to attack.

'Greetings, oh beautiful wood sprite,' he lilted. 'We meet again.'

Damn his eyes. Why was he always so romantic in his address?

'It is so, Lord King Owain. Might I ask however, why thou hast such a large entourage beyond our border? Tis quite a camp, I see.'

'A mere hunting party, oh, Queen. In keeping with our treaty, is it not?'

Cheeky opportunist. What treaty?

'Wouldst Milady consider joining my small band for a modest feast before continuing her journey?'

'And perchance wouldst thou be serving King Henry's venison?'

Owain's deep chuckle echoed in the trees.

I had a dilemma. I did not want to partake in any feasting with Owain Pendragon. As he had spies everywhere, so had Henry. We fought often enough as it was without adding tinder to the flames. I also did not wish to insult the king of the Welsh by refusing his offer. What to do?

I decided to confide in Antoine. His eyes widened as I quietly informed him of my condition, instructing him to pass it on to Owain with my apologies, but not to tell the men. The last thing I needed was a clucky Praetorian guard travelling at the speed of a tortoise.

Antoine sheathed his sword and approached Owain. He then quietly passed on my news to the Welsh king, who looked surprised. He stared while I tried to look suitably demure.

When I raised my head, Owain was staring at me with a strange expression: sadness, perhaps mixed with pity, before anger flitted across his handsome face, an expression I had not expected. Surely, it would not be unusual that Henry and I could be expecting another child. He urged his horse towards mine. I indicated to my men to let him draw near. He begged a moment of my time for a word in private.

'Ride awhile with me,' he said, reverting to Latin.

'Then let us continue in the direction in which we are travelling.'

'Your husband spends much time at Woodstock these days, does he not?'

'Yes, Archbishop Becket's activities seem to hover there, keeping Lord King Henry away from London.'

'Have you never questioned there could be another reason?'

'Why should there be any other reason? Becket is driving us to distraction, taking up time that should be spent on duties of the realm.'

'You should ask your husband about another, who could perchance be taking more of the king's time than Becket. And so, I take my leave, Queen Eleanor.'

With that he turned his horse's head, kicking the animal swiftly towards his camp.

I felt the blood drain from my face, and my pulse raced.

***

At the Ashwood's Manor I was treated with gentle, old-fashioned courtesy and homage. What a delightful couple. They told me they were honoured to have me as their guest. My maids and retinue were equally enchanted. I put Owain's words behind me, thinking he was being peevish because I would not accommodate his offer of hospitality. Nonetheless, I had a strange feeling of foreboding in the pit of my stomach.

We spent a few delightful days at the manor house. My guards could hunt and relax from their duties as my watch dogs. We all stretched our saddle-weary bodies. Lady Imogen had a vast and prolific herb garden of which I was mightily taken, as well as the beautiful flowers she grew. I confessed my condition to her, expressing how, with every child, I was plagued with morning sickness, which lasted for anything from eight to twelve weeks.

She sympathised, saying she had experienced similar symptoms, though she had only four children. She was amazed I was up to number ten, eleven, if I counted Phillip. She was concerned I was riding round the countryside as I headed towards my sixth moon. She begged me to take the rest of the journey carefully.

***

I was to return to London via Winchester, as arranged before I left for Shrewsbury with Aeled, but I changed my plans and headed towards Woodstock instead. It was, after all, a shorter route. I did not herald to Henry my intentions, perhaps to catch him unawares. But then, what was I looking for? It was a silly idea, really, not to send a courier, as if my long entourage would not draw attention in the villages and towns through which I passed. By the time I arrived at the palace at Woodstock, Henry had left for London. I heard he was annoyed with me because I had upset his plans to meet me at Winchester.

After my detour, I arrived in London. By now I had progressed to almost seven moons and was not feeling very well. Brynn put it down to me rushing around the countryside, but I felt this child was different. My bulge was sort of sideways, as if the baby lay across my body. Brynn said it was nothing to worry about, that in time it would flip over, head down. I tried to jest that my womb was so stretched, the incumbent could relax and put its feet up wherever it liked.

I had only a few words with Henry after he arrived back in London from Winchester before he was off again. This time to Windsor. I should have been resting, instead I had to attend to letters from Uncle Ralph. The first concerned me, because some vassals in the Aquitaine were having territorial disputes with their neighbours. He reported he and my justiciars were handling the situation. As I was in no state to travel out of England, I had to leave it in his hands. The second letter was more reassuring, thank

Chapter 10: Archbishop Becket

God, or Henry would be threatening them with hell, fire, and brimstone. I was not in the mood or the condition to have another argument about Anglo-Norman versus Aquitainean law. Heaven be praised, Becket kept him on this side of the channel. I sent letters to Uncle Ralph to be as strict as he thought necessary. As soon as this child arrived, I must return to my duchy. These territorial disputes might just be old rivalries resurfacing as they did from time to time. Nevertheless, after the Poitivin debacle, Henry had completely lost my people's trust, and they could have been testing him. The abandonment of Toulouse, although I think it was the wisest option, also had many of them disgruntled.

***

Joy, oh joy! Henry deigned to spend some of his oh so precious time with me! He arrived back from Windsor yester morn. This time I pinned him down before he galloped off again and insisted that we talk. This was the first opportunity I had to report on Owain's incursions across our border and I felt Henry was avoiding me.

'If you can be bothered, Henry, I need to speak to you. There are matters we need to discuss. And, before you utter a word, why are you evading me?'

'If you are referring to your excursion via Woodstock instead of returning from Shrewsbury to Winchester as planned, we would not have missed each other. You could have had the decency to courier me your change of plans.'

'Do not blame me, *'enri Plantagenet-a*. You were the one who galloped out of Woodstock – and everywhere else recently, I might add. Why was that? One could believe it was deliberate?'

'Your imagination is amazing, Eleanor.'

'It is not something I have imagined. You have said less than two words to me in weeks because we are never under the same roof. And stop using Becket as an excuse. I demand you keep me informed about your activities.'

'Look, I was told you are not as well with this child. So, I do not want to worry you with affairs of state.'

'Child or no child, getting information out of you regarding our kingdom is like getting blood out of a stone at the best of times. And, regarding my health, I am amazed you care.'

'God's teeth, Eleanor, you are impossible; if you are not criticising my Latin or my Anglo-Norman laws, you are nagging about my hair and beard and my temper. How about having a good look at yourself for a change?'

The list went on and on. I rose to my imperious best and stormed out. Henry roared off to Oxford. I packed up my brood and maids and returned to Woodstock by carriage. That was something I would normally avoid, but I felt so ill, I would have fallen from Rebel, even if I had managed to climb onto a side saddle.

Chapter 11. Estranged

I returned to Poitiers. It was six months since our son John was born. It was hell recording my thoughts. Henry, the adulterous bastard, and I were estranged. I left him and England although I still wear its crown as queen. It had taken time to be able to face the wretched truth of my humiliation. Inwardly my heart ached, but my rage twisted my guts.

While Henry was in York, in my revenge, I stripped every palace – my English homes – of their opulent trappings from the Aquitaine: every wall, every floor, every piece of furniture I loaded onto galleys on the Thames bound for Bordeaux. Every possession, gone! Henry was left with what he had before me. Nothing! Naught! Not even my perfume remained, heady, in our bed chambers.

***

John was born at Woodstock the day before Christmas in the Year of Our Lord 1166. I had little to do with him after his birth and never held him. I was too ill. Weeks later, Amaris imparted that, had it not been for Brynn, neither of us would have survived. She told me I was in labour for thirty-five hours.

John came into the world upside down. Firstly, a single foot appeared. Brynn managed to ease the second foot down which had been caught somewhere inside me. She instructed my maids, in turn, to support me, holding me over the side of the bed. Brynn urged me to allow the earth to gently draw my baby towards it. Eventually, she told me I could push with the final contractions to bring his head into the world.

Brynn told me he was blue when he arrived, not breathing straight away. When she smacked him, he eventually whimpered into life, but was feeble. I bled great clots. While I was unconscious, torn, Brynn used physics unknown to all, including Matthias, to treat me. Around my neck she insisted I wear Owain's whalebone talisman. Brynn thinks John could walk with a limp.

My parlous condition spread throughout the land. From monks and nuns in tiny monasteries to the mighty, from quaint Saxon churches to grand cathedrals, prayers were intoned. I heard that villagers moaned and wept, that the ecclesiastical hierarchy whipped themselves into a frenzy of religious zeal for the "French whore", probably wanting me dead. Since I had provided all that the country needed, heirs and a massive dowry, Eleanor of Aquitaine was expendable.

Henry was dragged from Rosamund Clifford's chamber to my bedside. Of course, I knew naught of this. When I opened my eyes, he was beside me holding my hand, terrified by how I looked, with my pallid face, black-ringed, sunken eyes, my lips blue, my copious, beautiful hair matted with sweat. He could not ignore the pile of bloodstained linen, and left, I heard, for his guilt.

I spent the next few days fighting for my life. Infection from my poor torn women's parts was feared, but again, thanks to Brynn's remedies, this was averted. Meanwhile, my body wracked hot and cold. One odd thing I do remember through the delirium was chanting. A choir of strange voices in a strange tongue. White robed, swaying individuals harmonised with a hypnotic mysticism. Amaris told me they were real; they were Druids. Henry was apoplectic. They were sent by Owain Pendragon. Brynn threatened Henry with a more than dire curse should he send them away. He allowed them to stay.

It was three months before I gained strength, before I could leave my bed without fainting. I heard my other children, my beautiful children, had regressed into fear and anguish. When I was well enough to have them in my bed chamber, they came shyly, led in by Hal I think they

Chapter 11: Estranged

were afraid I would disappear before their eyes. He was eleven, Matilda ten, Richard nine, Geoffrey eight, Lenore, five and baby Joanna, just a year. Their baby brother John, they said they had seen. He was with his wet-nurse. Geoffrey, in his usual forthright manner, told me he was sickly.

My maids had propped me up on my pillows. It took all my fortitude not to weep with happiness at their appearance. Such a joy it was to see them. They all babbled at once.

'When are you coming home, Maman?'

'Matilda, darling, I know not. When Brynn says I am well enough, I suppose.'

'We want you to come now. Papa only let us come to Woodstock for a few days because of our lessons.'

'Hal, it will not be much longer, I promise. I am getting stronger every day.'

'It is no fun without you. There is no music or games. London is just damn boring.'

'Richard, you must not curse.'

'Chess, chess! I want to play chess!'

'Geoffrey, stop yelling I cannot understand a word, and, yes, I promise I will play chess with you as soon as I can.'

'Baby John is puny, Maman. Papa let us see him, but we were not allowed any cuddles.'

'Well, maybe one day when he is stronger, Geoffrey. What was that Matilda? If you whisper, I cannot hear you. Betrothed to whom? Geoffrey, for God's sake stop yelling. Now say that again darling.'

'Papa has betrothed me to Prince Henry of Saxony,' Matilda sobbed. 'I am to live with his family till I am old enough to get married. But I—'

'And *I* am to marry Princess Margaret soon,' Hal interjected.

'Hal, what was that?'

'Papa wants me to marry Princess Margaret.'

'Oh, Hal,' I sighed.

Joanna bounced on the bed midst the cacophony of interrupting voices as they all tried to outdo each other.

'Joanna, darling, can you please stop bouncing.'

An ear-piercing scream issued from Joanna.

'Lenore you should not have hit her. Do not cry little one,' I said, hugging her to my bosom.

To my relief, Brynn intervened,

'Come now, all of you, off the bed. You can visit your Maman again tomorrow. She must rest. Out, now!'

Brynn shooed them still arguing out the door. By now, I was exhausted, but angry as to what had befallen my children without me being there to defend them against Henry's scheming; to have them parcelled off like property. I wept with frustration and heart-wrenching hurt. My lack of strength, which kept me from confronting Henry, infuriated me. I could only leave my bed for short periods. Brynn said it was the loss of blood that had made me so weak, and in time my body would catch up, but I must be patient. Huh!

Every now and then, Henry would appear at my bedside. Becket, he grumbled, was still making his life a misery. He asked if I enjoyed the children's visit. I had little vigour to argue with him, but I begged to know why was he sending them away? Why was he betrothing them off willy-nilly while I was too unwell to question the suitability of their future spouses? I called him a coward. With as much strength as I could muster, I asked him to wait till I was back on my feet before any of them were to leave my household. A little hysterically, I pleaded that he give me his word. Thank God he agreed.

***

Papa's desk, the library, my haven of security enveloped me. How I wished and prayed my memories could be salved away like the pain of birth.

Chapter 11: Estranged

After three months and a half, I was well enough to be carried in a carriage back to Westminster. I was gaining a little weight – as Jerome said, *'going from scrawny to skinny.'* Bless him! What would I do without him? My desk in London was piled with missives. Most of them carried prayers and wishes from the good people with whom I had become friends over the years: Malcolm of Scotland, Mother Joan, the Archbishop of York, big Geoffrey, Abbot Timothy, Aeled, dear boy, delightful Imogen and Reece, and others too numerous to mention. There were letters from clerics, barons and ordinary folk who went to priests or scribes to voice their love and their care. The Welsh seal I broke last.

My Dear Lady Eleanor, my Queen of the Wood Sprites,

It is with heartfelt relief that I hear you are well after your travail. Had the spirits outside our earthly realm, or our Lord God, taken you from this world, I would have been bereft. I hold you close to my heart and have done so ever since our accidental encounter by that mystical spring near Shrewsbury some years ago.

It distresses me that the man you hold dear treats you as he does. He deserves not to tread the ground on which you walk. Out of respect for you I will not challenge him in combat, instead, I pledge for as long as I live, I will keep the unwritten treaty between Wales and England. But, should anything befall you, it will be null and void, and your faithless king will face my wrath.

- A Druid.

The letter distressed me. Like his other epistles, I burned it and stared with heartfelt sadness as it flared in the grate.

I collected all the parchment and vellum together, to carefully bundle the generous thoughts and kindness into a small chest, when I found one missive bulkier than the others I had missed. I did not recognise the seal as I pried open the wax. To my surprise, a ring fell out. It was the one I had given Henry when we were crowned. The ring had belonged to Papa, given to him by my mother when they were wed. Henry always wore it, treasured it, so how come it was in this letter. How had he mislaid it? I opened the folded parchment.

This ring was found in the bed of Rosamund Clifford. We believe it to be rightfully the property of the Duchess of Aquitaine, rather than her deplorable, unfaithful husband.

I was found on the floor, where I had collapsed. Lucille thought I was unwell again, maybe over-taxing myself, till she picked up the parchment. Gently she sat me up, pushing my head between my knees. The others answered her frantic calls. I was carried to my bed. Ice ran through my veins. My teeth chattered. I vomited till I dry retched. The words Owain Pendragon wrote and what he had planted in my mind during my return from Shrewsbury flashed before me. But whatever suspicions I may have had, I put down to Henry's preoccupation with Becket's behaviour, and Pendragon's thwarted desires. Also, I was too ill to be bothered. My main concern now was to recover from John's birth for the sake of my other children. I decided not to give another thought to Henry's activities until I was stronger – or was I avoiding the obvious?

The piece of parchment went around my maids and to Jerome and Peter. The ring was put amongst my jewellery. As it turned out, they all knew, except for Jerome and Peter.

Lucille's face was red. 'We sort of guessed Milady. But how could we say anything when you were so unwell, even before Prince John's birth.'

'We did not want to worry you, did we, Amaris?'

'Marion is right Milady, and we thought it would all blow over, that it was just a fling because you were...'

'Because I was what?' No-one answered my rage because it was followed by Jerome's.

Chapter 11: Estranged

'By God's wrath, I will kill Plantagenet! Elly being unwell is no excuse. You should have said something. Well, I am not going to stand here and see the woman I... I care about more than my life hurt and humiliated by that Norman bastard.'

'Jerome, stop! Please, for my sake stop. Please.'

'No Elly! He will be singing higher than a descant by the time I finish with him. He will not be able to copulate again if he is still alive!'

'Peter, stop him please! Jerome stop!'

I was too feeble to stop him as he tore to the door. Peter grabbed him and there was a tussle between the two monks. Next thing I realised, Amaris was between them, yelling for them to calm down.

Peter and Amaris managed to force Jerome to stay within my chamber. He flung his arms around me, and we wept together. The scales had fallen from my eyes.

'So all that to-ing and fro-ing from Woodstock and Oxford and blaming Becket... You should have told me.'

My dear maids were now also in tears. 'We thought it was a momentary lapse, because Lord King Henry could not lay with you in the latter stages of your pregnancy, and you were not in a very pleasant mood. We believed he still loved you, and still does.'

But I found out from churls and pages from Oxford, he had to be dragged from Rosamund Clifford's bed to be with his wife when they thought she was dying.

***

By the time Henry returned to London, I had gone and so had my dower. My children accompanied me first to Bordeaux and L'Ombrière where I stayed to be comforted by dear, sweet, elderly Renée. I think it was in her arms when the floodgates truly opened.

I said nothing to my children except that I must take over the ruling of the Aquitaine to keep peace in the duchy, which was not far wrong as it happened. Once in

Poitiers, I had to decide about Joanna and John. I was not close to either child, who had been suckled and nurtured by their wet nurses and looked after by maids put in place by Henry when I was ill. I had rarely seen them.

Henry decided to send them to Fontevrault, to his Aunt Isabella. The children were settled, happy as it happened. I went to visit them but felt like a stranger. John, if I held him, screamed. I decided they were better off under Mother Isabella's care. I think she was amazed that Eleanor, the *Grande Maman*, the queen who suckled her own children, could now be heartless regarding her two youngest. She could not but notice a change in my demeanour.

Isabella took me to her quarters where she had refreshments for me and my small retinue. My expression prompted her to suggest a walk in her splendid gardens.

'What is it, Lady Eleanor? I can see you are burdened; you are not your usual self. I do not wish to be rude, but you appear distant, even a little haughty.'

What was I to say to her? She was Henry's favourite aunt. I was also afraid I would not be able to contain my emotions – self-pity and fury. My body, I knew, said much, with my fists clenched, my back as stiff as a pikestaff. Isabella was patient while I battled in my mind as to what to say. In the end, I told her the truth.

'I have left Lord Henry. I have discovered he has been unfaithful. He is having an affair.'

There was little point trying to keep my situation quiet because it would not be long before the world would be heralding my humiliating plight.

'I am shocked. Fool of a man!'

I thought she would be on Henry's side. After all, they were family. She was his father's sister.

I said, 'I need more time before I can bring John and Joanna into my household. I do not relate to them.'

***

Chapter 11: Estranged

Jerome was like Vesuvius. Now, back in Poitier. I knew he wanted us to talk, but I did not want to broach the subject with him. He was over-protective. It took all my willpower to order him and my Praetorian guard not to start a rebellious uprising. I told them to let me take my own revenge, that *'enri Plantagenet-a*, would rue the day he betrayed me. My chess tactics had always been superior. Jerome, however, could not be placated, so I was going to have to speak with him regardless of how much I desired to fume on my own. I sent a page for him to meet with me in the gardens. We walked towards the archery range. Both of us took out some of our pent-up frustrations and anger on the targets, then walked through the little wooded copse to a seat over-looking the River Clain behind the gardens.

Neither of us said a word. The silence was heavier than a rock of marble, then we gabbled over each other. I nodded to Jerome to go first.

'The man is a damned idiot. How could he treat you so? He is the luckiest bastard in Christendom to have you as his wife. You are talented and beautiful, and where would he be without the Aquitaine and everything else you have done for him? I am more than angry, Elly.'

'I do not know what to say, Jerome. I thought he loved me. Yes, we were arguing more often and viciously in recent years, but we always made up... in bed usually.'

Jerome blushed, then asked, 'Have you spoken to him?'

'No.'

'Do you know the woman Lord Henry has become involved with.'

'Yes, I know her name but that is all, and I have no intention of asking for more details.'

'Elly, would you like me to make enquiries, to find out what is amiss?'

'No, Jerome, most definitely not!'

'Would you forgive Lord Henry if, on realising his foolish mistake, he was to want you back?'

'You must be jesting. How could I ever trust him again? He is, was, the love of my life. No! No! No! I will be avenged in my own good time!'

My pride reared like a rampant tigress as I struggled with my emotions. Dear, good Jerome drew me towards him, his arms around me. I rested my head on his shoulder.

I listened in silence as Jerome started talking.

'When, Elly, you came back from Paris eons ago, you were embittered and angry, free, but not free. I understood that, because when your father died, my destiny too was set. I lost my freedom to be within your family. I was for the church. Your father gave me the education for a future I would never have had if my parents had lived through that tragic typhus epidemic. I would have become a shepherd, free, but not free from ignorance. Growing up in your household, I mourned for my parents, but every day, I gave thanks for what fate had given me – learning.'

Jerome paused, but then continued. 'When you had to marry King Louis, I was bereft. I could see how unsuitable your marriage was going to be. Without choice, I went to the Benedictines where I mourned not only Duke William, your Papa, but what fate had dealt you and me.'

Jerome's grip around me tightened. 'You asked me once had I ever loved a woman. I answered *yes*. At first, she was my little sister – a wild child, precocious, clever, outspoken, with a wicked sense of fun. Then, as we grew, not only did her cleverness stand out, but she also became a beauty. Her wealth was beyond my comprehension, but that was not important. So, lying there in my monk's cell, crying for the impossible, was not going to achieve anything, like forever mourning for my parents was not going to bring them back. I had to move on, to take what life had set me and to put out of my head what I could never have.'

We sat in silence. What could I say? It was obvious his feelings for me at one stage in our lives were more than brotherly. But even if my feelings for him had

Chapter 11: Estranged

been anything other than sisterly, the differences in our birth, our status, would have made any thought of being together impossible, like Abraham, my first love.

Jerome changed the subject. 'What about your duties as Queen of England? Have you thought about how Lord Henry will manage without you? You are an integral part of his reign, you know that. Many barons remain peaceful, more because of your influence than the king's. What about Pendragon? Will he now give England problems, Malcolm of Scotland too?'

'Like he plays chess, Jerome, he never thinks ahead to the end-game. He has sacrificed his queen. So be it!'

'It saddens me, Elly, that there appears to be no hope of a reconciliation coming from you.'

My heart and mind were roiling. Jerome had obviously thought deeply about this after his initial rage. After a few minutes, he continued, 'I think you are letting your contempt cloud your judgement by allowing your usually clear objectives to be muddied by spite.'

'I am not the only one who is betrayed, Jerome. What of his sons and daughters? Henry is using our children as pawns to advance his kingdom, and I am going to use every part of my being to stop him.'

'Elly, do not be naïve. That is the price you must pay for your nobility.'

My rigid determination surprised Jerome. I stood. My fists clenched like iron vices, my voice rasped, 'I will fight for my children's rights, Jerome, even if it is against their father.'

***

I plodded up the circular staircase to Uncle Ralph's solar. I had to tell him what had happened regardless of how humiliating.

'Ah, Eleanor, how lovely...'

I blurted out before he could utter another word, 'Uncle, this is difficult... I have left the king.'

'Where?'

'Not where Uncle Ralph! I have left. He is an adulterous bastard.'

I took a deep breath, 'As far as I am concerned, I am no longer his wife.'

'Dear God in heaven.'

He stood, leaving his desk to take my hands and sat me in a chair.

'Furthermore, I have stripped him of every comfort, every stick of furniture, every tapestry, every carpet – my dowery in other words. He can learn to live in poverty. He can survive on his whore's wealth, if she has any, instead of mine.'

'God's teeth... I sympathise my dear, but do not you think that was a bit extreme?'

'NO! And if he thinks he is getting another sou from the Aquitaine treasury, he can think again. I will countersign nothing.'

Uncle Ralph shook his head. 'Eleanor, my dear, as much as I am saddened by your predicament, what you are planning will miscarry, because King Henry must countersign monies we need from the treasury.'

'That will not affect us one iota: Henry knows nothing about my grandmother's fortune.'

'Ah... yes. My mother was good to you.'

Of course, Uncle Ralph knew about my 'other inheritance'. My grandmother was wealthy. She inherited much of her fortune from Grandfather William after his death in Jerusalem, and I suppose I received it as a reparation. For my uncle, though, it was like rubbing salt into a wound. Dangerosa, his mother and my grandmother who bequeathed it to me, was my grandfather William's mistress. It was complicated and, from the de Faye/Châtellerault family's point of view, something of which one did not speak. I had some of what was left of Nilla's dowry, too, and there was the Briolette diamond, but I said naught about that.

Chapter 11: Estranged

But, with blazing eyes, I continued ranting, 'Uncle Ralph, Henry has been getting every sou from my manors and their estates in England for years. I was granted queen's gold and had certain allowances, but I was never allowed to control my English income. Henry will now have to live off taxes and revenues from his kingdom and other domains. It may make him think twice when he next wants to gather an army to attack my people.'

My uncle shook his head. 'Is there not some way you can come to an agreement with Lord Henry, to reconcile your differences? By now, surely, he realises he has made a grave mistake.'

I stood. 'Mistake! He was in that woman's bed while I was bleeding, giving birth to John. It is a miracle that John and I survived. Was he hoping that I would die?'

I was close to tears. 'What is it with men, that they can have affair after affair, yet I am labelled the adulteress, the French whore, for falling in love before I met Henry. Those two men were well and truly out of my life by the time that wedding ring was slipped on my finger. I have never been unfaithful to Henry, when by God's teeth I could have been on more than one occasion. You know why? Because I loved him, and I thought Henry loved me. And you want me to come to a reconciliation!'

I was determined I was not going to cry in front my kinsman. I stood trying to breathe. Uncle Ralph was not a demonstrative man, so I was surprised when he put his arms around me, but I could no longer hold back. My shoulders shook as convulsive gulps wracked my body.

After he helped me back to my chair, he poured us each a goblet of wine. 'Elea, my dear. I feel your anguish. But the whole Duchy relies on our treasury funds.'

When was the last time he called me by my family diminutive?

He continued in a gentle voice, 'It is all very well for you personally to be well endowed, but could your inheritance of my mother's fortune sustain the Aquitaine and all its needs? If Lord Henry counters your revenge regarding his signature on Aquitaine treasury matters, where will the duchy be, the monasteries that rely on our alms, for instance, everything from the upkeep of all the palaces, to maintenance throughout the land for countless buildings, bridges, or sea walls like the one on the Garonne?'

I was pulled up in my tracks.

'Elea, if you take such drastic revenge on your husband, you take revenge on your own people, the people of the Aquitaine, Poitou, and Gascony. Think very carefully about that.'

Yes, I was being irrational, not looking at the board tactically. If I continued in this manner, I would be checkmated. Dear Uncle Ralph. I swallowed my wine and my pride. He poured me another.

I paused before I replied, 'Thank you for being so forthright.' Then I went on, 'Uncle Ralph I will heed your advice to do everything in my power to keep my duchy and counties well governed and solvent.'

'My dear Elea, you are more than capable of overcoming adversity. It is in your blood. After all, you were ordained Duchess of Aquitaine.'

He smiled and gave me a quick hug.

***

It was time to move. Instead of sitting around feeling sorry for myself, I had to take myself to every corner of my lands, something I had not done for many years. I was determined now. Richard, I would formally ordain as my heir, the future Duke of Aquitaine, then I would present him to his people. I would take all my children on a regal progress. They knew England well, but, except for Poitiers and L'Ombrière, they had seen little of the Aquitaine. It was time to introduce them to their relatives and their estates scattered throughout the countryside.

Chapter 11: Estranged

I busied myself with preparations for Richard's ordination. He would be soon turning eleven. I spent much of my time not just with him but with Hal also. I knew Henry would come for Hal one day to be crowned the Young King of England. It was imperative that I prepared him for his destiny, just as Papa prepared me for mine. I wanted him to understand there were many ways to govern other than going to war at the first sign of trouble. Henry's methods were honed by conflict and little else. I told both boys about Georgius, the head of the village of Rusuca on the Barbary coast, showing them on a chart where my foundering ship found a haven on my return from the crusades. I described how Georgius was a natural leader who ruled his people with wisdom and sensitivity. I explained how he listened carefully to their concerns, how he did not pass judgement till he knew all the facts. I told the boys he was a mighty advocate who had never read Cicero, who, in fact could not read. I told them how much I learned from this simple, good, and wise man.

All the boys had onerous responsibilities ahead of them. Each day, as their tutor, I emphasised to them they must be ready to talk, to negotiate, and above all to listen before they plunged into actions they may regret. I had to stress this point more to Richard than Hal. Geoffrey, I suspected, would be a law unto himself, but Richard was more like Henry, impulsive. He was inclined to rush in waving a sword before assessing the situation. The two eldest needed to be familiar with the laws of England and the Aquitaine. I found Papa's old copy of Cicero. We read it together and discussed legal argument. As Papa had made me, I insisted they learn our laws off by heart. I hoped to make advocates out of all my sons. Hal also needed to know Anglo-Norman law.

We played many games of chess. It was hard keeping Geoffrey away from the board. He could annihilate both his older brothers, which infuriated them. It was a challenge to keep ahead of him. I had to hone my wits to be razor sharp. Games were now taking days, often ending in a stalemate. Then he would argue the point about a move if I took one of his men. He often had me grinding my teeth like Henry. Hal said he was an obnoxious brat. Now where have I heard that before?

Matilda pouted when I left her out of the lessons, rebuking me, like a chanting monk, that girls should be educated, too. Of course, she was right, so I included her as well. But Lenore was still too young.

***

I knew I was running myself close to collapse. As well as the children's lessons, I had taken over the governance of my lands from Uncle Ralph. Writs, charters, petitions, and God knows how many missives were piling up on my desk. Uncle Ralph reminded me I had a panel of justiciars there to help. He suggested I follow my own advice to my sons, to listen, to consult. He also suggested I include the boys in some of the panel's discussions. Good advice.

I was trying to do too much, but I wanted to go to bed exhausted, so I did not have to think about Henry, collapsing into a dog-tired heap. There were nights, however, when no matter how spent I was, I lay staring at the canopy above my bed, yearning for his face, body, and odour. I ached for his touch and caresses. Aroused and frustrated, I would sob into my pillow. God's teeth, why did I still love him after what he had done to me?

I had too much pride to speak to Henry, nor could I trust myself to talk to him in a rational manner. Probably he did not want to speak to me either. We were too much alike in that respect. On my desk was a letter from Robert. With a sigh I broke the wax.

Dear Lady Eleanor,

It is with a heavy heart I pen this to you. Our world is cold and dreary without your grace and charm. It is as if

Chapter 11: Estranged

the bleak times of Stephen have returned as we cram together in one room at Westminster looking for the fires you lit with your personality as well as in the grates of your magnificent fireplaces. It is as if winter has permanently enveloped our lives.

Though he will never admit it, Henry is bereft without you. He knows he has been a fool. Henry has no-one to jest with, to bicker with, no-one to push him to be neat, or insist he not be slap-dash, no-one to love as you love. I know you are probably thinking, 'Well, what about Rosamund?' She is a pretty, meagerly educated creature, who appeals to his vanity by flattering him, and agreeing with everything he says, even when he is wrong. She strokes his ego by telling him how wonderful he is; something you would never do unless he deserved it.

I am not making excuses for him – he is, like many men, very clever, but lacking common sense from time to time. Not that he will admit it, but he fears his virility is being sapped; he sees his grey hair as a sign he is aging. But you continue to look beautiful and are as brilliant as ever. To make matters worse, you can achieve, with no apparent effort, what he cannot. Life has become for Henry a continuous joust he must win. He has to be seen to be powerful at all costs to keep his people under control. And force is the only law he knows.

Henry thinks, and it sticks in his craw, that all you do is bat your lustrous, dark eyes at an uncooperative baron and he is captivated, charmed. Henry cannot see that you urge the fractious to examine the futility of their actions, and appeal to their common-sense by encouraging them that it is in their best interests to conform to the laws of the land. Furthermore, you listen to their grievances. This, Henry should be doing instead of rattling their portcullises. He is jealous. All he sees is them drooling over his lovely wife.

Also, Henry fears you; he sees you as a competitor to his rule, to his authority. He leaves you as regent in England and you tame the country. He cannot control the Aquitaine, and your other lands, but you can.

He leaves England with pockets of rebellion from one end to the other, comes back, and the barons are eating out of your hand. But once he takes over the reins, they start revolting again.

You reinstated Malcolm of Scotland by clever tactics. Not a drop of blood was spilt when you freed him from his upstart nephew, David. It infuriates Henry beyond endurance when Malcolm sends you, instead of him, useful information.

What is more, Pendragon adores you, enraging Henry, who knows he cannot control the Welsh King except by waging war and then not doing it very well. It drives him insane he cannot keep peace with the Welsh. Henry believes the only reason harmony prevails on the border is because of the unwritten declaration of love between King Owain and the 'Queen of the Wood Sprites'. He also thinks Owain has been in your bed. I am sure this is untrue, but I cannot convince him otherwise. Then there is Becket, a constant thorn in Henry's side.

I am trying to persuade Henry to board a ship to Bordeaux, then to L'Ombrière. Would you consider coming back to England if he will not sail to you?

My love for you and Henry is deep in my heart and mind as I write. I believe he still loves you.

With deep fondness and respect,

– Robert de Lucy

I read and reread what Robert wrote, and I knew not what to think. I slipped the letter into my journal, so I would always have it for reference. Robert was the most honourable, chivalrous, and respected knight I knew. I had known him for as long as I had known Henry. Since they were small boys, he had been friend and companion to him, his loyal squire. In fact, Robert was more a brother to Henry than Geoffrey or William. In many ways he was like Jerome, dependable, and did not mince words when necessary. Robert had always treated me with kindness and respect, putting up with my fiery temperament with grace and good humour. He had helped me cross many a moat of despair when I was wracked with grief and sadness.

But what of Henry? From what Robert said he was not only jealous of other men in my vicinity, but of me? I tried to understand why. Yes, we looked at the duty of ruling differently. But then, I was brought up in the relative peace of the Aquitaine till I was thirteen; whereas, from aged ten, Henry had seen nothing but rebellion and civil war, a war he was still fighting when I met and married him. To Henry, threats and brutality were normal, hence the debacle of Poitou whereby I see violent conflict only necessary when diplomacy fails.

I knew we would never be able to agree. We were too headstrong, both wanting our own way. If we managed some sort of truce, the first disagreement could send him into the arms of the next woman who would flatter him. The tragedy was I saw myself in his misery like I was with Louis, searching for acceptance and understanding. Did I do that to Henry? Guilt reared its ugly head. But Robert believed Henry still loved me. I never loved Louis, I tried, but I could find nothing to love. Deep down, I thought I would always love Henry. But equally, I knew I did not want to subject myself to more anger and humiliation. Moreover, could I ever trust him again?

I penned a short reply to Robert, thanking him for his caring, enlightened thoughts, but, in answer to his final words, I wrote, *No. I cannot return to England. But I will speak to Henry if he comes to L'Ombrière.*

The shadows stretched across the library as the sun descended. I lit a candle and drank the flask beside me dry. Somewhat lurchingly, I made my way to bed. Amaris said naught as she helped me undress. She sat by my bed holding my hand till I stopped weeping and fell asleep.

Chapter 12. Heir Apparent

I decided to have Richard's ordination as Duke of Aquitaine at the Cathedral in Bordeaux. I could not bear the thought of having the ceremony here in Poitiers where Henry and I were wed.

The children were all excited. They loved staying at L'Ombrière just like Nilla and I did. For me it would be a gut-churning return with the memories of Henry's and my first meeting, as well as the last pleasurable time we were together. I would see, however Clotilde and Renée. My old nurse was as old as a tree, but still full of life.

As well as a fun part for the children, it was going to be an emotional experience for Richard. I had too much pride to invite Henry, or even let him know what was to take place. If others informed him, so be it.

Heralds were sent far and wide across the Aquitaine, Poitou and all my lands inviting nobles, relatives, and clergy to attend. I asked Mother Isabella to bring Joanna and John. She would be the only member of Henry's family to be in attendance. I sent a missive out of politeness to Empress Matilda, but she replied she was too old and frail these days to travel such a distance. No doubt she would be one of the first to notify Henry.

Our entourage through towns and villages stretched for leagues. We were hailed across the countryside. Richard rode beside me on a mighty steed. I let him choose the horse from our stables. He rides well, but I was concerned when he chose a prancing black stallion. He silenced my nagging by saying if I could ride one so could he. I still had Diablo, but he was not a young animal anymore, so apart from the odd outing around Poitiers, he spent most of his time fathering others. I was now riding one of his offspring, another beautiful, high stepping hispano. Like his father he had a devilish look in his eye, so I named

Chapter 12: Heir Apparent

him Beelzebub.

Hal was subdued, unusual for him. When I was able, I rode beside him.

'You are very quiet, Hal. Is there something worrying you?'

'Richard is being honoured before me. I think it is unfair, even though I do not want to be crowned the Young King.'

'I am sorry you feel that way, darling. I must have Richard ordained for stability in the Aquitaine. I thought you understood that.'

'I do... but... Oh, I do not know, Maman. I feel there is something you are not telling us about you and Papa, that is all. And I do not want to be crowned because it means we will have to go back to England and the title will not mean anything, anyway.'

'Oh.'

Dear God, what could I say to him? I took the coward's way out. 'Well, this is not the time or place for such a serious discussion. Do you mind if we put it to one side for now?'

'No, I suppose not,' sighed Hal.

***

When the day of the ceremony arrived, we paraded to the Cathedral in Bordeaux. Richard was taking it in his stride. It was Maman who was nervous. I was decked in my rites, as the up-and-coming Duke's mother, in scarlet and gold and wearing the crown of Aquitaine. A new one had been made for my ten-year old son in glinting gold.

Richard looked most serious. He was so handsome, though still little more than a child. The russet curls inherited from Henry we tamed with a good haircut. His eyes though shaped like mine are cornflower blue. He has my nose, but on him it does not look like it belongs on a Roman statue. My pride in my son and heir throbbed in my heart as we entered the Cathedral. Memories of Henry's and my Coronation flooded back. It was a struggle to remain dry eyed; my unbearable sorrow was mixed with the joy and delight in my heir. Hal's words niggled though.

I expressed these feelings to Jerome at the banquet, but I felt more than peeved when he told me I should have at least notified Henry about Richard's ordination to give him the opportunity to attend. Henry be damned, I thought.

From Bordeaux, the children, our entourage, and my beloved Praetorian guard progressed through our lands. We first travelled south to Gascony where I introduced Richard as my heir, Hal as the future King of England and Geoffrey as the future Duke of Brittany – if Henry ever got around to anointing his third son with the title which he was not keen about and which I have not had a chance to discuss with him.

John, being too young to travel, was back at Fontevrault. I had taken Joanna back into my court. It was bitter-sweet visiting my Châtellerault relatives as well as my father's kin without Henry. From Gascony, we made our way to Périgord, Limousin, Angouleme, then Poitou.

Back in Poitiers, we were all pleasantly tired after our successful journey covering many weeks. The children at times were a little fractious, wanting to explore and play away from the guards, or the three boys galloping their horses at breakneck speeds to see who could get to a castle or manor first. Shades of Henry, I was afraid. They were becoming quite competitive, especially Hal and Richard, who was going to outgrow his older brother. He was already taller and of a bigger build. I worried about their bickering and occasional punches. I had them taught archery and all were accomplished. By necessity, they had learned to handle swords and daggers. They were competent hunters. Geoffrey could out-argue anyone. While we were staying with Faydide, I discovered to my horror he had related to her with avid glee that I had left

Chapter 12: Heir Apparent

Henry. I was unaware he knew the real reason I was in the Aquitaine because I had not told the children why.

Faydide came to me in confidence, asking if it was true. I had to ask her from whom she heard the 'rumour'. When she said it came from Geoffrey, I was shocked, furious with him. There was no point in me denying it, so I asked her for a few private moments. She was sympathetic but questioned whether I was being a little too dramatic in my actions.

'Eleanor of Aquitaine,' she said 'I know it must be galling for someone of your beauty and intellect to be betrayed, but it happens. Men are men.'

I was struck speechless that my friend and cousin could think I should just put Henry's adultery out of my mind, and get on with my life as if nothing had happened. The hurt I felt could not be brushed away like an annoying fly. I related to her how on many nights I cried myself to sleep, heartbroken.

'Faydide, to know that the depth of my love for Henry, my commitment to his kingdom, and the responsibilities I have born as regent, are not good enough is unforgiveable.'

I told her what Robert had said about Henry being jealous. Some excuse! Of course, garrulous Geoffrey did not know where his father was while I was struggling to give birth to his brother. Whatever whispers he had picked up were not the whole gruesome facts.

Faydide was taken aback when she learnt those details. I sat with my head in my hands as I told her I could not forgive Henry. To think Henry's concern for me was so low, so thoughtless and uncaring, all I could think was that he wanted me dead. My feelings were in a turmoil of love and hate.

***

Once we arrived back in Poitiers, it was necessary to take clever clogs, *Monsieur Sabot Intelligents*, to one side.

'Geoffrey, a word.'

'Maman...?'

'Just hold your tongue and listen. I do not appreciate you prattling to my friends and relatives about a situation of which you know nothing about. You know nought as to what has occurred between your father and me. Yes, your father and I have had a disagreement, but it is private and in future I would appreciate you keep your mouth shut or you might find yourself in Fontevrault with John as his nursemaid. What do you have to say?'

'Yes, Maman. Sorry, Maman.'

'And so you should be. Just where did you hear these rumours?'

'It is all over the empire from Normandy to the Spanish border that you are refusing to speak to Papa or he to you.'

'Indeed. Well, in future, I expect you to respect my privacy – in fact our family's privacy. What happens within our palace and castle walls is not to be spread like dandelion seeds. Now, Clever Clogs, go. I do not want to set eyes on you for the rest of today.'

I felt like cuffing the cheeky, little smart-ass. And I still had to talk to Hal.

***

A missive arrived delivered by a breathless courier on an exhausted horse. Without looking at the seal, I knew who the author was. I avoided opening it out of cowardice more than any other reason. I was feeling the consensus was stacked against me. Almost everyone thought I should forgive Henry, give him another chance. Did I have the fortitude to remain estranged when I missed him so much? I have vowed I never will forgive him but... My heart was beating like a nervous filly.

What was I wanting, a letter full of contrition, begging me to return? Was I afraid this was not what it would contain? Was this why I dreaded opening it for fear he did not want me back knowing I was as unbending as a halberd?

Cowardice won out. I dragged Jerome away from a scripture lesson with Matilda and little Lenore, who was

Chapter 12: Heir Apparent

more interested in draping rosary beads round her neck than paying attention. Another Nilla!

Jerome followed my agitated gallop to the library. I pushed the letter in front of him pacing in circles, much like fidgety Henry.

'It is from the king,' I told him, as if he would not recognise the royal seals of England and Normandy!

'Why have you not opened it?'

'I fear what it might contain. I want you to open it.'

'Then what?'

'Read it,' I snapped.

'Hand me your knife. I will open it for you, but I am not reading the contents. They will be addressed to you. I will give you support should you need it.'

The rent of the seals tearing from the parchment sounded like a scream. As Jerome handed the parchment to me, my eyes scanned the page.

To Lady Queen Eleanor of England, Duchess of Normandy, Duchess of Aquitaine, Countess of Poitou, and Anjou, and Duchess of Gascony,

My Dearest Wife,
By the time you read this I will be on the high seas hoping to arrive at Bordeaux by early May. It is time for our eldest son, Hal, as Henry III, to follow his destiny to be crowned the Young King of our English Kingdom in Westminster Abbey. It is my intention to escort our son, Prince Henry, to his rightful country of England, for this ceremony.

It is my desire for you to bring him to L'Ombrière, where I will meet you, to prepare him for departure.

You may if you choose, return to England as my queen and wife to attend the coronation of our son and my heir.

I would have liked to have attended the investiture of Prince Richard as Duke of Aquitaine, but I was not invited. But I look forward to meeting with you in the near future.

Your husband,
Henry, King of England

I screwed the letter into a ball and flung it at Jerome, then swept everything off my desk in a furious arc. Jerome caught the pewter ink pot before it hit the floor, his hand splashed in blue.

'My dearest wife, indeed!'

The chair tumbled backwards as I stood. Jerome let me pace and roar.

After I had run out of abuse, he said, 'Elly, you knew Hal's crowning was imminent, and I understood you were not going to prevent it happening.'

My clenched fist slammed onto the desk, jarring my hand.

I thundered, 'It is the tone of the missive that angers me, not to mention the heartbreak of having to farewell Hal, who fears this inevitability. He is reluctant about the ceremony and does not want to go back to England. It will be a hollow title till his father dies, which of course none of us want.'

'You could have invited Lord Henry to Richard's ordination as your heir you know.'

'Whose side are you on?' I yelled.

'Yours. But revenge is making you bitter and resentful. I believe, Elly, you should rise above such sentiments.'

'Get out! How dare he judge me! Do you not understand my turmoil? I thought you sympathised with my position.'

The door shut behind him with a determined click.

I left the library after I had stopped shaking. With the letter in my hand, I strode to the school room. The children were busy working with their tutors. I excused myself for interrupting their lessons, saying I needed to speak to Prince Hal. He rose to follow me. There was an exchange of glances between Matilda, Richard, and Geoffrey, then heads bent back over their slates, while Maman's face expressed she was in no mood to be crossed.

Hal and I made our way to a quiet corner in the garden and sat on a bench. I gave him his father's letter. He read it, glanced at me, then scanned it again.

'I do not want to be crowned the Young King, you know that. I do not want to go home with Papa unless you come too, Maman.'

What could I say? After Geoffrey's revelation to Faydide, I knew my older children were aware that Henry's and my marriage was strained. Hal had hinted as such on the way to L'Ombrière. But I was certain they did not know the reason or the full details of my wrath, but it was getting harder to remain silent. I did not want them to hear the gory details from others' lips. But that was not the issue, now.

'Hal, darling, people of our birth and nobility have no choice but to execute our duties regardless of how reluctant or negative we might feel. It is paramount.'

'Maman, I will be happy and honoured to follow my obligations when the day comes. But I know Papa will crown me then tell me to keep my place. Just like he does with you. He will never give me any responsibilities. I will be twiddling my thumbs.'

'Hal, your father made me regent in England when he was absent and entrusted me with the administration of the Aquitaine, like now for instance.'

'Do you think I am an idiot, Maman? The only reason you are ruling the Aquitaine is because something serious has happened between you and Papa and you have walked out.'

'Hal...'

'Maman, you are miserable. When you are not looking sad, you are furious. You jump down everyone's throats, or you work yourself to exhaustion. Matilda, Geoffrey and Richard, we all know, Maman, we are not blind.'

I stood and walked away. I could not burden my children with my problems and taking my anger out on Hal would solve nothing.

Turning back, I said, 'I am sorry. Forget what you think regarding your Papa and me. You are destined to become the Young King. You have no choice, Hal. You will do your father's bidding. You will obey! When William died, your destiny was cast in stone just as mine was when my baby brother's life was taken. But I promise I will put your concerns to your father and do my best to persuade him to give you duties and offices you can fulfil.' I was dangling a carrot hoping to ease the tension. 'Hal, you are old enough to start training for your knighthood. I know you are keen to begin your preparations. You will now have that opportunity.'

Hal's face reddened, his voice strident, 'I want you and Papa back together – we all do, Maman!'

***

I sent Hal back to his lessons. What I did not say was his objections to Henry's demands would be placed at my door. The ache in my heart and the urge for vengeance twisting my gut fought with each other. To be honest, I felt alone, empty and burdened by my status.

Everyone wanted us reconciled, but I did not think I could do it regardless that in my heart I still loved Henry and I did not believe we could live amicably under the same roof as husband and wife. What was more, there was little to return to if I went back to England. Every vestige of comfort from my old homes was now stored here in Poitiers, and L'Ombrière. I supposed my manor houses would be liveable. But if I lived in isolation away from Henry, that would only push him towards further infidelity, which I could not abide which was probably what I was doing now.

I decided to travel to back to L'Ombrière. What would eventuate between Henry and me, I did not know. I tried listing the pros and cons of a reconciliation finding no answers. Our last argument became violent. Then there were Henry's black jealous rages. Moreover, I could not control my tongue when I lost my temper, and now he had given me greater ammunition. God's teeth, my self-

Chapter 12: Heir Apparent

control was close to non-existent.

I reread Robert's letter. That Henry thought I governed England and my lands better than he did answered some questions. I understood some of his resentment. But I could only see disaster ahead if he were so jealous of my abilities. I could refuse to be regent in England if I returned. Henry would probably never appoint me again anyway, but the day I retired as Duchess of Aquitaine would be the day I died.

***

I was avoided like a plague victim on what should have been a pleasant week's ride to L'Ombrière. No-one wanted their heads bitten off. All the way I mulled over how I was going to react to Henry and what I should wear. How would he respond? His letter, apart from his *My Dearest Wife*, was cold and I found that address insulting under the circumstances. Why all my titles, for God's sake. In the past he had never wasted words on that pomp.

I took to the old schoolroom when we arrived and let the children run riot through the gardens, giving them a break from their lessons. They were so excited, so looking forward to seeing their Papa they could not concentrate anyway. Before we left, I had John brought from Fontevrault so Henry could be with his whole family. John seemed a puny child. I had no idea what he thought of me. Mother Isabella said he was slow in his developments, teeth, talking, walking and so on. I could not tell who he looked like. There was perhaps a little of Henry's middle brother Geoffrey there. God help us if he had inherited that revolting man's personality. Not that I have helped John, being unable to relate to the child.

I could hear the children charging around the gardens with lots of squeals and laughter. So far no-one had come to blows. They deserved better than their irritable mother, which was why I was avoiding everyone including dear Renée and Clotilde. I knew they would eventually find me.

***

I could only hide for half the morning before Renée hobbled into view. Within minutes of her sitting next to me and taking my hands into her gnarled fists, I was six years old again sobbing on her shoulder,

'Renée, I am useless. I cannot hold onto the man I love; I am worn down by my duties and I cannot discipline my own children, so how can I rule my vassals? My life is a disaster.'

I soaked her gown and said, 'I know not what I want when it comes to Henry.'

Like yesteryear, she wiped my eyes and pushed my unruly locks from my face. 'You, darling child, can only play it by ear. Keep aloof. Your instincts will detect his mood, I am sure. It is up to him. After all, he is the one who has betrayed you. You will know if he is truly contrite.'

'Even if he gets down on bended knees and begs, I do not think I can forgive him.'

'Then you will have to do what you deem is dutiful for your status, your children and your people.'

'Jesus, Mary and Joseph!'

'Well, Elea, prayers to Them, too, might not be a bad idea.'

I think I detected a twinkle in her eyes.

***

My maids were not their usual exuberant selves as they laid out my gowns for selection. I walked along the line of shimmering silks and velvets, with their exotic embroideries and the scatterings of gems sewn with tenderness and skill by my clever seamstresses. In the end, a blaze of scarlet silk caught my eye.

My plaited mane was entwined with a red silk-bejewelled rope. I eschewed a veil but hung the Briolette diamond pendant round my neck. Was it to flaunt what Henry had, in my eyes, thrown away, or was it vengeance?

Chapter 12: Heir Apparent

Before I walked to Beelzebub, Amaris draped my cape around my shoulders to keep out the early chill. I mounted and my gown and cape were arranged over the horse. I adjusted the crown of the Aquitaine, to sit comfortably around my temples. I nodded to my escort; my gloved hands gathered the reins. Beelzebub, my beautiful hispano caparisoned to carry a queen, arched his noble neck and high-stepped with the grace of his breed through the courtyard onto the road that led to Bordeaux. In an easy canter, I rode towards my approaching king.

On a rise, half a league from the palace, we waited, scanning the road ahead. Dust plumes in the distance indicated horsemen travelling at speed. Only Henry moved at that rate. My nerves transferred to Beelzebub who danced about, snorting through flared nostrils, ears pricked. I pulled the reins tighter till his muzzle was almost on his chest. I watched the group of riders slow as they arrived ahead on a twin hill within shouting distance. Then my nerve deserted me. I turned Beelzebub for home and fled, scattering my guards. I could hear the thundering of Henry's small entourage behind me. I whipped my pounding steed across his withers. There was no way on earth I was going to let *'enri Plantagenet-a* catch me. He could ride like the wind, but by God so could I side-saddle, no less!

The grooms were amazed I was back so soon. I was off the horse and running, train looped over my arm, before they could wonder what was amiss.

Halfway to my quarters, Amaris grabbed me in her arms. 'Slow down! What have you done?'

'I panicked.' I was breathing in gasps, my heart pounding.

'Calm yourself! Milady, get yourself into the audience chamber. Your children are waiting.'

She removed my cape, straightened my gown and crown, and checked my flushed face for smeared kohl as a bevy of pages appeared from nowhere taking the weight of the train, and steering me almost without my feet touching the ground into the great hall.

My seven offspring were having a merry time, shoving, and tussling with shrieks of glee, being their revolting selves. Someone was screaming. It was John, overwhelmed by the brothers and sisters he hardly knew. I bellowed at them to stop their yelling and jostling and for Geoffrey to get down from my throne.

A cacophony of clattering hooves rose from the courtyard below, mixed with Henry's baritone, swearing. The children and I hastily arranged ourselves into a tableau of something akin to family bliss. I sat snotty-nosed and hiccupping John on my knee. He stuck his thumb in his mouth and stared into my face as if to say, 'Who, in Christendom, are you?'

Henry strode in, glowering like a winter's storm. John's thumb paused mid-suck. Joanna's bottom lip trembled, but the ensuing silence kept her from uttering a peep. I regained my hauteur. Henry's lips were stretched across his teeth. My eyes raked over him as he thundered, 'What in Satan's name was that about?'

The children froze.

'And you look beautiful, too, my dear Henry.'

But, before Henry could utter another word, Renée bustled in like a whirlwind, with John's nurse at her heels.

'All right, children! Out all of you. Nurse! Take care of the little one. Princes Hal, Richard and Geoffrey, there is a ball in the garden. Princesses Matilda and Lenore take care of Princess Joanna, all three of you can help me with some herbs. And, as for you two, make up or by Satan's breath, I will not be answerable for my actions.'

With that, Renée and the young Plantagenets left, not a whine, whimper, or argument from anyone.

Henry and I faced each other in icy silence.

As a tumult of emotions rampaged through my head, Henry's eyes scoured the room for wine, then limped to the flask and goblets arranged on a nearby table. His

Chapter 12: Heir Apparent

anger made him look desirable. Dear God, what was I thinking! I stood and descended from the raised dais. He handed me a brimming goblet, his hand knocking mine. His nostrils flared like Beelzebub's. I hoped it was my perfume. He eyed the diamond with narrowed eyes but said naught.

I tried not to swallow the wine in one gulp. It was hard to remember when I had been so lost for words. A Greek chorus chanted in my head, but not an utterance could force its way through my lips. We drained the goblets; he poured another round.

The great hall at L'Ombrière lived up to its name – great. I found myself pacing. The silence between us was frigid. I tried to calm myself with the next draft of wine. I could easily lose control if I allowed myself to drink too much. I stepped closer to the door.

'Where are you going?' Henry growled.

I found my voice. 'Nowhere.' The train of my gown was heavy. Without pages, it pulled me backwards.

'Why did you ride off like that?'

'Panic.'

Mental exhaustion was pushing emotions I had little control of close to the surface. I looked to set the goblet down on a side table, but my hand was unsteady. Henry rescued the goblet before it could spill. All I could do was look at the ground. Beside me, I could hear his breathing. The whole hall seemed hot and revolving.

'I feel faint. The crown is making my head ache.'

Henry disentangled my windblown hair from the wretched thing and placed it next to my goblet. Then he drew me towards him, his arms steadying me. I could not help but rest my head on his broad shoulder, breathing in his masculine, slightly horsey, odour.

'Thank you. I need to sit.'

Henry steered me to the steps of the dais and sat beside me. What was going through his mind? Were we both afraid of what could spew from our mouths? There was so much I wanted to say, to ask, but I could only think of furious, ugly words, even as my body craved comfort, and tenderness.

In the end, a cry squeezed from my throat. 'What are we to do?'

'About what?'

'About... *this*. Us.'

'I know not.'

I whispered, 'I love you and hate you. I could kill you for betraying me when my life was hanging by a thread. Revenge sustains me, enables me to survive. I cannot foresee a future for us together.'

Henry let out a roar. Was it pain? He groped to where my stiletto usually was. It was not there. I had not trusted myself to wear it. What was he going to do? I was shaking, struggling not to weep, so was he. It was too much. We wrapped our arms around each other.

'Why? Henry, why?'

'I do not know.'

I wanted to take him to my bed like we had always done. It was how we had solved our differences from the day we were wed, giving each other relief and pleasure in times of extreme stress and after our monumental arguments. My chamber was not far. Henry was begging me to forgive him. His right hand cupped my breast, his lips were on my neck, but just out of reach was trust!

www.ingramcontent.com/pod-product-compliance
Lightning Source LLC
Chambersburg PA
CBHW050133170426
43197CB00011B/1813